THE FUTURE OF THE BOOK

THE FUTURE OF THE BOOK

EDITED BY

GEOFFREY NUNBERG

WITH AN AFTERWORD BY

UMBERTO ECO

UNIVERSITY OF CALIFORNIA PRESS

BERKELEY LOS ANGELES

University of California Press

Berkeley and Los Angeles, California

Library of Congress Cataloging-in-Publication Data

The future of the book / Geoffrey Nunberg, editor; with an afterword by Umberto Eco.
p. cm.

Includes bibliographical references

1. Books and reading.
2. Written communication.
3. Databases.

I. Nunberg, Geoffrey, 1945-
Z1003.F9 1996 95-45441
028.5–dc20 CIP

ISBN 0-520-20450-6 (cloth)
ISBN 0-520-20451-4 (paperback)

Printed in the United States of America

2 3 4 5 6 7 8 9

The paper used in this publication is both acid-free and totally chlorine-free (TCF). It meets the minimum requirements of American Standard for Information Sciences—Permanence of Paper for Printed Library Materials, ANSI Z39.48-1984. ♾

THE FUTURE OF THE BOOK

Edited by Geoffrey Nunberg

Patrizia Violi	*Preface*	7
Geoffrey Nunberg	*Introduction*	9
Carla Hesse	*Books in time*	21
James J. O'Donnell	*The pragmatics of the new: Trithemius, McLuhan, Cassiodorus*	37
Paul Duguid	*Material matters: The past and futurology of the book*	63
Geoffrey Nunberg	*Farewell to the information age*	103
Régis Debray	*The book as symbolic object*	139
Patrick Bazin	*Toward metareading*	153
Luca Toschi	*Hypertext and authorship*	169
George P. Landow	*Twenty minutes into the future, or how are we moving beyond the book?*	209
Raffaele Simone	*The body of the text*	239
Jay David Bolter	*Ekphrasis, virtual reality, and the future of writing*	253
Michael Joyce	*(Re)placing the author: "A book in the ruins"*	273
Umberto Eco	*Afterword*	295

Patrizia Violi

PREFACE

The present volume grew out of a conference held at the Center for Semiotic and Cognitive Studies at the University of San Marino on July 28-30, 1994. Created in 1988 by the then newly established University of San Marino, the Center, under the direction of Umberto Eco and Patrizia Violi, organizes conferences, workshops and meetings, as well as short courses and summer schools, and promotes research and discussion on a wide range of topics related to semiotic theory and practices within a framework of the study of semiotic and cognitive processes.

Against such a background, the development of technology and its impact on the evolution and organization of social and cultural practices are a central concern, which affects many different areas of culture, society and the media. So it seemed singularly appropriate to organize a conference on the changes in, and transformation of, what is undoubtedly the oldest technologically mediated form of communication: the book and the act of reading.

What is the future of the book in this new era, as the end of the millennium approaches? The question raises issues that range from the transformation of the cultural institutions devoted to the storage and conservation of books to changes in the cognitive processes of reading and writing arising directly or indirectly from the introduction and use of the emergent technologies for reading and writing. Beyond this, we want to know how the structure of texts themselves will change, along with the socio-culturally mediated systems of textual genres and norms. How will text-based interactive systems for writing and interaction like the World Wide Web and MOO's affect the development and evolution of textual norms? Will the book as a material object still maintain some of its symbolic value, or it will disappear into the realm of merely virtual entities? Will new technologies enable us to look at ancient texts in a new way, discovering hidden structures?

Questions like these are important to researchers in a wide range of fields: philosophers, linguists, semioticians, historians, psychologists, experts in new technologies – not to mention authors, librarians, publishers, and others with a professional interest in the production and dissemination of the conventional book. This variety of perspectives and approaches was well represented by the participants at the conference.

During the conference, moreover, a special section was organized for the demonstration of electronic tools and products created for the support of genres like fiction, essays, and pedagogy.

The chapters of this book reproduce the papers that were presented at the conference, as revised in the light of discussions and comments. The proceedings of the San Marino Center have usually been published by Brepols; in this case, however, the widespread interest in the topic in the North American market suggested that we embark on a joint publishing venture with the University of California Press, who will copublish and distribute this volume outside of Europe.

Special thanks are due to Geoffrey Nunberg, who originally suggested the idea for the conference and whose many constructive suggestions and invaluable scientific assistance helped to make it a success, and also to the Rank Xerox Research Centre in Grenoble, which generously contributed to the organization of the conference, thus showing how a highly profitable collaboration between very different kinds of cultural institutions may be realized.

Geoffrey Nunberg

INTRODUCTION

One could be forgiven for assuming that anyone who talks about the future of the book nowadays will be chiefly interested in saying whether it has one. The public discussion has been dominated by prophesies of the people the press likes to describe as "computer visionaries." They give us a future where printed books, brick-and-mortar libraries and bookstores, and traditional publishers have been superseded by electronic genres and institutions; where linear narrative has yielded in all of its important functions to hypertext or multimedia; where the boundaries between traditional media and disciplines have been effaced; and where like as not print society has been replaced by a more harmonious and equitable discursive order. It is a vision calculated to provoke the indignant reactions of bibliophiles, like the declaration by the novelist E. Annie Proulx (cited by James O'Donnell in his essay here): "Nobody is going to sit down and read a novel on a twitchy little screen. Ever."

Still, the parties have more in common than either of them supposes. The bibliophiles' reactions are undeniably colored by fetishism, as witness their disproportionate concern about the difficulty of curling up in bed with a computer. (What's more, as George Landow astutely points out here, the fetishism is a little delusional, inasmuch as the morocco-bound ideal that bibliophiles tend to invoke has little to do with the form in which most students encounter the classical texts, in cheap paperback editions that will not survive even a single reading intact, and even less to do with the cobbled-together collections of photocopies in which they most often encounter the secondary literature.) But the enthusiasts of the new technology are not exactly innocent of fetishism either, both for their sleek new toys and for the obsessive, idle manipulations that they encourage. And it is probably these conflicting fetishisms that lead both sides to adopt a particularly concrete and implacable variety of technological determinism. They assume not just that the future of discourse hinges entirely on the artifacts that mediate it, but that artifacts and hence cultural epochs can only supersede one other – the doctrine most famously proclaimed by the archdeacon in Hugo's *Hunchback of Notre Dame* as "Ceci tuera cela." (As Umberto Eco observes in his afterword, no conference or collection of essays on the future of the book would be complete without someone citing these words, so I may as well get them out of the way at the outset.) In the story the visionaries tell, that is, the computer has to kill the book, rather than merely maim it or nudge it aside a bit. And because the partisans of the old order implicitly accept this point, they feel obliged not just to passionately defend the book, but also to disparage the technology that is supposed to replace it, "twitchy little screens" and all.

In its broad outlines, of course, the dialectic is not new. As Paul Duguid points out in his essay here, the doctrine of supersession has close affinities with the theoretical program of postmodernism, with its insistence that history moves by abrupt and sweeping discontinuities. It's clear, too, that most of the visionaries have been directly influenced by some version of Daniel Bell's notion that we are standing at the threshold of a postindustrial age, as the social order built around the production and distribution of goods yields to one determined by theoretical knowledge. And even closer to home, the program obviously owes an enormous debt to the paleo-post-Gutenbergianism of McLuhan. Indeed, if we take a longer view of things, as several of the contributors do here, the past can come to seem an unbroken stream of proclamations that man is living an epochal moment. As Proudhon once said, "La révolution est en permanence dans l'histoire."

Still, the current prophesies of the end of the book have some features that set them apart from the claims of a lot of the other millenarians. There is first the matter of periodization. Here the visionaries line up with McLuhan rather than with the postmodernists or postindustrialists, locating the beginning of the passing age in the fifteenth century rather than the eighteenth or early nineteenth, and explaining the crucial features of these later eras, like industrialism or the Enlightenment, as simply the delayed consequences of the introduction of print. (Or as people often put it, these things followed from the "logic" of the technology, a trope that implicitly reduces the needs and desires of human agents to a set of universal axioms.) The facile determinism of this picture is taken on here by Carla Hesse, who examines the parallels between the effects of the current digital revolution and the changes in publishing that were brought about in the wake of its rather more sanguinary predecessor of 1789. It was a period not unlike our own, she notes, which witnessed a pullulation of new forms, media, and institutions that underlay the "modern literary system," with its new conception of intellectual property. But what brought about these changes, she argues, was not technology but events like the Terror: "... there is no evidence of any clear link between the advent of printing and the emergence of the notion of the individual author as the source of knowledge or truths."

But unlike the postmodernists and postindustrialists – and indeed, unlike McLuhan – most of the enthusiasts of the new technologies have no real interest in advancing a historical thesis. The invocations of Gutenberg serve chiefly to demonstrate that the present situation is at least epochal, if not wholly unprecedented.[1] And the point of their historical determinism, you sense, is chiefly to establish their right to control the cultural moment and the material resources that it commands. This is how the future will be, they say, and the only choice we have in the matter is to get on board or to stand in the station as the train pulls away. People who say that tomorrow belongs to them are usually angling for a piece of today. (Thus are the words "vision" and "visionary" made banal, to the point where employees at some Silicon Valley companies are made to file "vision statements" as part of their annual review.)

It's important not to lose sight of this point when we evaluate the visionaries' prospective claims for the techology, which are anchored in immediacies far more than they are let on to be. No one doubts that digital technologies will have profound effects on the way our discourse is conducted and promise to lead to the emergence of a new "mediasphere," to use Régis Debray's term, a new regime of discourse. But the technology itself is changing so rapidly and unpredictably that even those who tend to think of it deteministically should have severe qualms about trying to predict what form it will wind up taking or what its cultural consequences are likely to be. When you hear someone making confident predictions about the state of the technology fifty or seventy-five years from now, you might think of some Eocene racetrack tout trying to call the winners of future Kentucky Derbies on the basis of observations about the herd of eohippi grazing about his knees.

Over the short run, to be sure, there are some technological predictions we can make with confidence. It is certain, for example, that the "twitchy little screens" will soon be replaced, perhaps by the amorphous silicon displays, which already exist in the laboratory, that rival offset in their contrast and resolution. And it's reasonable to assume that we will have displays before the turn of the century that are almost the equivalent of paper in their weight and flexibility, as well. Still, as Duguid and Debray both point out here, the utility and significance of the form of the book doesn't begin and end with the printed page. And we should bear in mind that the applications of digital technologies are not limited to the presentation of texts on screens, but promise to work fundamental changes in print publishing as well (the point tends to be neglected in these discussions, perhaps because ordinary consumers don't often see these technologies at work.) Digital printing, for example, eliminates a lot of the costs of production, storage, and distribution associated with previous methods of short-run printing, all to the immediate benefit of small presses, university presses, reviews, scholarly journals, and reprint houses (which now perforce include the proprietors of all the backlist titles and digitized library collections available for digital reprinting.) Initial printings can be smaller with additional copies made available on an on-demand basis, so that a small press, say, can publish more titles than would be feasible with traditional offset printing, and keep them "in print" indefinitely. (Small presses are also likely to profit from the advertising advantages of the web, where they can post catalogs that allow readers to sample a chapter or two of a prospective purchase.) Even with these new efficiencies, of course, these sectors will remain relatively marginal in the larger scheme of things, but so long as they remain healthy it would be hard to claim that "the book" is in its death throes.

Indeed, as Eco suggests, the very pervasiveness and generality of the technology make it difficult to identify any single digital *ceci*. You can see the problem in the way enthusiasts of the new technology have tried to locate its essence in each of its successive manifestations – the searchable digitized text, the bitmapped display, hypertext, multimedia, virtual reality, MOOs and MUDs, the Web – usually with a one-dimensionality that recalls those science-fiction worlds (the jungle planet, the desert planet) that are given over to a single ecology. And it is no less difficult to identify the predigital cela that the technology threatens to kill. After all, as Raffaele Simone observes here, the book is a heterogeneous form that can lodge a number of diverse textual guests. If we take the book in its broad sense to refer simply to bound, printed volumes, then most books will likely disappear soon, but the majority of these are the sorts of records whose existence in codex form has no particular cultural significance – parts catalogs, technical manuals, directories, regulations and legal records, and so forth. (And so much the better; as Eco notes, there are already too many books.) Among the books that people tend to care about as books, by contrast, the process of conversion is likely to be slower and much more selective. Scientific journals are almost certain to move to digital distribution, but for popular newspapers and magazines, the economic case for conversion is less compelling. CD-ROMs have already cut heavily into the sale of print encyclopedias, to the point where there are unlikely to be any left a generation from now, but the sales of print dictionaries seem largely unaffected by digitization (a recent edition of the *American Heritage Dictionary* wound up a bestseller in both print and digital versions). As for poetry reviews, novels, self-help books, political memoirs, critical editions, art books, travel guides... well it is simply too early to say. Some will probably continue to rest chiefly on printed supports, some will divide their lives between print and digital media, some will emigrate definitively, taking their place along a variety of utterly new digital genres.

Prediction, as James O'Donnell observes, is a mug's game. Still, I am willing to venture at least one more prediction here: by the end of the decade all our current talk of the "end of the book" will sound as dated and quaint as most of the other forecasts of this type that Duguid and Eco cite as historical precedents – photography will kill painting, movies will kill the theater, television will kill movies, and so on. ("Le cinéma va-t-il disparaître?" read the cover of a 1953 number of *Paris Match* that I saw at a bookstall not long ago, alongside a photograph of Marilyn Monroe of such evident glamour that a modern reader is left to wonder how the survival of the medium could have ever have been in doubt.) For one thing, the complexity and heterogeneity of the new mediasphere should by then be as evident as the heterogeneity of the world of film and television had become by 1960 or so. For another, these proclamations inevitably lose their value as positioning moves once the technology is no longer the property, material or intellectual, of a privileged faction. Indeed, access to the Internet has already become so widespread that many of the academics and technologists who pioneered its development have begun to complain about its vulgarization and to avoid its discussion groups; the Net has become like the fashionable restaurant about which Sam Goldwyn is reported to have said: "It's so crowded these days, nobody goes there anymore." Within a few years, there will be no predigital bourgeoisie left to *épater*.[2]

This will be all to the good, I think, since it will clear the air for other discourses about the future of the book that are likely to be much more fruitful. The shift is already evident in the technical and professional worlds. At the ubiquitous "digital libraries" conferences, for example, the Borgesian note has become almost inaudible against the buzz of discussions of client-server architectures, markup languages, middleware standards, and the like – all the questions that arise when we think of "the future" as a time we can actually plan for. (Or try to plan for, like the designers of new library buildings who find themselves in the position of having to accommodate the requirements of technology as much as 100 years in the future. You think of the challenge facing the city planners of the last *fin de siècle*, when the streets were just beginning to swarm with mass-produced bicycles.)

But the end of millenarianism makes place for another discourse as well, where we take the question of "the future of the book" as an occasion for critical reflection on the relation between technology and communication. For all their individual particularities, it's safe to say that all the contributors to this collection write with this object in mind. Certainly they are all enthusiastic about the possibilities opened up by digital technologies, and the majority of them have been actively involved in developing new technologies or applications (and while some have reservations about the technology, you will find no complaints here about "twitchy little screens"). But none of them takes "the book" for granted, in either the narrow or broad sense of the term. They may disagree about how central its future role will be, but none assumes that the digitization of discourse can be effected without some wrenching dislocations, and it's fair to say that none accepts the simplistic determinism of the visionaries. Ultimately, that is, the technologies cannot themselves determine how or where they will be deployed. This is left to us to decide, in the light of a far more nuanced understanding of the features of print culture that we invoke when we talk about "the book." Indeed, one reason why these technologies have attracted the interest of many writers, even those who have no immediate stake in their implementation, is that they provide such an excellent occasion for reflecting on the forms of discourse. (There is an obvious parallel here with the debates provoked by the ability of the computer to simulate other human activities, like perception or reasoning, which has naturally led to reflections on the nature of these capacities.)

In this sense most of the essays in this book fall in a long tradition of critical meditations on the cultural effects of new forms and new media, a line we can trace back through Raymond Williams, Carlyle, and Coleridge or through Benjamin and Baudelaire. Or, as James O'Donnell shows, well before that. Modern antitechnologists, he suggests, seem to take their model from "pragmatists of the old" like the fifteenth-century abbot Trithemius, whose *de laude scriptorium* was an extended criticism of the new technology of print, and who, though admiring print in the abstract, couldn't bring himself to accommodate it in a picture of monastic life. The visionaries can find an antecedent, less remotely, in a "theorist of the new" like McLuhan, whose extravagant prophesying and intolerance to any criticism of the new media ensured his media success and his intellectual failure. A better model than either, O'Donnell suggests, is in the "pragmatists of the new," like Cassiodorus, who undertook the practical enterprise (in the end, unsuccessful) of trying to adapt the new monastic culture to the preservation of the Christian Latin tradition. We might do the same, he says, by trying to adapt the new technologies to the preservation of cultural memory – which is, in the end, what we care for, rather than the books that have been its bearers.

I suppose it isn't surprising that classicists like O'Donnell (and Jay Bolter, as well) should be more readily disposed than most humanists to find the book ultimately dispensable, since the cultural tradition that most concerns them has already survived several fundamental shifts in its material support. For others, though, the prospect of the disappearance of the printed book raises considerable difficulties. As Paul Duguid points out, all the familiar talk of replacement and supersession presupposes that content is a kind of neutral substance that can be dislodged without change from its material base. This assumption underlies what he calls the "liberation theology" of technology, with its implication that, as he puts it, "a new Prospero will finally free the textual Ariel from the cleft pine – or at least from the wood products in which it is now trapped." But as he notes, echoing writers like McGann, McKenzie, Genette, and others, "all text relies to some degree on the very material embedding from which the technological liberation aims to give it independence." Social practice has turned the physical properties of the book – its bulk, its palpable inscription in space, its materially discrete pagination, its covers – into both interpretive and social resources. In fact, he suggests, the book may have a long life left in it.

Régis Debray makes a similar case, but in connection with the spiritual rather than the instrumental implications of the codex. He begins with a reading of the passage in Sartre's autobiography that recounts the writer's experience of his grandfather's library, and the importance of its essential physicality: "Even before I knew how to read I revered these raised stones, straight or slanted, ranged like bricks on the shelves of the library or lined in noble avenues like menhirs." In this "minuscule sanctuary," Sartre transformed himself through what Debray describes as a reverse eucharist into the "man-book," an inert object become a kind of gendered being. It is, Debray suggests, a microscopic cross-section of the history of this technology of memory: the codex as the symbolic matrix with which we link up with the world of meaning. In its permanence and fixity we, like Sartre, find an emotional stability, a shelter against the rush of time and death. "No culture without closure," he says, and suggests that the very capacities of digital media to overcome the material and temporal limits of print must lead to a kind of fundamentalist reaction to them. "The old man has not yet said his last word."

But what of the new electronic media that continue to emerge? Here, the challenge is to find modes of being that allow them to be true to their natures while preserving their cultural connectedness. As Carla Hesse observes, for example, the modern literary system was predicated on certain intrinsic properties of the mode of literary production, most notably its spatiality and objectification. In nineteenth-century France, only the book was exempted from prepublication censorship, because it took longer to produce and distribute and so was held to be more considered and less effective than newspapers or handbills, say, as an incitement to unreflecting action. But digital technologies, she notes, introduce a new mode of cultural production, in which the spatiality of print is replaced by a predominantly temporal mode of organization. In such a world, the categories of print discourse are inevitably reformulated. We may continue to talk about "books," for example, but they will no longer impose the physical and temporal distance between composer and reader that was an uneliminable property of their print antecedents. The challenge that faces us, she suggests, is how to reinvent the literary system and its mediators, books, libraries, and the rest, in the continuing service of "the cultural mission of civic humanism."

The librarian Patrick Bazin comes to much the same conclusion, if by a different route. He is concerned with one aspect of this new system, the development of the tools that will mediate our access to collections in a textual universe where we can no longer rely on the three types of boundaries essential to the printed text: "that of the text itself, in its spatio-temporal extension; that which separates reader and author; that, finally, which distinguishes text from image – that non-text *par excellence*." This "Copernican overturning" places greater prominence, he argues, on "tools of knowledge" adapted both to the form of the digital text itself, protean and elastic, and to the range of relationships that its various author-readers can assume. In short, he says, we have to create a system of "meta-reading" that transcends individual texts with their fixed boundaries, places, and roles, but which does not leave the reader with the sense of disorientation that can accompany the loss of all fixed reference points, the way one can feel, say, when wandering the Web. And in this, he adds, institutions like the library have a crucial role to play, not just as conservators, but by providing the kind of access that offers citizens – here there are close echoes of the conclusions of Hesse, Debray, and Eco – "the chance to reinvent together, in the context of relativism and virtuality, the public space of knowledge."

But the dislocations occasioned by electronic texts have to be addressed not just in the external means of access we impose on them, but also, at least to the extent the distinction makes sense in this domain, in their inherent form. To this end they require a new rhetoric and a new typography (taking the word in its broader, seventeenth-century sense.) And here, too, the technology must find a way to accommodate both its own material properties and the culturally determined modes of reading that it engages. This is the problem taken on in the essays of Luca Toschi and George Landow, each of whom draws on his experience in designing hypertext systems to try to arrive at the rhetorical principles that will govern the organization of such systems. Toschi in particular stresses the historical roots of this rhetoric. He begins by making the point, too often slighted, that the seeds of the new hypertextual forms are already present in the modernist tradition in a writer like Pirandello and adds that "electronic writing requires among other things good philology and an awareness of rhetoric, aesthetics, and of the history of writing, considered in its most diverse forms... By means of the language of hypertext, it is finally possible to make manifest what has always been done in practice, to create systems where the connections that paper can only suggest to the mind... are physically realizable and accessible to manipulation." In this sense, he suggests, hypertext can serve among other things as an ideal medium for collating and presenting textual variants that lead to the establishment of an authoritative literary text (and so, by-the-by, of overcoming one of the putative limitations of print that Trimethius noted five centuries ago). Above all, he suggests, a literary hypertext remains an authorial text, shaped by a single consciousness.

Landow, by contrast, tends to stress the discontinuities in new forms like multimedia and hypertext, which take us "beyond the book" by creating new modes of reading and "new forms of intellectual and cultural interchange." It may be that most of what is out there now is crude and self-indulgent, but then it is early days yet (after all, he points out, it took a hundred years after the introduction of the book for people to come up with the title page). And as opposed to Toschi, he stresses the collaborative nature of hypertext and the Web, which permit the creation of texts which "embody multiple points of view" and which blend genres and modes. This is an idea developed in a slightly different context by Raffaele Simone, who sees in the future of the book a dissolution of the membrane that has surrounded the historically constructed "closed text" – original, authorial, perfected, a space that resists all intrusion – and a return to the medieval notion of the "open text," an object that is "penetrable, copiable, limitlessly interpretable." Unlike Landow, who comes the closest to technological determinism of any of the authors here, Simone sees the premonitory signs of this shift in the emergence of print forms like the nonbook (for example, user's manuals or compilations of phrases, jokes, or citations), which set the stage for the interactive books and book-games that the computer makes possible. But for him, as for Landow, the shift presages a new textual consciousness and the disappearance or at least the occlusion of the author: "Sooner or later no one will remember the closed and protected text."

Still, it may be a mistake to make too much of the apparent differences among these approaches to the new media. The writers have had, after all, different aims: Toschi has been concerned with producing a synoptic critical edition of a classical printed text, Landow with creating a new text to be built by accretion by numerous contributors, and with the uses of hypertext in literary creation. Taken together with Simone's, these essays make the point that a medium like hypertext does not impose a unique rhetoric or mode of application independent of its application or the social construction of particular modes of reading.

Landow closes his essay with some remarks on virtual reality, a form that may seem to allow us to "dwell in fiction," as one writer has put it. But Landow notes too that so immediate a form of experience poses the risk of taking us not just beyond the book, but beyond language, with its necessary abstraction. This is the theme that Jay David Bolter develops at greater length in his essay. Bolter suggests that the emergence of multimedia and virtual reality represents a progression toward increasingly more "natural" signs, a process that is already well under way in the "breakout of the visual" that is evident in newspapers like *USA Today* (another nice reminder of the extent to which the effects of these technologies have been prefigured in recent print discourse.) Indeed, some have seen in the technology of virtual reality the advent of a wholly natural and unmediated system of signs – for example, in representations of height that can induce genuine symptoms of fear in acrophobics. Bolter agrees that these media clearly favor the ascendancy of the visual, to the point where they may even signal the end of prose (as daring a prediction as ventured by any of the contributors here), but he also avers that no representation can escape the sign entirely. There is no road back from semiosis. And indeed, the hypertext novelist Michael Joyce makes a similar point in a meditation on the phenomenology of digital reading occasioned by a poem by Milosz. Joyce argues that one of the effects of the "infantile seamlessness" of virtual reality is to arouse in the viewer the desire to violate the illusion, "running full-speed for the edges of the representation, boundary testing, bursting through, blowing away the whole wireframe world." Perhaps there will someday be virtual worlds that can contain our flight, he says, "but they too will be a structure of words; everything we see from now on is made of words." (Indeed, they may still be chiefly words in the literal sense. At least Umberto Eco refuses to accept Bolter's assumption that the technologies militate for the predominance of the visual. McLuhan's fundamental mistake, he says, was in insisting that image was coming to dominate alphabet in the new media, a mistake repeated by the theorists of digital technologies. Whereas in the computer, he claims, we have an ideal tool for manipulating information in its alphabetic form.)

But these differences in approach come with the territory and mirror the emergent heterogeneity of the subject matter. And they remind us too how much the category of "the book" is itself the result of a fortuitous concourse of institutions, genres, and technologies. The one thing that is certain is that the introduction of new technologies will be accompanied by a dispersion of the cultural and communicative functions we associate with the book. There was never any essential reason why we should consign our novels and parts catalogs to the same artifacts, or why we should sell poetry and cookbooks in the same retail outlets, and now that we can imagine doing things otherwise, the contingency of the present is brought home to us. It leads us to a view of the future that is far from the determinism of the visionaries: when everything is possible, nothing is forgone.

Notes

[1] One widely known enthusiast is fond of saying that the analogy to Gutenberg doesn't do the computer justice; what we should really invoke, he says without apparent irony, is the domestication of fire or perhaps the evolution of opposing thumbs. (And what, you want to ask, of the bicycle?) But this is just the other side of the doctrine of supersession as a means of establishing the exceptionality of the present moment: not just "never again," but "never before."

[2] Access to digital technology is likely to be a middle-class prerogative for some time to come (in the United States, PCs are right now about four or five times as frequent in white households as in black), and as these technologies become increasingly important as vehicles of cultural transmission, the cultural divisions between classes may become still further marked. It is true that the absolute cost of computational power has been declining at a sharp and constant rate, but this does not presage the end of technological disparities between rich and poor, since access to each new level of digital communication – the Web is the latest example – requires a correspondingly greater capital investment.

Carla Hesse

BOOKS IN TIME

1. Introduction: The medium is not the mode

What can the history of the book tell us about its future? What must we understand about the cultural and historical roles of traditional literary institutions – such as, the author, the book, publishing, and the public – in order to design the systems and institutions that will mediate the uses of new electronic technologies? Since the publication of Lucien Febvre and Henri-Jean Martin's *L'Apparition du livre* over three decades ago (1958), there has been what can only be described as an explosion of research into the history of printing, publishing, reading, and "the book" in early modern Europe, and particularly early modern France.[1] Historians should thus be in a good position to offer some illumination of the central issues this forum raises.

Let me begin by underscoring the fact that despite the technocratic bias of much of this research, the historical record makes unquestionably clear that the most distinctive features of what we have come to refer to as "print culture" – that is, the stabilization of written culture into a canon of authored texts, the notion of the author as creator, the book as property, and the reader as an elective public – *were not* inevitable historical consequences of the invention of printing during the Renaissance, but, rather, the cumulative result of particular social and political choices made by given societies at given moments.

Indeed, for this reason, the term "print culture," to my mind is not only inadequate for comprehending both the emergence and the complexity of modern literary culture, but is also misleading in that it implicitly carries with it a technological determinism that conflates the history of a *means of cultural production* (the printing press) with the historical development of a *mode of cultural production* which Roger Chartier has called "le circuit du livre" and that I would render in English as "the civilization of the book," or better still, for reasons I hope soon to make clear, "the modern literary system." Careful discrimination between these two different, though clearly interrelated, historical phenomena – the means and the mode – as well as an assessment of the nature of their interdependence is, I think, critical to our comprehension of both the complexities and the possibilities presented by the development of electronic media. My opening theoretical axiom, then, is that the medium is *not* the mode.

2. A brief genealogy of the modern literary system

The printed book, authored and owned and transmitted to a reading public through the nexus of a commercial market, was not a self-evident consequence of a technological change, but rather the expression of a cultural ideal whose key elements have been elaborated slowly in western societies since the Renaissance, but which crystallized into what I would call the "modern literary system" with the advent of the modern western democracies at the end of the eighteenth century.

Recall, first, that the codex book became the dominant form for preserving and transmitting the written word in the West almost a millennium before the advent of movable type or the emergence of the notion of the individual author as a source of ideas. And while it is clear that the introduction of printing accelerated, intensified, and extended the reach and exchange of literate culture, there is no evidence of any clear link between the advent of printing and the emergence of the notion of the individual author as the source of knowledge or truths. This idea seems much more clearly linked, rather, to the changing political, institutional, and cultural demands of the Renaissance states and their absolutist successors, which developed the need for new sets of skills and a new notion of individual accountability. Indeed, while the Renaissance elaborated a new discourse celebrating man as creator, a discourse which contributed to the social elevation of the artist and the intellectual, it was not until the eighteenth century that the author was recognized in western Europe as a legal entity. And even then s/he was not seen as the proper creator of his or her ideas, but rather as a handmaiden chosen by God for the revelation of divine truth.[2] It was only slowly, over the course of the eighteenth century, and in a highly limited manner, that the author became legally recognized as the originator of his or her works (in England in 1710; in France in 1793; and in Prussia in 1794).

Moreover, as Geoffrey Nunberg (1993) has recently reminded us, books have never been the exclusive, or even the most prevalent form of printed matter, though they have been the most privileged and most protected. It may thus be concluded that the authored and owned book is an expression of a cultural ideal which the modern West has cherished but which has had very little to do with the technology that has produced it. Indeed, it is a ideal that was not at all self-evident even to the founders of the great modern democracies, who more than anyone cherished the printing press as the great agent of Enlightenment and human progress. In fact, one of the most striking facts to the historian of the book is how closely the current discussion of the future of the book in the electronic age resonates with debates among the eighteenth-century Enlightenment *philosophes* and their revolutionary heirs.

John Locke, for example, was deeply skeptical about the value of books as a source of knowledge. In his eyes they were as likely to be repositories of falsehoods and superstitions as of truths. Indeed he saw real dangers in the illusion that books were containers of knowledge. He was aware that the very form of the book, by fixing, tends to reify the information inscribed in it. The only true source of knowledge, he maintained, is that disclosed directly to the senses. Books must be seen merely as a mechanism of transmission, a fulcrum between sender and receiver, rather than as a repository or container of fixed truths.[3]

And in France, Condorcet argued more radically still that the notion of authorship itself was an archaic creation of the absolutist monarchy, bent on dispensing privileged commercial and honorific monopolies to favored subjects rather than on facilitating the spread of light. From a radical sensationalist viewpoint he argued that knowledge from the senses does not, and should not, belong to anyone, because knowledge inheres in nature itself, not in the mind that perceives it. Unlike physical property (such as land), he argued, two people, or for that matter an infinite number, can think of, inhabit, and make use of the same ideas or information at once. How then could one of them have an exclusive claim to be the source of those ideas or that information?[4]

Thus, long before the advent of the digital revolution in publishing, a central strand of Enlightenment thought had already condemned the book as an archaic and inefficient cultural form. As knowledge came to be seen as derived from experience, it also came to be seen as ever-expanding, and as opened-ended as experience itself. To fix knowledge between two cardboard covers, and to attribute ownership of that slice to someone was to constrain its circulation. The best way to spread knowledge, according to Condorcet, was through authorless and opened-ended texts, circulating freely between all citizens: he imagined the periodical press supported through the mechanism of subscription rather than through the institution of royalties to authors or monopolies to publishers. Indeed, what Condorcet conceived of as an ideally transparent mode of exchange through the deregulation of print publishing looks a lot like a mechanical version of the Internet.

There are striking resemblances, as well, between current descriptions of the new electronic text and the modes of textuality invented and explored by the periodical press of the eighteenth century: the free play with formatting, the excitement about the combining of image, music, and text, the reassertion of the editorial over the authorial voice, the notion of the text as bulletin board, and, alternatively, as a transparent network for the exchange of letters. The eighteenth century also witnessed experimentation with microtechnologies as a means of putting the power of publication into the hands of every individual citizen. In 1789, Condorcet had the fantasy of using these new technologies of print and modes of textuality to, as he put it, "bring all of France into a dialogue with itself." And, in fact, he became a key player in the formation of a multimedia publishing group that experimented with all of these modes of publication and circulation.[5]

Interestingly, it was not the technological limits of mechanical printing that prevented Condorcet and his eighteenth-century collaborators from realizing their dream of a perfectly transparent free-form exchange between citizens through the medium of the printed word. Rather, the experiment was abandoned because of the political terror they experienced as cultural forces were unleashed with this new textuality after the French Revolution of 1789.

With the battle cry of "freedom of the press," in 1789 cultural revolutionaries like Condorcet spearheaded a movement to liberate print culture from the repressive institutions and regulations of the former regime. The declaration of "press freedom" encompassed far more than simply an end to prepublication censorship. It brought down the entire literary system of the old French regime, from the royal administration of the book trade, with its system of literary privileges and its army of censors and inspectors, to the monopoly of the Paris Book Guild on the professions of printing, publishing, and bookselling. Between 1789 and 1793, the mandate to liberate the Enlightenment from censorship and to refound cultural life on enlightened principles translated itself into a massive deregulation of the publishing world. By 1793, anyone could own a printing press or engage in publishing and bookselling. What is more, with the abolition of royal literary privileges and the end to prepublication censorship, it appeared that anyone could print or publish anything. Thus, the first few years of the French Revolution saw the corporatist literary system of the old regime entirely dismantled and replaced by a free market in the world of ideas.[6]

These changes did not, however, inaugurate the kind of cultural life their authors had envisioned. Cultural anarchy ensued in the wake of the "declaration of the freedom of the press." The collapse of royal regulation put the notion of authorship itself into question. Pamphleteers reveled in anonymity while literary pirates exploited the demise of authors' "privileges." Far from propagating enlightened ideas, as Condorcet had dreamed, the freed presses of Paris poured forth incendiary and often seditious political pamphlets, as well as works that appeared libelous or obscene to the new men in power. Once legalized and freed for all to copy or to sell, the great texts of the Enlightenment went out of print. The revolutionary reading market demanded novels and amusement, not science and useful knowledge. More profoundly, without any commercial protection of the author or publisher, book publishing became economically unfeasible. In the wake of these first consequences of the deregulation of print culture, the cultural policy makers in successive national assemblies came to recognize that laissez-faire cultural politics was utopian, and that they would have to find a means to regulate the world of print if their ideal of an enlightened republic was to be realized.

The cultural terror Condorcet experienced in the first few years of the Revolution led him to radically revise his dream of a totally deregulated, authorless, free exchange between citizens through the medium of print. Indeed, it led him to play a leading role in initiating legislation in 1793 to restore a cultural order centered in the "civilization of the book," by legally recognizing the principle of literary property as a means of holding individual authors accountable for what they published and by reregulating print commerce to make book publishing, as opposed to ephemeral printed matter, again commercially viable. The book-centered culture that emerged from the French Revolutionary legislation was, however, radically different from that of the old regime. Through the legal notion of a "limited property right," the National Convention reshaped the political and legal identity of the author, transforming that cultural agent from a privileged creature of the absolutist state into a property-owning civic hero, an agent of public enlightenment. And it transformed the publishing industry as well, abolishing corporate monopolies on the means of production, the printing and publishing world, as well as perpetual exclusive privileges on the literary inheritance of France. Publishing was thus regrounded in the principles of market commerce. These legal and institutional changes aimed at ensuring the dominance of the book – a cultural form that encouraged slow, reasoned reflection upon events, rather than the spontaneous and rapid interventions made possible by newspaper and pamphlet production. The author of books, who had property rights in his or her work, could therefore be held legally accountable for what he or she published.

However, it is nonetheless important to note that the "property rights" of authors, legislated by most western European countries by the end of the eighteenth century, were not unlimited in scope. French, English, and Prussian law all recognized that "public interest" dictated that after a fixed period following the author's death, all books should enter into the "public domain" and thus become freely reproducible by anyone licensed to print. After this period heirs or publishers could no longer claim exclusive reproduction rights to these texts, but only to their *particular edition* of a given text.

This has meant that for the last several centuries the lion's share of profits in commercial publishing has inhered not in the limited "property right" claims to an author's text, but rather in the claim to a particular edition of the text or, as Gérard Genette (1987) has called it, the "paratext" (format, notes, introduction, illustrations, etc.). Indeed, it is for this reason that even to this day most European bookstores are organized by publishing houses (Pléaide, Seuil, PUF, etc.) as well as by subject and author. Significantly, John Seely Brown and Paul Duguid (1993) have recently renewed interest in the intellectual and commercial value of paratextual apparatuses and their elaboration within the digital environment.

The legal notion of the "public domain" has preserved even within the modern book publishing world a critical element of Condorcet's ideal of universal access to a common literary inheritance. The modern "civilization of the book" that emerged from the democratic revolutions of the eighteenth century was in effect a regulatory compromise among competing social ideals: the notion of the right-bearing and accountable individual author, the value of democratic access to useful knowledge, and faith in free market competition as the most effective mechanism of public exchange.

The more conservative French regimes which followed the revolutionary period took further legal and administrative steps to favor "the book" over the pamphlet or the newspaper as the dominant form of printed publication in our time. In France, for example, between 1800 and 1880 only book-length publications were freed from prepublication censorship. The political implications of this cultural policy were immediately apparent to the liberal philosopher Benjamin Constant:

> All enlightened men seemed to be convinced that complete freedom and exemption from any form of censorship should be granted to longer works. Because writing them requires time, purchasing them requires affluence, and reading them requires attention, they are not able to produce the reaction in the populace that one fears of works of greater rapidity and violence. But pamphlets, and handbills, and newspapers, are produced quickly, you can buy them for little, and because their effect is immediate, they are believed to be more dangerous. (Constant 1814: 1)

It is significant to note here that what Constant sees as the critical distinction between "the book" and other forms of printed matter is not the physical form of the printed word, or the implicit set of social actors that it requires (author, printer, publisher, and reader), but rather the *mode of temporality* that the book form establishes between those actors. The book is a slow form of exchange. It is a mode of temporality which conceives of public communication not as action, but rather as reflection upon action. Indeed, the book form serves precisely to defer action, to widen the temporal gap between thought and deed, to create a space for reflection and debate. The book, as Marcel Proust recognized, is a fulcrum that creates space out of time.

* * *

The parallels between the debates and policy questions of the late eighteenth century and those of today are to my mind very striking. Like Condorcet in 1792, we seem to be facing the anxieties that attend the possibility of losing the means of associating a particular work or text with an individual agency, or of losing the writer's and even the reader's individuality; the possibility of a disappearance, perhaps, of the Enlightenment sense of self and of a sociability based upon a Rousseauesque model of intellectual community and of a liberal model of public life rooted in individualism and private property. These cultural institutions, I hope I have demonstrated, were not consequences of printing, but rather of sociopolitical choices, embodied in legal and institutional policies that ensured the realization of that cultural ideal.

For this reason, I would assert that the current debate over the electronic book should be a debate as much about the *modes* as about the *means* of cultural production and consumption. I do not think that technologies are the only, or even the main, issue at the center of the debate. The kind of textual destabilization and experimentation apparently made possible by the advent of new electronic technologies – hypertext, electronic bulletin boards, the Internet, and so forth – are less a consequence of these new media *per se* than of the process of determining the appropriate and desirable forms of their institutionalization. Indeed, I might speculate that the kind of experimentation that we are currently witnessing in electronic publication is a symptom of an underregulated or rather, relative to print media, unregulated communications medium that has evolved alongside of or beyond the reach of current regulatory frameworks rather than a consequence of the technological possibilities opened up by the digitalization itself.[7]

The *modern* literary system, the "modernized civilization of the book," that emerged from the democratic revolutions of the eighteenth century represents a particular vision of cultural life which embodies the ideals of the autonomous, self-creating and self-governing, property-owning individual, universal access to knowledge, and the assurance of cautious public reflection and debate. What we must determine, then, in the remaking of the literary system in the electronic age, in our choice to either challenge or affirm those ideals through the legal, political, economic, and institutional policies we implement, is what kind of cultural agents we envision for the future: put somewhat tendentiously, are we to sustain self-constituting and accountable citizens of a democracy or are we going to advance the future of continuously and spontaneously recomposing postmodernist subjectivities, inhabiting an increasingly imaginable, technocratically managed empire? An account of what is at stake in these choices, in my opinion, is more adequately expounded in the *Late Histories* of Tacitus, which chart the transition from republican to imperial Rome, than in the descriptions to be found in recent publications concerning hypertext, cyberspace, or virtual reality. And once we have designated a clear cultural task for the future, the questions of which tools and what modes of institutionalization and regulation are appropriate to that task will follow easily.

3. The remaking of the literary system in the electronic age

The striking parallels between the late eighteenth and late twentieth centuries' cultural debates suggest to me that what we are witnessing in the remaking of the "modern literary system" at the end of the twentieth century is not so much a technological revolution (which has already occurred) but the public reinvention of intellectual community in its wake. The electronic revolution of the past half century has not so much changed modes of human inquiry as it has rendered opaque some of the most seemingly transparent and fundamental cultural choices faced by modern societies: how we determine – as individuals, communities, and nations, and perhaps as a globe – to use these information technologies and toward what ends.

The introduction of these new technologies has radically destabilized and transformed the legal, economic, political, and institutional infrastructure of modern knowledge exchange – permitting, most significantly, the circumvention of traditional mechanical pathways of publication and communication. But these cultural consequences have less to do with the design of the microchip than with the forms of knowledge and modes of exchange that the *introduction* of microchip technologies has both wittingly and unwittingly made possible.

Indeed the process of reinventing the modern literary system in the wake of the microchip is already well under way. And, perhaps not surprisingly, some of the dimensions of the cultural landscape that are beginning to emerge in this digital environment are comfortingly familiar. Thus, for example, we can detect in the new electronic municipal library project in San Francisco a reprisal of the cultural mission of civic humanism carried forward from the Renaissance Italian city states to the postmodernist Pacific rim. And the new Bibliothèque Nationale de France, which is rapidly reconfiguring the French cultural map, despite its extraordinary architectural and technological innovations, is recognizably anchored in the universalist and encyclopedic traditions of the Classical, Republican, and even Socialist French state. Finally, we can recognize the hand of old-fashioned pragmatic American federalism in the massive project sponsored by the United

States Library of Congress to convert the Cold War satellite networks of the Radio Free Europe headquarters in Munich into an international bibliographic database for emerging Eastern European parliaments.[8]

* * *

This is not to suggest, however, that nothing new is occurring as a consequence of the electronification of the modern literary system. Most striking to the historian, in witnessing the remaking of the literary system in the present age, is the almost unwitting impulse to reconceptualize the key institutions of modern literary culture – the book, the author, the reader, and the library in terms of time, motion, and modes of action, rather than in terms of space, objects, and actors.

This recasting of knowledge forms in temporal rather than spatial terms can be detected across a surprisingly diverse range of recent library architecture projects. Most notably, Dominique Perrault's great rhetorical achievement in the design of the Bibliothèque Nationale de France is a despatialization of the library's form, the articulation of an "architecture of the void," a building without walls, a library that is a nonspace. But it is very interesting to observe that a similar set of rhetorical moves is made by an architect working on a library project in a radically different architectural idiom and with a frame of reference and a set of aims that are local rather than global in nature. Thus Cathy Simon, the architect of the new municipal library for the city of San Francisco, also repudiates a rhetoric of space, conceiving of her new library as exemplifying an "architecture of motion," a "kinetic architecture," comprised, weblike, of nodes, intersections, and passages, rather than volumes delimited by walls. And, more radically still, the international project to create libraries for the new parliamentary bodies emerging in eastern Europe is being conceived simply as a series of globally coordinated satellite networks linking far-flung databases that are not really located anywhere at all except in the hands of their users.

As with the rhetoric of architecture, so, too, with the rhetorical construction of the knowledge that will no longer lie within, but rather circulate through, these nonspatial libraries: the language used to describe the forms of knowledge of the electronic library metaphorically draws our gaze from the spaces delimited by classificatory grids to the lines of the grids themselves, to the trajectories of those boundary lines, and to the relations constituted at their points of intersection. In fact, knowledge is no longer conceived and construed in the language of forms at all ("bodies of knowledge," or a "corpus," bounded and stored), but rather as modes of thought, apprehension, and expression, as techniques and practices. Metaphors of motion abound. "Information flows between its creators and users", in the words of Paul Evan Peters (1992). Knowledge is no longer that which is contained in space, but that which passes through it, like a series of vectors, each having direction and duration yet without precise location or limit.

The availability of Boolean search through vast full-text databases, as the librarian Robert Berring (1986) has observed, renders obsolete the need for indexers and fixed indexes of texts, or even for subject catalogs. Each individual user can construct a unique search path through any given database. Moreover, information specialists and computer scientists see that the advanced application of algorithms is leading a breakdown of the very boundary between information and method itself. Thus the computer scientist Allan Newell writes:

> As anyone in computer science knows, the boundary between data and program – that is, what is data and what is procedure – is very fluid. In fact... there is no principled distinction in terms of form or representation of which is which. (Newell 1986, cited in Lyons 1992: 89)

In the future, it seems, there will be no fixed canons of texts and no fixed epistemological boundaries between disciplines, only paths of inquiry, modes of integration, and moments of encounter.

The notions of the writer and the reader are being recast within this temporal idiom as well. The designers of the workstations for the Bibliothèque Nationale de France, for example, redefine the reader in terms of the kind of reading s/he practices. Gone are the social (learned versus popular), political (public versus private), or economic (fee paying versus nonfee paying) categories that once described the constituencies of literary life. The imagined writer-readers in the electronic age are conceived, instead, in terms of their mode of action in time. The crucial distinction in the world of electronic writers and readers, according to the designers of the Bibliothèque Nationale de France and the librarian Robert Berring among others, will be between long- and short-term researchers.[9] Thus the long-term researcher will move in an ever-expanding web of vectors. S/he will have a sense of direction, because s/he will be competent in the technologies of research, but like an explorer who at once creates and charts a path, the electronic reader will not yet know where s/he is going to end up. Metaphorically, then, to enter this cyberspace – the new electronic literary system – is to journey out of space, and into the dimension of time.

What appears to be emerging from the digital revolution is the possibility of a new mode of temporality for public communication, one in which public exchange through the written word can occur without deferral, in a continuously immediate present. A world in which we are all, through electronic writing, continuously present to one another. There is, I would like to suggest, something unprecedented in this possibility of the escape of writing from fixity. What the digitalization of text seems to have opened up is the possibility for writing to operate in a temporal mode hitherto exclusively possible for speech, as *parole* rather than *langue*. New modes of reading-writing are emerging: E-mail communication in "real time," the on-line public forum, certain forms of interactive hypertext, the development of dynamaps in genetic and bibliographic research, and so forth.[10] The implications of these performative modes of electronic writing are potentially profound. Such modes make it possible to imagine a world in which writing loses its particular relation to time, in which the space created by the structure of deferral gives way to pure textual simultaneity, to what we might want to call scripted speech. Interestingly, though perhaps not surprisingly, it is lawyers who have been the first to seize upon the social implications of this development, and who have begun to advance new regulatory models for electronic reading-writing-publishing as performance and service rather than commodity.[11]

Digitalization, then, I am suggesting, is introducing a new mode of temporality into the modern literary system. It does not, and will not, however, impose new cultural forms. It is not inevitable that fixed forms of writing and modes of textuality such as the book will become extinct, or that we will all soon be living within a transparent utopian present constituted through scripted speech. Digitalization, rather, has created a new terrain upon which the literary system will now operate; it is a terrain that reconceives our mental landscape (both forms of knowledge and modes of apprehension and exchange) in performative rather than structural terms. What kind of literary system we (re)invent upon that new terrain is still for us to decide. The story of how the modern literary system will be remade in the face of these new temporal possibilities, and with what consequences, is one that historians are not yet able to tell. It is possible to speculate, however, that if performative modes of writing supersede structural ones, the history of the book will become nothing more than memory.

Notes

[1] Some main landmarks of this historiography include Febvre and Martin (1958), McLuhan (1962), Bollème et al. (1965), Martin (1969), Davis (1975; 1983), Roche (1978), Eisenstein (1979), Darnton (1979; 1982), Chartier and Martin (eds.) (1983), Chartier (1987; 1992), Chartier (ed.) (1987). For some of my contributions to this literature, see Darnton and Roche (eds.) (1989) and Hesse (1991).

[2] See Post et al. (1955), Davis (1983), Woodmansee (1984), Rose (1988), and Hesse (1990).

[3] See John Locke, *The Educational Writings of John Locke*, a Critical Edition with Introduction and Notes by James L. Axtell (London: Cambridge University Press, 1968); John Locke, *An Essay Concerning Human Understanding*, Peter H.Nidditch (ed.) (Oxford: Clarendon Press, 1987); and also John Locke, *A Commonplace Book to the Holy Bible...* (London: printed by Edw. Jones, for Awnsham and Churchill..., 1697).

[4] See Marie-Jean-Antoine Caritat, marquis de Condorcet, *Fragments sur la liberté de la presse* (1776), in M.-F. Arago (ed.), *Oeuvres de Condorcet* (Paris: Didot, 1847, vol.11: 253-314); see also Hesse (1990).

[5] See the fascinating study of this publishing group by Kates (1985).

[6] For a more extensive discussion of this story, see Hesse (1991: esp. chapters 1-2).

[7] The literature on the issue of current legal and regulatory questions raised by electronic media is very large and constantly expanding. I am basing my remarks here principally upon the special issue of *Serials Review* edited by Grycz (1992), Ginsburg (1993), and Schlachter (1993).

[8] See Bloch and Hesse (eds.) (1993). See also Maignien (1993).

[9] See Grunberg and Giffard (1993) and Berring (1987).

[10] On new modes of writing, see Levy (1993) and Bolter (1993).

[11] See Grycz (1992), Ginsburg (1993), and Schlachter (1993).

References

BERRING, R.

1986 "Full-text databases and legal research: Backing into the future," *High Technology Law Journal*, 1, 27: 27-60.

1987 "Legal research and legal concepts: Where form molds substance," *California Law Review*, 75, 15: 15-27.

BLOCH, H.R., AND HESSE, C. (EDS.)

1993 *Future Libraries,* special issue of *Representations*, 42.

BOLLÈME, G., ET AL.

1965 *Livre et société dans la France du XVIIIe siècle*, Paris: Mouton.

BOLTER, J.D.

1993 "The architecture of electronic writing," paper delivered at the workshop "The electronic book: A new medium?", Xerox Research Parc, Grenoble, France, September 9-10, 1993.

BROWN SEELY J., AND DUGUID, P.

1993 "Keeping it simple: Investigating resources in the periphery," in Terry Winograd (ed.), *Exploring Software Design*, Menlo Park: Adison Wesley.

CHARTIER, R.

1987 *Lectures et lecteurs dans la France d'Ancien Régime*, Paris: Seuils.

1992 *L'Ordre des livres*, Paris: Alinea.

CHARTIER, R. (ED.)

1987 *Les usages de l'imprimé (XVe-XIXe siècle)*, Paris: Fayard.

CHARTIER, R., AND MARTIN, H.-J. (EDS.)

1983 *Histoire de l'édition française*, Paris: Promodis, 4 vols.

CONSTANT, B.

1814 *De la liberté des brochures, des pamphlets et des journaux*, Paris.

DARNTON, R.

1979 *The Business of Enlightenment: A Publishing History of the Encyclopédie, 1775-1800*, Cambridge (Mass.): Harvard University Press.

1982 *The Literary Underground of the Old Regime*, Cambridge (Mass.): Harvard University Press.

DARNTON, R,. AND ROCHE, D. (EDS.)

1989 *Revolution in Print: The Press in France, 1775-1800*, Berkeley: University of California Press.

DAVIS, N.Z.

1975 "Printing and the people," in *Society and Culture in Early Modern France*, Stanford: Stanford University Press: 189-226.

1983 "Beyond the market: Books as gifts in sixteenth-century France," *Transactions of the Royal Historical Society*, 33: 69-88.

EISENSTEIN, E.
1979 *The Printing Press as an Agent of Change*, Cambridge: Cambridge University Press, 2 vols.

EVANS PETERS, P.
1992 "Making the market for networked information: An introduction to a proposed program for licensing electronic uses," *Serials Review*, 18, 1-2: 19-24.

FEBVRE, L., AND MARTIN, H.-J.
1958 *L'apparition du livre*, Paris: Albin Michel.

GENETTE, G.
1987 *Seuils*, Paris: Seuils.

GINSBURG, J.C.
1993 "Copyright without walls? Speculations on literary property in the library of the future," *Representations*, 42: 53-73.

GRUNBERG, G. AND GIFFARD, A.
1993 "New orders of knowledge, new technologies of reading," *Future Libraries*, special issue of *Representations*, 42: 80-93.

GRYCZ, C.J. (ED.)
1992 "Economic models for networked information," *Serials Review*, 18, 1-2.

HESSE, C.
1990 "Enlightenment epistemology and the laws of authorship in revolutionary France, 1777-1793," *Representations*, 30: 109-137.
1991 *Publishing and Cultural Politics in Revolutionary Paris, 1789-1810*, Berkeley: University of California Press.

KATES, G.
1985 *The Cercle Social, the Girondins, and the French Revolution*, Princeton: Princeton University Press.

LEVY, P.
1993 "The electronic book or navigation in hyperspace? Toward virtual worlds of shared meanings," paper delivered at the workshop "The electronic book: A new medium?", Xerox Research Parc, Grenoble, France, September 9-10, 1993.

LYONS, P.A.
1992 "Knowledge-based systems and copyright," *Serials Review*, 18: 1-2.

MAIGNIEN, Y.
1993 "La constitution de la collection numérisée de la Bibliothèque de France: Vers un nouvel encyclopédisme?" paper delivered at the conference "New Technologies in the service of literature," Oxford University, October 1-3, 1993.

MARTIN, H.-J.
1969 *Livre, pouvoirs et société à Paris au XVIIe siècle*, Geneva: Droz, 2 vols.

MCLUHAN, M.
1962 *The Gutenberg Galaxy*, Toronto: University of Toronto Press.

NEWELL, A.

1986 "The models are broken the models are broken," *University of Pittsburgh Law Review*, 47: 1023, 1033.

NUNBERG, G.

1993 "The places of books in the age of electronic reproduction," *Representations*, 42: 13-37.

POST, G., ET AL.

1955 "The medieval heritage of a humanistic ideal: 'Scienta donum dei est, unde vendi non potest,'" *Traditio*, 11: 195-234.

ROCHE, D.

1978 *Le Siècle des lumières en province. Académies et académiciens provinciaux (1680-1789)*, Paris: Mouton.

ROSE, M.

1988 "The author as proprietor: Donaldson V. Beckett and the genealogy of modern authorship", *Representations*, 23: 51-85.

SCHLACHTER, E.,

1993 "Cyberspace, the free market and the free marketplace of ideas: Recognizing legal differences in computer bulletin board functions," Comm/Ent. *Hastings Communications and Entertainment Law Journal*, 16, 1: 87-150.

WOODMANSEE, M.

1984 "The genius and the copyright: Economic and legal conditions of the emergence of the author," *Eighteenth-Century Studies*, 17, 4: 425-448.

James J. O'Donnell

THE PRAGMATICS OF THE NEW: TRITHEMIUS, MCLUHAN, CASSIODORUS

First a little late news from the net. Books are here to stay:

> *Books are forever*, says author: Fiction Pulitzer Prize winner E. Annie Proulx says that the information highway is "for bulletin boards on esoteric subjects, reference works, lists and news – timely, utilitarian information, efficiently pulled through the wires. Nobody is going to sit down and read a novel on a twitchy little screen. Ever." (*New York Times*, 5/ 26/ 94, A13)[1]

Of course, a successful novelist has a certain conflict of interest that might distort judgment. Whether the fictions that we can and will read on screen will be known as "novels" is a question I leave for others. I have no reason to think that books will disappear within a reasonable future, but the status of the book is surely labile now as it has not been in five hundred years. My purpose in this essay is to meditate on some of our experiences in such labile past times and to venture to extract a few morals.

Let me begin with a story that played itself out a few miles from San Marino, on the strand at Rimini. The pope was not happy. He had been summoned from Rome by the government at Ravenna to face accusations, not for the first time, of irregular election and unseemly conduct. To be sure, he had not yet been called, as he was later to be called, to pay back a rather substantial loan made by a Milanese banker taken to sustain the costs of doing business with the grasping functionaries of the government; but on the other hand he had not yet been raised, as he would later be raised, to the formal rank of saint of the universal church. He was this day breaking his journey to Ravenna at Rimini, walking on the beach and taking the air, when he saw a carriage pass by on the high road to Ravenna carrying women he recognized. They were the very women with whom he had been accused at Rome of illicit association, and he knew at once that they had been summoned to Ravenna to testify against him. Keeping his knowledge to himself, he waited until nightfall, took a single aide, and fled back to Rome, muring himself up in Saint Peter's to hold out against the world.[2]

My point is not to tell the story but to call attention to the way we come to know it.

Sometime in the early sixth century, it began to be the practice at Rome for the life of each succeeding pope to be added to a collection of short lives of his predecessors in what came to be known as the *Liber Pontificalis*. The orthodox collection of these lives was continued well into the Middle Ages and is a standard historical source, whose value for popes, from the late fifth century onwards particularly is wells known. But this story does not come from the orthodox collection, the one that helps make Symmachus a saint. It is found on the first three folios of a sixth-century manuscript preserved today at Verona.[3] The single life of Symmachus, written according to the rules of the genre embodied in the official *Liber Pontificalis*, is followed by short entries, also generically resembling the larger *Liber*, about the other popes down to Pope Vigilius, whose death ca. 555 gives the manuscript a likely approximate date.

The fifth and sixth centuries were a period in which Latin Christianity was making remarkable strides in adapting to its use the power of the written word.[4] It was not that Latin Christians were beginning to write, but that they were now using the written word with sophistication to organize and control their world. In particular, the papacy itself emerges in this period as a textualized artifact: the lives of the popes are one piece of evidence, their chancery-collected letters that begin to survive in substantial numbers are another. The affair in which Symmachus found himself embroiled, the so-called Laurentian schism (named after his rival), testifies to the new power of the written word as well. First, the very survival of this "Laurentian fragment" suggests that not only was the papacy itself publishing official lives, but it was doing so well that it made it worth somebody else's while to write the counterhistory, to put together a collection in which Symmachus appeared, but in no good light. *That* text, with which I began, was probably written in ill grace by the losers after the fact. An even more interesting collection of texts came from the winners in the course of the action: the so-called Symmachan Apocrypha are four texts, none exactly what it seems, written at the height of the controversy between Symmachus and Laurentius. The texts purport to be historical documents, for example, a papal decree, the records of a synod, an account of a trial, dating from as far back as two hundred years earlier, all bearing in one way or another on the history of the papacy. What they have in common is that they provide elegantly forged *precedents* for various points of argument that Symmachus was making against his rival. The coherence and consistency of these four texts, and the very different faces they are made to wear, make us confident in saying that these were not cases of idle stories told to good effect, but of deliberate creation of textual authorities whose authors had to know that they were literally cooking the books.[5] The main point is obvious: it must have been *worth* forging those texts in the eyes of the makers, and there must have been an audience in place already conditioned to judge ecclesiastical legitimacy in documentary, textual terms.

There is much else from that period alone to show how the "library of the Fathers" was coming into existence, with all manner of supporting documentation, and to show how far the public and spiritual life of Christianity was beginning to be regulated by authoritative texts. Vincent of Lérins, author in the 430s of a *Commonitorium* that attacked (discreetly and anonymously) the authority of Augustine of Hippo, may himself have been the first author to speak of the "fathers" of the church as figures of textual authority.[6] In one sense this was inevitable, for the generation of Ambrose, Jerome, and Augustine had a very thin collection of Latin texts on which to rely and could not depend on authority of that kind. Those writers and their contemporaries left behind by comparison a vast body of work of imposing power and persuasiveness, and those who read such books had to begin to make sense of what it was like to live in a Christianity where the bishop in your church's pulpit was surrounded by a moat of dead *writers*. By the sixth century, the power of dead writers was felt strongly enough that it began to make sense to condemn them. A vital issue at and before the second Council of Constantinople of 553 was whether authors who had died in the peace of the church could be subject to retrospective condemnation. In one sense it is outrageous that such postponed judgment should be imposed. But if it is no longer a question of the living deeds, but the dead textual word of an author that lives on after him, then condemning *authors* was only an acknowledgment that *books* had begun to dominate discourse.

The late antique Latin experience in the making and shaping of power and community through the written word had a technological basis in the adoption of the codex form of the book,[7] but the real change was cultural and social. So too, at other moments of transformation, the impulse, often very powerful, can be technological, but what saves the process from determinism is that thousands of small and particular choices are made by individuals and institutions to channel that force to shape society and its institutions. The Latin Christian "textual community"[8] that emerged in late antiquity is one of the most powerful and long lasting of such communities. In many ways it was more powerful than that of Greek, Hellenistic, and Roman antiquity, inasmuch as the direct line from Mediterranean antiquity was broken decisively in the destruction of the ancient libraries, while there are still today physical collections of books that have been kept together and valued for their contents from the sixth, perhaps the fifth, century.[9] The organon that we inherit, though influenced by ancient models in various ways, is that created in late antiquity, where it is no longer poetry that forms the center of the collection, but "nonfiction" – scripture and its supporting texts.[10] The modern skeptical scholar works in research libraries that share exactly that preference for non-fiction and enshrine it in their cataloging systems, cataloging systems that in other ways reflect the late antique and medieval, but not specially the ancient ways of organizing the mental world.[11]

We will return to late antiquity for further meditation after considering some more recent upheavals. The introduction of movable type made a revolution, no question. That story has been often and movingly told.[12] It bears remarking that the story of that revolution is regularly told in *print* and by partisans of the revolution. It may very well be that this revolution was a good thing, but any historical event recounted entirely by partisans is open to reconsideration. What I have to say now began when I asked those partisan narrators a question they were not very well equipped to answer: who *didn't* like the technology of print, and why didn't they like it?

The applicability of the question to our own time is obvious. If we can return to the last comparable watershed between ways of recording and distributing words and look for the history of resistance to the new technology in that period, we can gain some advantage of perspective on controversies in our own time, when it is far from clear to many people that the revolution that is upon us will be a benign one. To find the answer to that question is not easy, precisely because the partisans wrote the history of the revolution. The occasional mentions that are made of resistance to print are for the most part inaccurate, and thoroughly patronizing.[13] I persisted, and found more than I expected to. History, it should come as no surprise, repeats itself repeatedly.[14]

A good place to begin is with a standard popularization published forty years ago in a Penguin edition. There we read of another great man who passed time in the neighborhood of San Marino, Duke Federigo of Urbino, legendary bookman and father of the duke *fainéant* who figures in Castiglione's *Il Cortegiano*. In the memoirs of his agent Vespasiano da Bisticci, ca. 1490, we are told that in the Duke's library "all books were superlatively good and written with the pen; had there been one printed book, it would have been ashamed in such company."[15] The argument is one made on esthetic rather than utilitarian grounds, and the Duke must be given full credit. The Urbino manuscripts now in the Vatican Library give ample evidence of an elegance and an artistry of presentation that few printed books before the late twentieth century have ever rivaled, and that, in some cases, none will ever rival. The "Urbino Bible," for example, is an elaborate and massive triumph of manuscript illumination. A theologian may well prefer a more workaday copy of a philologically sound critical edition of the scriptural text, and may even prefer a text in some language other than Latin, but few would argue that the devout are at least as well served by the grandeur of this book as by the shabbiness of modern puritanical black binding and fine print.[16] But Federigo also had numerous lesser works copied into manuscript from printed sources.[17]

In the same Penguin we read of Cardinal Giuliano da Rovere, later Pope Julius II, patron of Michelangelo and father of the modern Saint Peter's Basilica, who had Appian's *Civil Wars* copied in 1479 from the Speier edition of 1472. He retained the colophon and changed it only from "impressit Vendelinus" ("Wendelin printed") to "scripsit Franciscus Tianus" ("F. T. wrote/copied"). That brings us to one of the things that everyone who works in this period knows casually and imperfectly, that there were people having printed books copied by hand. Why?

The authoritative study of the topic is that of M.D. Reeve,[18] who makes several points:

1. Printing so multiplied the number of copies available that the old technology, looking for a book to copy, was more likely to hit on a printed than a handwritten exemplar.

2. Further, if the *Consolatio ad Liviam* (a fifteenth-century discovery, and perhaps creation, since recognized as spurious) is printed in the works of Ovid, there will have been many who wanted just *that* poem and copied it out, rather than buy the whole book. For these first

two reasons, at least 10 of 16 and possibly 12 of 16 manuscripts of the *Consolatio ad Liviam* come from printed editions.

3. What is clear is that the fifteenth century did not sing the praises of printed editions on textual grounds, indeed had reason to be suspicious of them (see below), so they were not chosen as models (or cannot be proved to have been chosen) on those grounds.

4. A few idiosyncratic owners account for most of the manuscripts made from printed books. Apart from Urbino, the two bibliophiles Bartolomeo Fonzio and Raphael de Marcatellis loom quite large in the literature on surviving examples of this type of book.

Raphael de Marcatellis has been the object of two important studies by Albert Derolez.[19] Marcatellis was abbot at Ghent and died in 1508. What is clear from Derolez's studies is that two considerations were foremost in the minds of such a patron. First, luxury – and a preference for luxury is *often* a preference for an older, handmade product without any prejudice toward the general utility or inevitability of mass-produced goods – and second, access, for hand copying was also a way of getting books not yet circulating in your own country. In the case of Marcatellis, more than half the incunabula that served as models for his manuscripts are not to be found in any present-day Belgian collection. They were probably not on the book market in the Low Countries, and he would have borrowed them from Italian friends. We may also note that hand copying was the only way to obtain a coherent corpus on a given subject. We now praise electronic texts for their malleability in this way, forgetting sometimes that the relative stasis, not to say intransigence, of the printed book is the anomaly in the history of the written word, and that user-made anthologies are the norm.

But if we can explain away some of this resistance to the new technology of print, or at least minimize its force, we must accept the greater validity of other complaints. The earliest known call for press censorship was from a classical scholar, Niccolo Perotti, upset about Andrea de Bussi's shoddy classical editions being printed in Rome. Perotti asked the pope, in a 1471 letter, to establish prepublication censorship to ensure that editions were carefully edited (the appeal was unavailing, and de Bussi became Vatican librarian.) And the correspondence of the Basel publishing house of Amerbach[20] is full of letters to Johannes Amerbach contrasting his careful work with most printers' cheap output.[21]

The wisest men foresaw as well that the superabundance of books would lead to the promulgation of uncomfortably divergent opinions. The famous chancellor of the University of Paris, Jean Gerson, had already complained of overabundance and the seeds of error in 1439, and voices were heard as early as 1485 in Nürnberg lamenting that it was not only the wide distribution of error but the uniformity and consistency of error in print that made it powerful.[22] All the copies of the printed book are alike, and *therefore* it is impossible to compare and correct copies one with another. An error inserted in one is in all, and there is no control as there was in collating individually prepared manuscripts.

Worse, an abundance of words would lead to confusion – of this, men were certain already in the *fourteenth* century. Nicholas of Lyre, in his second prologue to the literal commentary on the Bible, was mistrustful of the limited hypertexting of the glossed manuscript page:

> Although they have said much that is good, yet they have been inadequate in their treatment of the literal sense, and have so multiplied the number of mystical senses that the literal sense is in some part cut off and suffocated among so many mystical senses. Moreover, they have chopped up the text into so many small parts, and brought forth so many concordant passages to suit their own purpose that to (some degree they confuse both the mind and memory of the reader and distract it from understanding the literal meaning of the text).[23]

Old and new were uncomfortably assorted in other ways. There were defects in presentation for a long time, often eerily resembling those of our own day: the scholar who struggled to get the right Greek font for his printer will sense a kindred spirit in the printer whose incunabular edition of Servius left blank spaces in which Greek words and phrases could be written in by hand. At what date contemporaries became sensitive to the loss of historical value in their treatment of manuscripts is an open question. Not until the mid-sixteenth century were large numbers of medieval manuscripts scrapped once they had been supplanted by print, and to be fair, it was not their means of production but their contents that rendered them liable to destruction: law texts and the Latin Aristotle had other reasons for obsolescence than the form in which they were presented. At the time of the Reformation, service books of the old liturgy suddenly faced rapid destruction.[24]

The patron saint, so to speak, of critics of print is the immensely (if not always prudently) learned Abbot Johannes Trithemius, of the Benedictine house of Sponheim near Frankfurt (later of Würzburg). Few who pass this way will fail to have heard of his book, *printed* in 1492, *De laude scriptorum*;[25] the ironical will also have recalled that years later in his chronicle of the monastery of Hirsau (1515), he praises printing, "ars illa mirabilis et prius inaudita imprimendi et characterizandi libros." What do we make of this marvel of erudition in an age of transition who cannot make up his mind? Shall he be *our* patron saint of indecision?

Some of his criticisms make him out a typical footdragger. Anything prepared on paper will not last very long, he alleges. (There *were* already manuscripts on paper, but he is correct that the lighter, cheaper material was more commonly used by printers.) "For if writing is placed on skins, it can last for a thousand years; but print, when it is a thing of paper, how long will it last?"[26] The shelf life of paper he estimates at two hundred years, and of course he is not entirely incorrect.

The higher quality of the manuscript artifact and the value added by the scribes and illuminators also merit his dispraise for print. Scribes are more careful than the slapdash artisans of print, and so the spelling and the other features of books are much more carefully looked after.[27]

Let me pause now to observe something about the criticisms of print that I have so far cataloged, both from Trithemius and from others. They are all true and valid. Every negative claim made about print is correct, and every negative prophecy came true. Take the argument about the likeness of copies making collation and correction impossible: a perfectly valid point. Why did it not derail print in its glorious career? I suggest two reasons.

First, the point, though valid, is not decisive, that is, for all that we idealize correctly made books, we do put up with a light admixture of error. The value of the book is not seriously degraded by its errors; indeed, if that were the case, then the written manuscript book would have been insufferable, but users were well acquainted by the fifteenth century with the praxis of deciphering imperfect books.

Second and more important still: the system of communication introduced by print was so large, so fast, so powerful, and ultimately such a source of wealth that the defects of the system could be remedied as far as need be. Proofreading was labor-intensive and wasteful in a manuscript scriptorium, but quite cost-effective in a print shop; and if the print shop is busy preparing stock prospectuses where tens of millions of dollars are at stake, proofreading of a madly obsessive-compulsive nature is both cheap and sane in view of the possible losses from error. If the collection and comparison of errors are important, then the nineteenth century could in due course perfect the strategy of the "critical edition," gathering and cherishing precisely the variant readings of manuscripts, multiplying and then freezing them in print, and perpetuating whatever informational value they have to offer.

In short, in the end, the defects of print and the criticisms they drew didn't matter. This is a lesson worth mulling at length.

I want to suggest, however, that Trithemius, in particular, was no mere Luddite, voicing fears drowned out by the roar of progress. For the pieces of criticism of print that I have extracted here, as others have done before me, are only a small part of his whole treatise. His true topic is the undermining of the ethos and culture of the monastic scriptorium. Writing is the spiritual manual labor *par excellence*, and that way of life was threatened by print:

> ... In no other business of the active life does the monk come closer to perfection than when *caritas* drives him to keep watch in the night copying the divine scriptures... The devout monk enjoys four particular benefits from writing: the time that is precious is profitably spent; his understanding is enlightened as he writes; his heart within is kindled to devotion; and after this life he is rewarded with a unique prize.

There then follows the story of a dead Benedictine who was such a passionate copyist that after they buried him, *post multos annos*, it was found that his three writing fingers were miraculously preserved while the rest of his body had rotted away.[28]

Furthermore, the technology of writing had worked its way deeply into the social and economic structure of the community. The monks who didn't know how to write were put to work binding, rubricating, making pens, and the like. The life of the monastic community had been permeated by the technology and the spirituality of writing. To let it go was to let go something that was perhaps not essential to the monastic ideal, but that had become integral to its practice. It is the undermining of the monastery that Trithemius most feared.

And of course he was right. Benedictine monasteries show a growth curve from A.D. 500 to 1000 ticking sharply upward toward the end, then roaring forward with a lusty growth and sustained prosperity from 1000 to 1500, but the last five hundred years have shown at best mixed results. At the very least, the social and cultural domination of much of European society by monasticism and allied institutions (I here count the friars and other extraclaustral religious orders, who paid their own tribute to monasticism by the care with which they withdrew from it and rivaled it) faded rapidly in the sixteenth century. I make no determinist suggestion here, but only observe that the ability of the institution to survive depended on its ability to adapt itself to the new technological environment (universities did much better, until now at least, than monasteries, after all, though in the fifteenth century they shared many common traditions), and that was an adaptation that Trithemius could not bring himself to theorize. If in practice he approved of print and used it, he could still not find a way to bring print into his picture of the monastic life.

He was not alone. A few places maintained scriptoria and print shops in the same house, such as an Augsburg monastery where the two coexisted ca. 1471-76, but most such arrangements lasted only for a short time. So, for example, at the house of the Strasburg Carthusians, Heinrich Eggestein worked a while to print the life history of Ludolf of Saxony, their prior, and taught some of the monks the new technique.[29] In practice, print was a business that flourished in less salubrious parts of town, among grubby businessmen unafraid of dirty hands. It was there that a new information order was created, and the social order found itself wrenched, sometimes agonizingly slowly, sometimes shockingly quickly, to align itself with what technology had created.

* * *

To see what became of the technology, its critics, and the social order at the time of the introduction of print to Europe, and to see this not only as a triumphant, but also as a complex tale of fractioning and regrouping, would put us in a much better position to see the way forward from here in our own time of transition. The exciting contemporary work on the history of the book is of great intrinsic interest, but, like all of the best historical writing, tells us important things about ourselves as well.[30] I will leave that story for others to pursue and move once again disconcertingly quickly forward through centuries nearly to our own time.

The most visible anti-Trithemius of our time was undoubtedly Marshall McLuhan.[31] There are other prophets even still among us (I think of Ted Nelson and his vision of Xanadu), but McLuhan seized the high ground of public visibility at an opportune moment. Even George Steiner (1963/1970) in those days, while finding very little *specifically* to praise or agree with, found him worth reading for reasons he could not well articulate. Every lesson that Trithemius failed to grasp, McLuhan had learned at an early age. It was perhaps precisely his lavish impatience with any criticism of new media of communication that most shocked his readers; and it was his eager willingness to imagine large-scale social transformation far ahead of the curve that distinguished his contribution to our common vision. He was both of his time and ahead of his time, of course; if we do not yet live in a global village, we still live in a world bound closer by satellites and CNN than was the case even thirty years ago. Think of the film *The Gods Must Be Crazy*, where the artifact of mass consumption culture dropped from the sky offers a first link between the bushman and the greater world; only thirty years ago, locations far less remote were at least as cut off from the marketing strategies of Atlanta and New York.

It was the prophetic role that McLuhan cut out for himself that represented his greatest success and his lasting failure. Though it may seem self-evident that new media of communication bring a powerful set of forces into play, McLuhan did not succeed in seizing the high ground of intellectual discourse, did not succeed in creating a line of successors, disciples, and pedantic periphrasts to follow him, and did not finally achieve the respectability that would have guaranteed that his ideas had been rendered harmless.

What I say is obvious and commonplace, and I will not prolong it. I think two points can be made in explaining the anomaly, that the prophet who most explicitly and for the most part the most successfully addressed the conditions of knowing and communicating in our time is still so largely without honor.

First, prophecy is a mug's game. Aeneas could have told McLuhan that. He had seen all the Roman future before him in his visit to the underworld, but whatever he saw there did him precious little good in what followed. The prophets of Israel were famously ineffectual in shaping the behavior of their people. Prophecy embodies a high and definite example of that style of telling the truth which assures that it will not be believed. (Prophets say many untrue things as well, McLuhan his share of them, and that is no help; but *everyone* speaks untruths, yet we don't make that fact an absolute disqualification for credibility.) Prophecy is very gratifying to the prophet, especially if and as he has the fortune to live to the stage of seeing his prophecies come true (though often the prophet's personal status and even health may be made to decline at the point of verification: Cassandra found that out quite clearly), but it is far from clear what useful social function the prophet plays. Does he shape behavior usefully? Evidence is hard to come by. The true usefulness of a prophet is for us to digest his theorized future *after the fact*, and it is early days yet to put McLuhan to this use.

There is a more interesting point. The intellectual domain that McLuhan inhabited is one that is unusually difficult to master satisfactorily. For it is striking that scholars who address the questions McLuhan did, whatever the historical period under review, find it hard to conduct their discussion of the history of the *conditions* of intellection in a way that satisfies the ordinary criteria of intellectual discourse. McLuhan, Ong, and Havelock knew one another and found solidarity in their mutual experience of marginalization, and it might almost be enough to explain that marginalization by some defect they shared. The problem runs deeper. The categories by which we *do* our intellectual business in the academic world are so deeply ingrained in us that to turn our power to relativize those categories, historicize them, and leave them as it were *sous rature*, intact but relativized, is, and *rightfully* is, unsettling and disturbing. Consequently, to work our way fairly into other mentalities is in the end a fantasy impossible of realization. It is no more possible than the task of imagining that I am someone I am not. In the end, a McLuhanite or Havelockian reconstruction of technology-influenced mentalities of other times is and will remain a fiction by the terms of the system of discourse in which it is practiced; "Plato's doctrine of the forms" is, by contrast, hard, cold, reassuring positivist fact. I say, "by contrast": that is, within the terms of our world of discourse, we may interpret Plato's texts to the point of extracting a doctrine from them, and we may show that the steps we take to do that are all valid. Reasonable minds may very well remark that the product, "Plato's doctrine of the forms," is something that Plato could not possibly recognize or approve of, but within the terms of our world of discourse, that does not matter and has not mattered – the transformations are licit ones, therefore the results are licit ones. The problem with the intellectual challenge of McLuhanism in all its forms is that it insists on asking us to perform transformations that our own senses tell us are illicit, to engage in a kind of magic thinking about the past or even about the immediate future. We may agree with every certainty that the newly literate Greeks were very different from the scholars of the era of the dawn of print, but we have not the tools to bring those two systems of discourse in line with each other. We have only a system of discourse of our own, time bound and technologically conditioned.[32]

And so we fall away from McLuhan's visions unpersuaded, and rightly unpersuaded, even as we accord him prophetic status and prophetic dishonor. If we are circumspect, we see that the problem is not unique to the history of communication media, but is also the underlying problem in the history of mentalities.[33] Whether a self-consciously postmodern reconstruction of mentalities will prove in the long run any more successful is perhaps to be doubted; if it succeeds, it will have been because it begins so self-consciously, so self-doubtingly – precisely the feature that makes such forms of investigation and discourse so rebarbative to the *bien pensant* cultural community beyond.

In short, I am saying two things about McLuhan: his work is of great value, but does not have the value it seems to have. It is instructive, stimulating and maddening – and perhaps most effective when most maddening. But its prophecies do not lend themselves to guide practical applications. If judged as myths, they are high-quality myths; if judged as history or sociology, they fail.

So if we find ourselves in a whirlwind of conflicting ideas and new technologies, what then is a better way to proceed? Clinging cautiously to older social institutions is bad for those institutions themselves; bellowing prophecies into the whirlwind persuades few and leads to no concrete advances. Both roles have their important functions and will find practitioners, but we may be forgiven for pressing on to seek out a *via media*.

For my last exemplar, let me come back and arrive where I started and know the place for the first time (so to speak). Cassiodorus suffered the indignity of serving as my dissertation topic and lent his name to my first book – quite passively in both cases.[34] I came to him in part because of a reputation that I later was at some pains to demolish, his reputation for having snatched declining classical civilization from the barbarians, locked it up in the cloister, and having taught the monks how to copy the classics – a Romantic image, and entirely untrue.[35] I did not realize at the time that I had stumbled upon someone with his own eerie appositeness to the issues I have been discussing here.

Cassiodorus belonged to that century or so of Latin Christian writers who were inventing Latin textual Christianity. He knew personally figures like Dionysius Exiguus, who founded canon law and calculated the dating scheme B.C./A.D.,[36] Eugippius of Naples, who produced the first one-volume edition of what one might call *The Essential Augustine*, and of course Boethius. Toward the end of a long career as statesman, Cassiodorus had in mind a very conservative educational program of innovation: the establishment of a Christian school (a "university," but the word is wildly anachronistic) at Rome, with the support of Pope Agapetus (535-36). Given his own way, Cassiodorus would have patronized this place into his declining years. It is important to note that he had in mind to found such a place, not because he thought it time to unseat the classics, but because he thought the classics could take care of themselves, and that it was Christian textual study that lacked funding. (I would argue that such Christian textual study needed to be invented before it could be lacking in support, and it was Cassiodorus' own age that was more or less finishing the job of invention.) But war broke out, the war Justinian fought to restore Italy to the Roman Empire, the war that shattered Italian political unity for the next thirteen hundred (or more?) years, and Cassiodorus found himself an honored guest, that is to say a political refugee, in Constantinople, writing a commentary on the Book of Psalms. When the war ended, he returned to Italy, not to any of the important cities where he had spent his career, but to his remote Calabrian estate of Vivarium, where he had founded a monastery on the family property. There ca. 554 he picked up where he had left off twenty years earlier, with what is visibly and expressly the same intellectual project that he had thought to pursue at Rome. His *Institutes* are the intellectual schematic diagram of that project and a precious piece of evidence for early medieval Christian Latin culture.

In many ways, the project there was a misfire. If it has been made out to be a turning point, it is because our narratives of the past *insist* on having turning points. There is no sign that Cassiodorus did a very effective job at inculcating Christian textual culture into his monks. He left Pelagius's own Paul commentary to be expurgated after his example (he did Romans himself, left the rest for them), and they made a cheerful hash of it, with the engaging result that this detailed commentary on Paul's epistles, still full to brim with Pelagian assumptions and interpretations, but sanitized of the most objectionable slogans, went forth into the Middle Ages as though it had a guarantee of orthodoxy about it, and it boasted stray quotations here and there from Augustine: in this way, Augustine was made the unwilling and unconscious guarantor of the survival of Pelagius' ideas in this particular pervasive form.[37] The last we see of Cassiodorus, he is still trying to train his monks as scribes by compiling a treatise on spelling, but the enterprise seems to have gone for naught: a few years after his death, the monks are seen squabbling with the local bishop and their community subsides into oppressed obscurity. Enough copies of Cassiodorus' works survived to circulate in the Middle Ages, with varying effect.[38] It was at least 150 years after his death before serious monastic scribal culture took root in Britain, and the spread thereafter was slow and uneven. In many important respects Cassiodorus was a failure.

I have come also to see that this deflated savior of western civilization I learned to mistrust when young had nevertheless had the right idea. He did not despise the new, but used it wholeheartedly; he did not reject old social institutions, but found new ways to adapt them, and when thwarted one way, found another, odder but still functional, way to use them; and he did not tarry to prophesy a new age of learning and wisdom. Most of all, he did things. The larger scheme within which he did them was not widely imitated, nor was it imitable. Even to say this is to reveal what is so often wrong about our expectations of ourselves and our cultural heroes: we dream of strong leaders, men on white horses, people who change history. Those are the fools and the demons of our past. The most effective change is that wielded by those who do not expect to create or manipulate a closed system, but those who recognize that effective change takes place in an open system, in one where it is the accumulation of shrewd and collaborative actions of the many that generates unexpected harmony. The monastic Latin Middle Ages were predicted by no one, chosen by no one, built by no visionary hand.[39] At a distance we can all argue how we could have built a better Middle Ages. But that neglects the true merit of an age that out of unpromising materials achieved far more than it had reason to expect, and did so because it had stumbled upon forms of enhancing and institutionalizing autonomy and local responsibility, and if it is not obvious that I am thinking here of the large social movements conventionally labeled "feudalism" and "monasticism," then in just that failure of obviousness is our failure to imagine successfully how complex societies really are, how slowly they change, and how impressive coherent change of any kind really is.

So where does that leave us? By implicitly excluding the pragmatics of the old (Trithemius) and the theoretics of the new (McLuhan), I consciously rule out two forms of behavior that academics in particular are fond of. What the partisans of the book are less instinctively good at is just the pragmatics of the new. I suggest that Trithemius makes a good patron saint for our conservatives, and McLuhan an equally good patron saint for our theoreticians. In Cassiodorus, I would rather find not a patron saint, but a colleague, a practitioner who innovated, failed, innovated again, and did so on a scale and with a modesty of purpose that guaranteed him not only that he would eventually suffer the indignity of a young whippersnapper paying him the tribute of a debunking, but also that an older, more subdued practitioner of the new would recognize him at last as a colleague. Cassiodorus solved nothing: that is his virtue.

I mean by this construction no disrespect, I should emphasize, for "theory," but perhaps a repositioning. When the great lady *Philosophia* appears in Boethius' chamber, the Greek letters pi and theta on her garment and the ladder ascending from the former to the latter inscribe the precept that *Theoria* follows on *Praxis*. A true pragmatics is not theoryless, but seeks indeed the apotheosis of theory arising out of practice. The pragmatician is the person who rather hopes that at the end of the day the morning's theory will not have been vindicated but enhanced, even transformed, ready to reinvigorate practice and at the same time ready to be transformed again.

So Cassiodorus found ways to use the modern[40] codex book to display the novel kinds of texts of his time.[41] We cannot now reconstruct fairly just how novel, just how annoying, what he did might have seemed. The younger Cassiodorus seems as much a man of his time as the elaborately mannerist Ennodius, as the elaborately erudite Boethius; the older Cassiodorus goes clearly beyond their traditionalism, and at any rate he abandoned their world of civil and ecclesiastical careers for a different kind of textual life. Would Boethius have gone to live in a monastery on the Ionian Sea? Ennodius, a social climber on the fringes of Boethius' circles, wrote his own educational prescription for young men of his time:[42] to read Ennodius side by side with Cassiodorus is to see the difference between old and new in a single generation.

It also seems to me no coincidence that Cassiodorus is a name

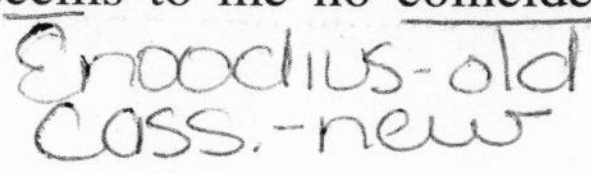

more readily recognized by graduates of library schools than by Ph.D.'s. For the task he undertook, of imposing the most transparent possible intellectual organization on the body of texts before him, is quintessentially that of the librarian. In ages when knowledge was scarce, those who created it were the heroes of the tribe, and librarians their acolytes. But in an age of information overload, production and even dissemination of knowledge will be child's play. Publishers hope that I will still be willing to pay for special pieces of information in the future, but I wonder if they are not too optimistic, not too much like Trithemius hanging on desperately to an obsolete social structure. What I am sure that I *will* be willing to pay for as the oceans of data lap at my door is help in filtering through that flood to suit my needs. Of the participants in the production, dissemination, and consumption of knowledge today, it is the librarians who have already made that kind of skill their specialty. The librarians of the world have, moreover, already led the way, for academics at least, into the new information environment, not least because they are caught between rising demand from their customers (faculty and students) and rising supply *and* prices from their suppliers, and so have already been making reality-based decisions about ownership versus access, print versus electronic, and so on. In short, they are just now our leading pragmatists.[43] Can we imagine a time in our universities when the librarians are the well-paid principals and the teachers their mere acolytes in a distribution chain? I do not think we can or should rule out that possibility for a moment.

Pragmatism is a difficult discipline. To reconstruct *ourselves* to fit the world in which we find ourselves is often a distasteful chore. I like to invoke the image of Saint Jerome in his study, that familiar topic of Renaissance painting. We look at one of these paintings and even today, those of us who inhabit traditional academic fields (or even only feel a nostalgia for them) find it easy to project ourselves into them. In my favorite, that of Antonello da Messina in the National Gallery in London, recent scholarship sees that the projection of present into the past was already part of the original program;[44] what is presented as Jerome in his study is also probably a flattering implied portrait of the polymath cardinal Nicholas of Cusa. To project ourselves into the same setting is too easy; likewise, when I read the familiar lines of Machiavelli about putting on the robes of state and retreating to study the classics of an evening,[45] I am too easily seduced into thinking that my own relation to these old texts is a similar one. The difficulty is to recognize that we are *already* impossibly far from Jerome and even impossibly far from the Renaissance, and that our work lies elsewhere.[46]

Perhaps one way to make that self-awareness easier is to make ourselves deliberately more conscious of the unnaturalness of this whole affair our culture has had with books. We long ago ceased to see the oddity of textuality and its institutions – publishers who produce books, libraries who treasure and make them available, scholars who pass on the mystic arts of interpretation to students. Is it not strange that we take the spoken word, the most insubstantial of human creations, and try through textuality to freeze it forever; and again, try to give the frozen words of those who are dead and gone, or at least far absent, control over our own experience of the lived here and now? Cultural continuity resides in memory, which is to say, in the keeping in mind of that which does *not* exist, not any longer. That is an extraordinary way to be human, and we may very well find someday a species in a remote corner of the galaxy that manages something like humanness without that elaborate construction of continuity. For now, perhaps it suffices to realize that everything we do in this line has something of the Rube Goldberg construction about it. Every now and then the complex and gawky constructions will be rebuilt, may perhaps even partially collapse of their own gaudiness. The genuine spirit of our culture is not expressed in applying small pieces of cellotape to hold together the structure we have received, but in pitching in joyously to its ongoing reconstruction. In that vein, I would suggest that for all the passion and affection I bring to books, I have very little business caring for the future of the book. Books are only secondary bearers of culture. "Western civilization" (or whatever other allegorical creature we cook up to embody our self-esteem) is not something to be cherished. "Western civilization" is us, and making it and remaking it is our job. The thought that we have come here in a generation that will have as many opportunities to botch the job as we will have had might be frightening – or it might, better, be exhilarating.

Books are secondary
civilization is in us.

Notes

[1] This utilitarian information comes from the network itself, from the useful service called Edupage, dated May 26, 1994.

[2] "Fragment Laurentien", in L. Duchesne, *Le Liber Pontificalis* (Paris, 1886, tome premier: 14).

[3] The manuscript is Verona XXII (20); see Lowe (1947) and the discussion at Duchesne, (*ib.*: xxx-xxxi); the same manuscript contains two other patristic collections of lives of worthies (those of Jerome and Gennadius) and then a miscellany of documents relating to ecclesiastical controversies of the early sixth century germane to those in which Symmachus found himself entangled.

[4] See the pathbreaking work of Vessey (1988; 1991: 341-54; 1993a: 135-45; 1993b: 175-213) and O'Donnell (1994: 19-31).

[5] See Richards (1979: 69-99). The documents in question have still not had editions more recent than the eighteenth century and would repay closer study.

[6] Even scripture itself was gaining new *textual* status as a written artifact in this period. Leaving aside the important contribution of Jerome, self-constructing as the Christian Origen (see Vessey 1993a), in fixing scripture in Latin and surrounding it with commentary, a recent study by Hahneman (1992) argues strongly that even the so-called Muratorian Canon is no older than the late fourth century, and with that downward redating all the earliest catalogs of the Christian scriptural canon date to no earlier than the fourth century, and only two of those (Eusebius and the Codex Claromontanus) come from earlier than A.D. 350. In a Latin world in which there was no such thing as a "Bible" (that is, a complete collection of scriptural books in one set of covers – this was apparently first seen in Latin at Cassiodorus's monastery in the mid-sixth century and the oldest surviving example is the Codex Amiatinus that was in some way modeled on Cassiodorus's own work – see O'Donnell 1979: 206-7), a good handlist of canonical books was a vital tool for acquiring accurate knowledge, but it only became vital when the written text and not the written-text-as-mediated-by-authorized-interpreter began to take on a central position of its own.

[7] See O'Donnell (1993).

[8] The phrase of course is that of Stock (1982).

[9] That sixth-century Verona fragment is part of a small, famous collection rediscovered in that city in the early eighteenth century by Scipio Maffei, but it is reasonable to assume that the oldest continually managed collection of books in the Latin world is that of the Vatican Library.

[10] On the shaping of medieval libraries, see McKitterick (1989: 165-210).

[11] The roots of our ideologies of knowledge, especially in their educational application, in late antique neo-Platonism, deserve to be better understood; the seminal work is Hadot (1984).

[12] The classic modern studies are Febvre and Martin (1958), McLuhan (1962), Eisenstein (1979, 1983), and now again Martin (1988) takes a broader view with pride of place for printing (1988); see also next note.

[13] The important exception is Giesecke (1991); of great interest also is the less-focused but rich collection of studies of Milde and Schuder (eds.) (1988).

[14] Giesecke (1991: 705, n. 3) quotes Ong (1987: 82): "Es wird die meisten Menschen sehr verwundern daß die gleichen Einwände, die heute gewöhnlich gegen Computer vorgebracht werden, von Plato in *Phaidros* und im *Siebten Brief* gegen das Schreiben angeführt wurden."

[15] Steinberg (1955: 44).

[16] There is an irony here that should not be missed. In early 1993, a small and select collection of precious books from the Vatican Library traveled to the United States for an exhibit at the Library of Congress. I was among the few fortunate thousands who saw the books while they were there, and vividly recall the display of the first page of the Book of the Apocalypse in the Urbino Bible just as I came into the exhibit hall. But that is now for me only a memory, and even from San Marino the book itself is many miles away and access is restricted. It is accordingly of great value that the Library of Congress undertook to make digitized images of the book pages on display in its exhibit and to make them available on the Internet. That very page of the Urbino Bible may now be consulted from any suitably connected place on any of the seven continents (follow the trail to "Vatican Library," then "The City Recovers," and finally "Urbino Bible"). On a properly equipped machine, the image can be enlarged, cropped, and enlarged again, with remarkable accuracy of detail: I have seen it enlarged on a projection screen to several times its original size with brilliant representation of the fine details of manuscript painting. Even, I think, Duke Federigo would be impressed; though I grant that both the aesthetic and the devotional effect are somewhat swamped by the technological wizardry.

[17] Thus Vat. Urb. lat. 353 contains seven works, of which at least four are copied from editions published in 1474 and 1475, and the same could be true of the other three works the manuscript contains; it was written for the Duke of Urbino between 1474 and 1482 (details apud Reeve, see next note).

[18] Reeve (1983); see also Bühler (1960: 34-39), still praised by Reeve, but Bühler's generalization (p. 16: "experience has taught me that every manuscript to the second half of the fifteenth century is potentially and often without question a copy of some incunable") is tantalizing but still unsupported. See Lülfing (1981) and Lutz (1975: 129-38) (describing such miscellaneous copies in the Beinecke Library at Yale).

[19] Derolez (1979) and especially Derolez (1986: 140-60).

[20] See Hartmann (ed.) (1942-1974).

[21] See Monfasani (1988); I owe this reference to Brian Ogilvie of the University of Chicago.

[22] See Giesecke (1991: 169-75).

[23] Quoted from Minnis and Scott (1988: 269); Minnis instances the work of A. Mary and R. Rouse, now conveniently available in Rouse and Rouse (1991), who have shown at length how the distinctive applications of print to the organization of knowledge were often anticipated by indices and concordances in medieval manuscripts, devices that needed print for full realization of their potential.

[24] The most meticulous study I have found on evidence for this practice is Ker (1954); I have profited as well from discussing the subject with learned friends who handle incunables all the time, especially G.N. Knauer and Barbara Halporn (the latter points out that the Amerbach letters "indicate that he and Koberger had a lot of copies made for their use in preparing text for the press. In the publication of the Bible with commentary of Hugo of St. Cher they ran into a lot of heavy weather with the lending monastieries because they worried about not getting their MSS back or getting them back damaged" [personal communication, 9/ 93] – which suggests that care for the old was common as long as the old had value in itself). Nicholson Baker, in the *New Yorker* (April 4, 1994: 68 ff), attacks the destruction of the old card catalogs in contemporary libraries in just the terms that students of the Renaissance used for the destruction of old manuscripts in the sixteenth century. In both cases, the critic values the old cultural artifact as a thing in itself, full of information that neither producer nor owner ever meant to be there. What was a transparent guide, in the case of the manuscript of Aristotle, to the wisdom of the ancients, and in the case of the card catalog, to the contents of a building's collection, becomes for the humanist scholar an opaque and fascinating cultural phenomenon in its own right. One may accept the validity of the humanist approach while refraining from condemning others for not cramming their attics with *every* cultural artifact ever produced.

[25] K. Arnold (ed.), with introduction and German translation (Würzburg, 1973). For a more cautious reading of this text than that ventured here, see Brann (1982: 144-74).

[26] *De laude scriptorum*: 7; cf. also chapter 1.

[27] *Ib.*

[28] *Ib.*: 5-6; so a thousand years earlier, Cassiodorus, *Institutiones* 1.30: "tot enim vulnera Satanas accipit, quot antiquarius Domini verba describit."

[29] Giesecke (1991: 182 and 229).

[30] To name only a few favorites by which I have been influenced, see Chartier (1987), Hunt (1993), Jardine (1993), and Darnton (1982).

[31] McLuhan (1962) contained all *in nuce*, while McLuhan (1964) was the explicit *summa* and McLuhan (1967) was as it were the *summa pauperum* of this cult.

[32] Here is the point to acknowledge that I have had much profit in reading and rereading Lanham (1993), which I have reviewed in *Bryn Mawr Classical Review* 94.6.13; Lanham is a theoretician of the new who has learned much from McLuhan's example, and from deeper springs of the rhetorical tradition that originate in ancient Athens as well.

[33] The last generation or so of patristic scholars has worked very hard indeed to figure out what a "miracle" is, and the results have been, candidly, a massive failure. Gregory the Great has scandalized the moderns with especial effectiveness here; the

best study, a glorious failure past which successors make no real advance, is Boglioni (1974: 1): Brown (1981: especially 17-22), on what he calls the "two-tiered model" that has distorted modern appreciation, puts the difficulties well; best is Rousselle (1990), who succeeds by refusing to address the question of miracle in its familiar form and observing instead structures of practice.

[34] See O'Donnell (1979).

[35] In its extreme form, the view appears in Hammer (1944-1945); but the *expectation* that Cassiodorus would be some such figure implicitly underlies the magisterial review of my book by Cameron (1981), and indeed a decade later, in her textbook Cameron (1993: 42, in a sentence footnoted with reference to my book) reverts to the old orthodoxy and says exactly what she knows to be untrue. I have also had the experience of hearing the book praised publicly by an eminent scholar who went on to say that it was a very "depressing" book. Clearly, the traditional Cassiodorus fills a *need* in our mental furniture of his time of transition, a need that persists beyond all reasonable refutation.

[36] Cassiodorus is himself apparently the first figure we know of to have used that scheme, in a treatise on calculating the date of Easter, but it was Bede who put it into general circulation a century and a half later.

[37] Johnson (1989).

[38] So Benedict Biscop found copies of some books (including the Bible that in some way inspired the *Codex Amiatinus*) in Rome to take back to Northumbria, while at the Carolingian monastery of Murbach, Cassiodorus' *Institutes* provided a basis for the library catalog: see O'Donnell (1979: 238-55).

[39] One may debate the self-consciousness of reformers like Charlemagne and Alcuin, but best to see now Wright (1982) for implicit sober critique of the latter and the *destructive* power of his vision of "Latin".

[40] The word is apposite; Cassiodorus is the first figure we know of to use the word *modernus* in a way approximating our modern sense: see Freund (1957).

[41] Two examples may be given: the way marginal *notae* are used to tag passages in his Psalm commentary for their relevance to the study of various aspects of the seven liberal arts (these may be seen, in a grossly inadequate edition, in the Corpus Christianorum edition of that commentary); and in the way the mnemonic illustrations are used in the *Institutes* to organize material on the page: see Troncarelli (1986: 22-58).

[42] Ennodius, opusc. 6, *Paraenesis didascalica* (MGH ed.: 310-15).

[43] Take, for example, Okerson (1994): the map is not the territory, but creation of a good map (and this directory is an excellent map) often has the effect of giving the territory a self-conscious identity and opening it up to exploration by many others.

[44] Jolly (1982) arguing from details of the cardinalatial costume in which Jerome is portrayed.

[45] De Grazia (1989) has the great merit of disiconification and hence (paradoxically) perilously enriches our sense of the possibilities of self-identification with the Florentine.

46 Such an iconic representation of the scholar has its uses. Can we imagine a future in which the professor becomes a variety of software, an icon you click on in order to get access to the network of information he surveys? That future is close at hand: for description and demonstration of such a pedagogy as it is now possible and practiced, see http://ccat.sas.upenn.edu/teachdemo.

References

BOGLIONI, P.
1974 "Miracle et nature chez Grégroire le Grand," *Cahiers d'études médiévales*, Montréal.

BRANN, N.L.
1982 *The Abbot Trithemius (1462-1516): The Renaissance of Monastic Humanism*, Leiden.

BROWN, P.
1981 *The Cult of the Saint*s, Chicago.

BÜHLER, C.F.
1960 *The Fifteenth-Century Book*, Philadelphia.

CAMERON, A.
1981 "Cassiodorus deflated," *Journal of Roman Studies*, 71: 183-86.
1993 *The Mediterranean World in Late Antiquity AD 395-600*, London.

CHARTIER, R.
1987 *The Cultural Uses of Print in Early Modern France*, Princeton.

DARNTON, R.
1982 *The Literary Underground of the Old Regime*, Cambridge (Mass.).

DE GRAZIA, S.
1989 *Machiavelli in Hell*, New York.

DEROLEZ, A.
1979 *The Library of Raphael de Marcatellis, Abbot of St. Bavon's, Ghent, 1437-1508*, Ghent.
1986 "The copying of printed books for humanistic bibliophiles in the fifteenth century," in *From Script to Book: A Symposium*, Odense.

DUCHESNE, L.
1886 *Le Liber Pontificalis*, Paris.

EISENSTEIN, E.
1979 *The Printing Press as an Agent of Change*, Cambridge, 2 vols.
1983 *The Printing Revolution in Early Modern Europe*, Cambridge.

FEBVRE, L., AND MARTIN, H.-J.
1958 *L'apparition du livre*, Paris.

FREUND, W.
1957 *Modernus und andere Zeitbegriffe des Mittelalters*, Köln and Graz.

GIESECKE, M.
1991 *Der Buchdruck in der frühen Neuzeit: Eine historische Fallstudie*, Darmstadt.

HADOT, I.
1984, *Arts libéraux et philosophie dans la pensée antique*, Paris.

HAHNEMAN, G.
1992 *The Muratorian Fragment and the Development of the Canon*, Oxford.

HAMMER, J.
1944-1945 "Cassiodorus, the saviour of Western civilization," *Bulletin of the Polish Institute of Arts and Sciences in America*, 3: 369-84.

HARTMANN, A. (ED.)
1942-1974 *Die Amerbachkorrespondenz*, Basel, 8 vols.

HUNT, L. (ED.)
1993 *The Invention of Pornography*, New York.

JARDINE, L.
1993 *Erasmus, Man of Letters*, Princeton.

JOHNSON, D.W.
1989 "Purging the poison: The revision of Pelagius' Pauline commentaries by Cassiodorus and his students," Princeton Theological Seminary, Ph.D. thesis.

JOLLY, P.H.
1982 "Antonello da Messina's 'St. Jerome in his study': A disguised portrait?", *Burlington Magazine*, 124: 27-29.

KER, N.R.
1954, *Pastedowns in Oxford Bindings with a Survey of Oxford Binding c. 1515-1620*, Oxford.

LANHAM, R.
1993 *The Electronic Word*, Chicago.

LOWE, E.A.
1947 *Codices Latini Antiquiores 4.490*, Oxford.

LÜLFING, H.
1981 "Die Fortdauer der handschriftlichen Buchherstellung nach der Erfindung des Buchdrucks. Ein buchgeschichtliches Problem," in L. Hellinga and H. Härtel (eds.), *Buch und Text im 15. Jahrhundert*, Hamburg: 17-26.

LUTZ, C.E.
1975 "Manuscripts copied from printed books," in C.E. Cora, *Essays on Manuscripts and Rare Books*, Hamden: 129-38.

MARTIN, H.-J.
1988 *Histoire et pouvoirs de l'écrit*, Paris.

MCKITTERICK, R.
1989 *The Carolingians and the Written Word*, Cambridge.

MCLUHAN, M.
1962 *The Gutenberg Galaxy*, Toronto.
1964 *Understanding Media*, New York.
1967 *The Medium Is the Message*, New York

MILDE, W., AND SCHUDER W. (EDS.)
1988 *De captu lectoris: Wirkungen des Buches im 15. und 16. Jahrhundert*, Berlin.

MINNIS, A., AND SCOTT, A.B.
1988 *Medieval Literary Theory and Criticism c. 1100-c. 1375*, Oxford.

MONFASANI, J.
1988 "The first call for press censorship: Niccolo Perotti, Giovanni Andrea Bussi, Antonio Moreto, and the editing of Pliny's natural history," *Renaissance Quarterly*, 41: 1-31.

O'DONNELL, J.
1979 *Cassiodorus*, Berkeley.
1993 "St. Augustine to NREN: The tree of knowledge and how it grows," *The Serials Librarian*, 23, 3/4: 21-41.
1994 "The virtual library: An idea whose time has passed," in Okerson/Mogge (eds.) (1994): 19-31.

OKERSON, A.L. (ED.)
1994 *Directory of Electronic Journals, Newsletters, and Academic Discussion Lists*, Washington: Association of Research Libraries, 4th edition.

OKERSON, A.L., AND MOGGE (EDS.)
1994 *Gateways, Gatekeepers... and Roles in the Information Omniverse*, Washington.

ONG, W.
1987 *Oralität und Literalität. Die Technologisierung des Wortes*, Opland.

REEVE, M.D.
1983 "Manuscripts copied from printed books," in J.B. Trapp (ed.), *Manuscripts in the Fifty Years After the Invention of Printing*, London: 12-20.

RICHARDS, J.
1979 *The Popes and the Papacy in the Early Middle Ages, 476-752*, London.

ROUSE, M.A. AND ROUSE, R.H.
1991 *Authentic Witnesses: Approaches to Medieval Texts and Manuscripts*, Notre Dame, Ind.

ROUSSELLE, A.
1990 *Croire et Guérir: la foi en Gaule dans l'Antiquité tardive*, Paris.

STEINBERG, S.H.
1955 *Five Hundred Years of Printing*, Harmondsworth.

STEINER, G.
1963/1970 "On reading Marshall McLuhan," *Language and Silence*, New York.

STOCK, B.
1982 *The Implications of Literacy*, Princeton.

TRONCARELLI, F.
1986 "Con la mano del cuore. L'arte della memoria nei codici di Cassiodoro," *Quaderni medievali*, 22.

VESSEY, M.
1988 "Ideas of Christian writing in late Roman Gaul," Oxford, Ph.D. thesis, unpubl.
1991 "Patristics and literary history," *Journal of Literature and Theology*, 5.
1993a "Jerome's Origen: The making of a Christian literary *Persona*," *Studia Patristica*, 28, Leuven.
1993b "Conference and confession: Literary pragmatics in Augustine's 'Apologia contra Hieronymum,'" *Journal of Early Christian Studies*, 1.

WRIGHT, R.
1982 *Later Latin and Early Romance*, Liverpool.

Paul Duguid

MATERIAL MATTERS: THE PAST AND FUTUROLOGY OF THE BOOK

1. Goodbye the book?

With barely the flick of a digital switch, the long era of the "coming of the book" appears to have given way to the brief period of its going.[1] For it is going, predictions insist, like the telegram, the Bakelite phone, the vinyl record, or the analog computer before it. United only in a shared sense of inevitability, gloomy bibliophiles and triumphant technophiles wave the book goodbye.[2] As elegies are read, eyes turn from history to the future. To be concerned with the past risks appearing like Shakespeare's Salisbury, vainly trying to "call back yesterday, bid time return," while to talk about the continued relevance of the book can single you out as a modern Erewhonian.[3]

I want to argue, however, that there are good reasons beyond either nostalgia or an insurmountable hatred of technology to question the apparent choice between leaping to the new or drowning with the old. If nothing else, futurologists do have a habit of announcing both deaths and births prematurely. Talking machines, domestic robots, automated language translators, and a host of other "new technologies" have, for forty years or more, been perennial examples of "vaporware," always coming yet never coming "within the next decade." Even the paperless office, long on the timetable, still shows little sign of arriving. Indeed, many digital offices can't even do without the typewriter, though its "Nunc Dimittis" was sung years ago. The forward thrust of predictions tends to insist that we don't look back. But past predictions, particularly failed predictions like these, deserve more attention than they get. The point of reexamining them, though, is not to gloat. Rather, it's to understand where predictions go wrong.

With technological predictions, I suggest, assumptions about the relation between past and future, on the one hand, and simplicity and complexity, on the other, make claims more plausible than they should be.[4] If we accept the past as simple and the future as complex, we tend not to question the idea that complex new technologies will sweep away their simple predecessors. So, for example, in 1938 the *New York Times* could easily assume that the heavily engineered typewriter would do away with the simple pencil (Petrosky 1990: 331).

Or take, as another example, the matter of the door. Since the twenties, one way people have known they were watching a film about "the future" (and not merely about people who reveled in Spandex *avant la lettre*) was the inevitable presence of sliding doors. The supersession of the simple hinge by automated sliding technology long ago became a visual synecdoche for the triumph of the future. Yet while the sliding door still appears on the futurological screen, the millennia-old manual hinge endures all around us (even on our laptop computers and cell phones). One reason it survives, I suggest, is that despite its technological simplicity, time has given the hinge a rich social complexity that those who foresee its imminent demise fail to appreciate.[5] Hinged doors, after all, are not just to be passed through; they communicate polysemiously. We can, for instance, expressively throw them open or slam them shut, hold them or let them swing, leave them ajar and hide behind them, satisfyingly kick, punch, or shoulder them, triumphantly barge them open or defiantly prop them shut.

The survival of pencils and hinges (and even typewriters), long after the development of alternatives, argues that, in forecasting technological conquests and describing the march of technological complexity, we have a tendency to underestimate what Raymond Williams (1974) calls the "social-material complex" of which technologies are only a part. Like an exasperated gardener, we snip triumphantly at the exposed plant, forgetting how extensive established roots can be. Pencil and hinge survive technological cuts on the strength of their deep social resourcefulness. And for similar reasons, we may find that the simple hinged book will prove as enduring. The closed cover, turned page, broken spine, serial form, immutable text, revealing heft, distinctive formats, handy size, and so on offer their own deep-rooted and resilient combination of technology and social process and continue to provide unrivaled signifying matter.[6]

So, to explore issues concerning the past and the futurology of the book, I start from the simple fact that, despite lugubrious elegies and triumphant dismissals, the book, like the hinge, is still here. Its continued presence raises these related issues of the resilience of artifacts and the frailty of predictions and allows me to suggest that to design robust new artifacts (design being itself an act of prediction): it may be important not to dismiss survival as cussed and irrelevant resistance, but instead to consider, in social and historical terms, the sources of endurance.

Unfortunately, the necessary task of addressing the relation between old and new technologies can be difficult. If, as Benjamin (1969: 257) suggests, the Angel of History goes backward into the future, "face turned towards the past" and wreckage piling at its feet, technology's angel usually advances facing determinedly the other way, trying to sweep objects and objections from its path.[7] There is much to be gained, I believe, from getting the two angels to see eye to eye. Unfortunately, as I shall argue, this has recently become only more difficult. Technology's angel is engaged in a passing flirtation with "critical theory," which harbors much of what Jameson calls postmodernism's "deafness to history." To add deafness to blindness is not what McLuhan expected when he foretold a return to the synergy of the auditory and the visual, though it may explain why the volume of debate and, in particular, of the demonization of the book has, as a result of this flirtation, been raised a notch or two.[8]

In particular, any idea that old technologies can tell us anything about new ones has been discouraged by two futurological tropes (supported in varying degrees by critical theory) that I intend to examine in some detail. The first is the notion of *supersession* – the idea that each new technological type vanquishes or subsumes its predecessors: "This will kill that," in the words of Victor Hugo's archdeacon that echo through debates about the book and information technology. The second is the claim of *liberation*, the argument or assumption that the pursuit of new information technologies is simultaneously a righteous pursuit of liberty. Liberationists hold, as another much-quoted aphorism has it, that "information wants to be free" and that new technology is going to free it. The book, by contrast, appears never to have shaken off its restrictive medieval chains.

Together, ideas of supersession and liberation present a plausibly united front. But this front, I want to suggest, conceals some significant conflicts. First, cultural arguments for supersession lean heavily on the language of postmodernism, while liberationists' arguments about emancipation are laden with the ideas of postmodernism's great antipathy, "the enlightenment project." And second, technological ideas of supersession understandably expect progress through technology, while liberation looks for freedom from it.

The latter conflict in particular reflects, I go on to claim, uncertainty about relations between form and content, information and technology. In general, both supersession and liberation assume that information stands aloof from the technology that carries it. Whereas I argue that if books can be thought of as "containing" and even imprisoning information, that information must, in the last analysis, be understood as inescapably a product of bookmaking. Books, I conclude, are not a hide bound alternative to the freedoms of the multiply linked items of hypertext, but an important social, political, and historical solution to problems raised by the particularity of such linked items.

So in the end, I suggest, to offer serious alternatives to the book, we need first to understand and even to replicate aspects of its social and material complexity. Indeed, for a while yet, it will probably be much more productive to go by the book than to go on insistently but ineffectually repeating "goodbye."

2. The supersession of the book

The idea of supersession is never too far from discussions of the book, where the words of Hugo's archdeacon are repeated again and again: "This will kill that. The book will kill the building... The press will kill the church... printing will kill architecture." (Hugo 1978: 188-189). And though the book notably did not "kill" architecture, these words are now read against it. The gloom of the archdeacon is transformed into the triumph of the digerati: computer architecture is set to take revenge. Thus it seems fitting that the Dean of Architecture at MIT should envisage a future in which the book will exist only as a sort of methadone treatment, irrelevant except to those "addicted to the look and feel of tree flakes encased in dead cow (and prepared to pay for it)" (Mitchell 1955).[9]

Of course, futurological predictions that the past is slipping into irrelevance encompass much more than just books. Following Toffler's announcement that society was crossing the greatest divide since barbarism gave way to civilization (a change driven, as he saw it, by the "great growling engine of technology"), the rhetoric of technological revolution and dismissals of the *ancien régime* have become quite unexceptional. Talk of breaks and disconnections, of paradigm shifts and social transformations, of waves and generations, and of disjunctions between old and new abounds. It's now merely a reflex, more obligatory than provocative, for Negroponte to tell us we're entering a "radically new culture" propelled by the technological movement from "atoms to bits." Under the cumulative weight of these proclamations, it becomes increasingly easy to believe that to fall behind in the technological race is to fall behind in the human race. Technology's path, in this view, is "inevitable and unavoidable," Negroponte (1995: 4) tells us.[10] To demur or look back could be a symptom of "lunacy," according to Lanham (1994: 23), of isolation "in a quaint museum of the intellect," in the view of Feigenbaum and McCorduck (1983), or of clinical "future shock," those morbid symptoms of the inadequate individual in the face of progress (Toffler 1971: 21).[11]

But if the reach of this revolution concerns humanity as a whole, the book nonetheless forms an important centerpiece. Nor is it merely a symbol of reaction. Accepted by many as an "agent of change" in the Gutenberg revolution, the book is easily cast as a force of reaction in the information one.[12] Its material lineaments stand accused of foisting a vast amount of ideological baggage on innocent people. Thus Landow (1992) sees its "center and margin, hierarchy and linearity" as fostering a malign "conceptual system." The book is something, he insists with some urgency, "we must abandon" in order to go through "this paradigm shift, which marks a revolution in human thought."

In such accounts of a textual revolution, voices of critical theorists and postmodernists join those of technologists in proclaiming supersession. Undoubtedly, they are well suited for this role, for, in Jameson's words (1994: ix), postmodernism "looks for breaks" and when it finds them it usually portrays them in suitably supersessive terms. Thus Olsen, who is credited with the first use of "postmodern," sought complete secession from the past: "had we not, ourselves (I mean postmodern man) better just leave such things behind us?" (Olsen, quoted in Ford 1995). More famously, Lyotard (1979: 3) announced the "postmodern condition" by unequivocally dismissing precedent: "the status of knowledge is altered... the general situation is one of temporal disjunction." Perhaps nowhere is the sense that culturally the past has been left behind more evident than in Baudrillard's writing, which repeats on page after page that things are "no longer," "no more," "never again," the way they were: "*ne... plus,*" "*ne... plus,*" "*ne... plus*" echoes through his writing.[13]

"Only disconnect" seems to have become the united rallying cry of contemporary cultural and technological theorists alike, and this apparent convergence is sometimes offered as independent and cumulative evidence of an epistemological or even ontological shift. I contend, however, that it is more a case of coincidence and opportunism.

To understand what drives the claims of both technologists and compatible cultural theorists, we should notice that, while recalling the archdeacon's sense of patricide, they invert his attitude toward it. His was a cry of loss and regret. These new cries of supersession are, to the contrary, triumphantly dismissive. They celebrate escape from the clutches of the past and in so doing reveal that most assertions of supersession are at base declarations of independence. This desire to secede from history and set to work on a newly cleaned *tabula rasa* involves both settling accounts with the old and selling accounts of the new.

To take the latter first, claims of supersession are, above all else, a significant marketing ploy. Rapid technological development has increased pressure to sell the new on the heels of the old, no matter how durable the old. Sales departments no longer offer just a new car, but a new type of car. The new, by implication, doesn't merely replace the old; it supersedes it. The recurrent advertising theme of a "revolution in technology" insists that the machine we have is out of date and the one we need is in the showroom. In the process, establishing a break to reestablish year one of the postrevolutionary era both distracts from the resilience of the old and neatly bids up the future of the new, as if to claim, so Henry James noted in apostrophizing the ever-renewed "New World," that "since you had no past, you're going in for a magnificent, compensatory future" (James 1987: 66).[14]

We should not be too surprised, then, to find technological debate opportunistically embracing the idea of supersession. And we should also acknowledge that intellectual movements, too, need to exploit their own short model years with all the energy of a sales force. The "posts" have indeed promoted themselves as a revolutionary departure from a narcoleptic past. And as with technological marketing, such promotions have dealt handily with much of history's awkward clutter. An assertion of postmodernity promises, as Jameson (1994: xiv) points out, "to get rid of whatever you found confining, unsatisfying, or boring about the modern, modernism, or modernity." History can undoubtedly be one of those confining issues, and facets of postmodernism attempt to cast it off in the name of *posthistoire*.[15] But escape is never easy. Dismissals of history always recall the history of dismissal. Claims of supersession have, in fact, a well-documented history mapped by, among others, Walter Jackson Bate (1970), Harold Bloom (1975), Raymond Williams (1973), and Stephen Toulmin (1972).[16]

Bate's study (1970: 4 *passim*) traces various strategies for dealing with the "burden of the past," and claims of supersession and new beginnings are among the most significant. Moreover, Bate notes an intriguing relation between such cultural claims and technological innovation. He suggests that whenever techniques of cultural preservation (the development of printing, libraries, and museums, for example) improve, the perceived increase in the cultural burden prompts a new generation to try to find ways to throw off the old.

On occasion, technology can be seen playing a double role in this process. Where established technology prompts secession by threatening to suffocate a new generation with the legacy of the old, "new" technology, if sufficiently distinct, can be invoked as a means of escape. Marinetti's "Manifeste de Futurisme," a classic claim for supersession ("We stand," he declares, "at the high peak between ages!"), provides a clear precedent for this double involvement of technology. Its vision was propelled, as Banham (1976: 100) notes, by a desire for "the overriding of an old, tradition-bound technology, unchanged since the Renaissance, by a newer one without traditions". The old, along with "Time and Space," Marinetti insisted, must be annihilated by the speed of new technology. Museums and academies, which Marinetti dismissed as "the graveyards of vain endeavor," were to be swept aside to allow the Futurists to set out unburdened. In particular, Marinetti insisted to his followers, "Go and set fire to the stacks of the libraries".[17]

If the past cannot easily be physically burned to the ground, it can at least be theoretically or ideologically reduced to ashes. Raymond Williams explores ways in which this has been done. Tracing ideas of temporal disjunction back to Heisod, Williams (1973: 13-33) shows that claims about the utter newness of the new long antedate both postmodernism and modernism.[18] (Declarations of separation may actually be one of the ties that perennially binds one generation to another. So regularly do generations insist on their utter newness that the first to be truly different may in fact be the generation that does not claim this distinction.) Within this tradition, certain ways of dismissing the past recur. In particular, as Williams argues, the past is repeatedly portrayed in a version of "pastoral" that extracts idyllic and simple aspects of an earlier age only to contrast them with the assumed complexity and sophistication of the present.[19]

This strategy emerges in contemporary dismissals of the book. Characterizations of the present "condition" often portray the past, either directly or by implication, as a time in which, for instance, the prelapsarian sign and referent walked hand in hand on their amiable way. For Baudrillard (1981: 5) this was the childlike phase of history in which "l'image... est le reflet d'une réalite profonde." By contrast with our own, in these pastoral societies the author was apparently both alive and suitably authoritative, and the reader naive and suitably subordinated. The inhabitants of the past saw the book, some have claimed, as "the natural and only vehicle for a written text" and the text simply "a transparent window into creative thought" and consequently they suffered beneath the "tyrannical" voice of print.[20]

We should always be suspicious of the contempt that flows beneath a surface of idealization and concern. And we should note how often the characterization of "them" is in fact a self-aggrandizement of "us." Roger Chartier (1991: 90) describes a similar world "in which the book was revered and authority was respected" until the book "lost its charge of sacrality" and "reverence and obedience gave way to a freer, more casual way of reading." What distinguishes Chartier's account from these other claims, however, is that he is describing the attitudes of eighteenth-century urban élites towards the pastoral innocence of their rural counterparts and forebears. Significantly, a skepticism we have been led to believe characteristic of the postmodern reader was, it seems, evident even at the start of the enlightenment project. In this light, our claims to a new, technologically mediated epistemological disillusionment seem particularly hollow.[21]

In the end, the apparent convergence of technological futurism and cultural theory fails to distinguish itself with decisive clarity from the very past it attempts to escape. Instead, it primarily recapitulates what it sought to supersede. Of course, we all know that those who forget the past are condemned to repetition, primarily of Santayana's tedious aphorism, but the problems of supersession may require stronger remedies. As a practical matter, naive ideas of supersession may actually be making some forms of repetition difficult rather than inevitable. While our technological superiority has long been taken for granted, high acid paper and silver nitrate film are silently destroying significant regions of twentieth-century cultural production with much more success than Marinetti had destroying the nineteenth. Meanwhile, the rapid, predatory supersession of both hardware and software is rendering recently created digital documents and archives inaccessible or unreadable. To save significant products of our digital being, we may have to move, some suggest, from bits back to atoms.[22]

We need to be cautious about the trivialization and dismissal of the past, however, not simply because we may lose particular documents or artifacts, but because we are also losing valuable cultural insights gained through old communicative technologies, just as we are trying to build new ones. Disinheriting the present from the past rejects a legacy of many and varied strategies that our actual as opposed to idealized predecessors engaged to deal with the problems of the sign, of narrative, of linearity and nonlinearity, of deferral and *différance*, or of authority – problems which the past, pastoralization to the contrary, was insufficiently benign to obscure from its inhabitants. Just as archivists are now resurrecting apparently otiose paper documents to help fathom unreadable digital archives, so we may need to reassess earlier communicative artifacts and forms to revive some of the newer ones.[23]

Of course, it's easy to portray such an attitude as no more than nostalgia and resistance in the face of progress – a nostalgia that fails to appreciate, moreover, how different the past is from the present and that clings naively to a seamless view of history, which the sophistication of "critical" critiques has long since made problematic. Undoubtedly, Bachelard's notion of *coupure*, disseminated by Althusser and Foucault, has made simple ideas of historical continuity and recovery untenable. Equally, Foucault's caution against searching for "origins" has rendered searches for historical precedent highly suspect. But there is no need for those who seek, in Johnson's words, to "explore times gloomy backwards with judicious eyes" to cede the theoretical high ground too readily. Indeed, many who assert the utter newness of the new need themselves to pay more than lip service to the force of these arguments. Claims of supersession, for instance, often escape portraying history as seamless only by the factitious insertion of a single seam, which often falls just behind the claimant. Beyond this single, uniform rent that frees the claimant from the past, history usually looks not the complex of tessellated breaks or ruptures we are led to expect, but placidly smooth and undifferentiated. Portrayals of a postmodern rift occasionally appear to be no more than a grossly naive reading of Althusser (1990) or Foucault (1972; 1977a) that hopes to sweep aside problematic issues from the past simply by declaring a new *problématique*. Ozenfant (1952: 43-83) nicely parodies such cataclysmic analyses by calling the first section of his history of painting and sculpture "From Before the Deluge to 1914."

In particular, the broad, parallel rents in the social and technological fabric produced by theories of the simultaneous transition of technology and culture into a new era assume a process of remarkably even, parallel development. These look quite naive beside more thoughtful analyses of uneven development.[24] Where supersessive rifts do allow some room for uneven development, it is usually only to lend unexamined support to widespread notions of "culture" and even biology lagging behind "technology" and needing to catch up. Thus to keep up with technology's autonomous unfolding, Vannevar Bush, the father of hypertext, feels we need to develop a new language (Bush 1945a), De Landa (1993) suggests a new form of "synthetic reasoning," Schrage (1995), a more advanced gene, and Jameson (1994: 39), new organs.

Similarly, it is claims of supersession rather than appeals for improved historical analysis that seem primarily concerned with origins. To the extent that technological and critical-theoretical triumphalism declares a supersessive break between past and future, it implicitly makes itself the new origin. Like Satan's autochthonous army, it wants to "Know none before us, self-begot, self raised" and so set the terms for future debate.[25] To resist simple ideas of supersession, by contrast, encourages richer investigation of those very genealogies supersession makes untraceable. Though prone to declare unbridgeable rifts himself, Althusser, in his critique of Hegelian ideas of supersession, argues that only by rejecting supersession, by refusing to succumb to the banalities of Hegel's all-subsuming progress can we "retreat" (as Althusser 1990: 76-79 calls it) to the genuine complexities of history.

In all, then, I suggest it's important to resist announcements of the death of the book or the more general insistence that the present has swept away the past or that new technologies have superseded the old. To refuse to accept such claims is not, however, to deny that we are living through important cultural or technological changes. Rather, it's to insist that to assess the significance of these changes and to build the resources to negotiate them, we need specific analysis, not sweeping dismissals. Indeed, as Williams (1973: 21) argues, proclaiming our distance from the past only prevents "the reality of a major transition" from being fully "acknowledged and understood."

In the case of the book, it's helpful to note Foucault's (1977b) remarks on the author function: "It is not enough to repeat the empty affirmation that the author has disappeared... we must locate the space left empty by the author's disappearance, follow the distribution of gaps and breaches, and watch for the openings that this disappearance uncovers," (Foucault 1977b: 121) and again, "Themes destined to replace the privileged position accorded the author have merely served to arrest the possibility of genuine change." (*ib.*: 128). A similar case can be made against unguarded assumptions of the death of the book. The theory of technological supersession too easily suggests that there will be no space left empty, no gaps or breaches to worry about, and (as I argue in the following section) that all technological change is progress toward the removal of privilege. Technology, it is assumed, is projecting society into a postmodern, posthistorical plenum where the only problems are caused by Luddites.

3. Liberation technology

Except at their most vaunting, assumptions of supersession tend to run beneath the surface of debate as pressures and tendencies that shape discussion rather than as topics that appear within it. One symptom of this subterranean presence, however, may be the claim of liberation. Leo Marx has argued that, unless protected by claims for simultaneous emancipation, deterministic visions of technological development quickly turn dystopian. Information technology in particular is often painted as either the panopticon or the beacon of liberty. (The famous Apple advertisement during the Superbowl of 1984 presented both by opposing imprisoning Big [Brother] Blue to the liberating rainbow of Macintosh.) The idea that supersession brings with it liberation provides a bulwark against the darker side of this opposition.[26]

So where statements about supersession are often muted, the cry of liberation tends to ring clear. Hence the wide currency of Stuart Brand's extravagant aphorism that "information wants to be free," which has been picked up by many who want to chase off the imprisoning book. Bolter talks about the "revolutionary" goal of "freeing the writing from the frozen structure of the page" and ultimately "liberating the text." Barlow claims information "has to move," Nelson suggests that only with new technology can emerge the "true structure and interconnectedness of information," while Sterling argues that information "wants to change... [but] for a long time, our static media, whether carvings in stone, ink on paper, or dye on celluloid, have strongly resisted the evolutionary impulse."[27]

This language of liberty moves quickly to such icons of freedom as the market and the frontier. Thus Rheingold evocatively subtitles his book on electronic "communities," "Homesteading on the electronic frontier". The Electronic Frontier Foundation, with which Brand, Barlow, Sterling, and Rheingold are connected, brings many related ideas of liberty together, associating "electronic" technologies with the frontier and the "marketplace of ideas" and in so doing casting doubt on preelectronic technologies like the book. Intriguingly, such proclamations occasionally transfer attributes of liberty from people to information. Freedom of information, once a citizen's right to gain access to information, by a sleight of argument becomes the right of information to move freely, free of material impediment. This is not to deny the important First Amendment issues taken up by the Electronic Frontier Foundation. But for a variety of reasons, the language of personal freedom is being attached to information, which as a result is given autonomous desires and an independent existence and evolution. Technological futurology occasionally transfers autonomy and rationality from people and societies to machines. Here, there's a similar exchange. Information is endowed with human attributes and simultaneously a certain independence from human control.[28]

This transference ultimately rests on dualistic assumptions. Where once we had ghosts in machines, now we have information in objects like books. Technology is thus called upon to do for information what theology sought to do for the soul. But this liberation technology is quite distinct from liberation theology, for where the latter turned from tending the soul to tending the body, liberation technology turns in the opposite direction, away from the text's embodiment toward information's pure essence. When the young Wordsworth let out the impassioned cry against the book,

> Oh! why hath not the Mind
> Some element to stamp her image on
> In Nature somewhat nearer to her own?
> (*The Prelude* [1850], V, 45-49)

his more down-to-earth associate replied calmly that this "was going far to seek disquietude" (*ib.*, L. 53). But now the question is being asked again and more earnestly, and digital information technology is being offered as the answer. The book, no longer its incarnation, has been reduced to the incarceration of the word. But a technological Prospero seems at last to be at hand to free the informational Ariel from the cleft pine (or wood products) in which he has been trapped.[29]

Barlow, an influential popularizer of the electronic future, uses the idea of a wine or spirit stoppered in a bottle as a metaphor for this entrapment. The image goes back at least to Milton's *Areopagitica*: "books... do preserve as in a vial the purest efficacy and extraction of that living intellect bred in them." But as that last phrase indicates, Milton resisted any simple image of the book as mere container: "books are not absolutely dead things, but do contain a potency of life in them to be as active as that soul whose progeny they are". Barlow, however, disdains such qualification. The container, as he sees it, is thoroughly superseded, and, like a good genie, the contents once free will not go back.[30]

Many present this release in near apocalyptic terms. Electronic text will, Lanham argues, "disempower... the force of linear print" and "blow... wide open" social limits imposed by the codex book, in the process democratizing the arts and allowing us "to create that genuine social self which America has discouraged from the beginning." Landow agrees it will liberate readers from the "tyrannical, univocal voice of the novel" and create the sort of intertextuality that, in Thaïs Morgan's words, will free "the literary text" from "psychological, sociological, and historical determinisms". While for Bolter it will remove a veil of distortion so that "what is unnatural in print becomes natural in the electronic medium."[31]

A fair amount of poststructuralist theory is being ingested to provide intellectual support for what is, in fact, the demonization of the book. In particular, Barthes's (1974) powerful distinction between the "work," servant of one master, and the "text," an item of pleasure for many, is invoked directly or indirectly to confirm the idea of books as procrustean containers. Electronic technologies are spoken of as if they would shake the "text" free from the "work" (though Barthes 1979: 34 himself held "it would be useless to attempt a material separation"). And more explicitly, Barthes's concept of the *lexia* has proved an influential and tendentious term for the unit of liberated text.

Yet the invocation of Barthes raises some doubts about the convergence of theorists and practitioners. For Barthes, the *lexia* was the arbitrary unit into which he separated text in order to disrupt "blocks of signification of which reading grasps only the surface, imperceptibly soldered by the movement of sentences, the flowing discourse of narration, the 'naturalness' of ordinary language." Starting with these *lexias*, and with the errors of his structuralist-scientistic past clearly in mind, Barthes (1974: 13 *passim*) sets out to explore "several kinds of criticism (psychological, psychoanalytical, thematic, historical, structural)" which collectively destroy any notion of "totality" and deny "naturalness" to the work. As a result of the ensuing dramatic reconstruction of the text, the work is revealed to be an impossibility, a denial of its own assertions.

Barthes's dramatic strategies undoubtedly challenge those who accept the book as writ. But, as I've suggested already, the ideally naive reader envisaged here is, above all else, a pastoral idealization. In fact, Barthes's ideas seem to challenge more forcefully many of the enthusiasts of electronic hypertexts. For while Barthes's poststructuralist legacy merges easily with the general demonization of the book, it does not fit so easily with ideas of pure, natural information or the grand information-retrieval concepts put forward by, for example, Vannevar Bush and Ted Nelson, the great forefathers of practical hypertext. (Nor is it quite at home with the fairly conventional pedagogical goals of, for example, Lanham and Landow.) Many who embrace poststructuralist forays against the codex to support their arguments for the electronic emancipation of information or society too easily forget that these forays were launched to a significant degree because the book was presented not as a prison, but as a key technology of the grand narratives of emancipation. Dominant strains of postmodernism and ideas of posthistory have long insisted that all such emancipatory narratives, whether they concern books or information technologies, are illusory.[32]

Critical theory aside, the idea of liberation technology superseding the entrapments of the past has its own internal problems. The argument that supersession and liberation belong together rests on the paradoxical prediction that freedom from technology can be achieved through technology. Here it's perhaps possible to detect the shadow the military has cast over a great deal of technological futurology.[33] The desire for a technology to liberate information from technology is not far from the search for a weapon to end all weapons or the war to end all wars. The idea that the latest weapon is an agent of peace, that the latest putsch will be the last, is seductive. But ultimately it is both corrupting and misleading. As with so much optimistic futurology, it woos us to jump by highlighting the frying pan and hiding the fire. In the face of such arguments, we do better to remember Andrew Marvell's ambiguous celebration of Cromwell's conquest and liberation of Ireland

> The same art that did gain
> A power must it maintain

or how Ariel quickly discovered that the same magic that liberated him from the tree indentured him to Prospero.[34]

4. Material information

The tangles supersession and liberation get into result, I think, from the dualistic assumptions I referred to earlier. In this section, I suggest that, if we avoid the assumption that information and technology, the "semiotic" and the "perceptual," in Bolter's (1991: 13) terms, are as distinct and separable as wine and bottles, we avoid the problematic tangles. After discussing this idea of dualism and its connection to the trope of the pastoral a little further, I outline an alternative way to think of information. This alternative, more systemic approach emphasizes the role of material artifacts in both making and warranting information.

Ideas of supersession, I argued, often rely on a pastoral characterization of the past (or future), and this can help explain both the source and the nature of the problematic dualism. William Empson argued that the pastoral attempts but always fails to depict a reconciliation of the inimical products of mind and matter.[35] It's not surprising, then, to find pastoral visions in debates about the book and its past and future. Ideas about the reconciliation of conceptual and physical, mind and matter, sign and signified provide the common ground between pessimistic and optimistic views of technological development. Extreme pessimistic views suggest that the coming of the computer is destroying previous reconciliation achieved by the book. Extreme optimists hold, by contrast, that any prior sense of harmony was a delusion and that the computer will both dispel those illusions created by the book and in its place achieve true reconciliation, offering the "real character of information," "the genuine social self," and so forth.[36]

A significant alternative position shares the optimists' view that the past was an era of delusion, but distinguishes itself by denying the promise of future reconciliation. Harmony, this view suggests, is always a deception; attempts at reconciliation can only end in contradiction. (This view explains why pastoral, like the Queen's jam, is something never achieved today, but only projected into yesterday or tomorrow.) This position escapes the disappointment of the one and the hope of the other, but it nonetheless shares the dualism of both optimist and pessimist. It argues less against their dualistic assumptions than their vision of harmonious reconciliation. So Empson and Barthes, for example, see a pastoral landscape seeded by the intentions of Marvell or Balzac but producing only self-annihilation and contradiction.

Varied though their destinations may be, there is evidently one way to avoid starting down any of these paths and that is to reject the dualism with which they all begin. In the next few paragraphs I sketch an alternative position.[37] Rather than to think of wine in bottles, each of which has a separate identity, it is more useful to consider information and technology as mutually constitutive and ultimately indissoluble. Apt images then would be rivers and banks, Yeats's example of dancer and dance, or Newman's of light and illumination: you don't get one without the other. In this view, information is undoubtedly less autonomous than liberationists would hold; on the other hand, books appear more productive and less like the passive constraints supersessionists make them out to be. Indeed, it can be helpful to think of them as Richards (1960: 1) did when, somewhat uncharacteristically, he declared that "a book is a machine to think with."[38]

Viewing the book as a machine, we quickly bridge the supersessive chasm some have dug between new technology and the book, as if one were a machine and the other not. Indeed, the idea of the book as a "machine to think with" makes it seem much closer to what are standardly called information technologies than either those who idealize it in Miltonic vein as "the Soul's progeny" or those who demonize it in Mitchell's terms as "tree flakes encased in dead cow" seem to believe. In the end all information technologies and the information they carry – whether made from trees and cows or sand and petroleum – are not independent, but interdependent.[39]

If books and the information they carry are interdependent, then, as a machine, the book is clearly more than a conduit for ideas produced elsewhere.[40] It is itself a means of production. This concept goes beyond the simple idea of an individual book producing the information it contains. Books are part of a social system that includes authors, readers, publishers, booksellers, libraries, and so forth. Books produce and are reciprocally produced by the system as a whole. They are not, then, simply "dead things" carrying preformed information from authors to readers. They are crucial agents in the cycle of production, distribution, and consumption. This is why, as McGann (1991: 10) puts it, "readers and audiences are hidden in our texts, and the traces of their multiple presence are scripted at the most material levels." Recent work by McGann and other "bibliographic" critics such as McKenzie, Chartier, Genette, and Darnton increasingly acknowledges this systemic relation of the work, the author, and the audience and the role played by the passage of physical books in creating, maintaining, and developing this literary system. Their work and related ideas about cultural production and consumption of cultural artifacts offer fuller and more complex accounts of the book than those implicit in claims of supersession and liberation.[41]

For instance, arguments of Michel de Certeau (1984) and Richard Johnson (1986) help explain how easy it can be to idealize information technology and demonize the book as if the two were not, indeed, both machines. De Certeau and Johnson hold that in attempting to understand cultural artifacts traveling a social circuit, it is essential to distinguish the different cardinal points of the system. To take one and ignore the others inevitably misrepresents the system as a whole and the role of the artifact within it. Similarly, it is a mistake to contrast analyses made from two different points on the circuit. Arguments against the book, for example, often characterize it not in terms of the whole cycle, from writers to readers and back again, but from the point of authorial production alone. Isolating this position allows the book to appear to exert malign, authoritative influences over passive audiences. (Indeed, as de Certeau argues, the isolation of production more generally both leads to and ultimately vitiates many of Foucault's arguments about the efficacy of power.)

Information technology, by contrast, is often characterized in terms of the circulating text or of cultural consumption, but not of production. Privileging the circulating text makes information seem remarkably self-sufficient and the book, by contrast, imprisoning. In the past, "practical," "new," and structuralist critics looked from this point of view, granting the text an autonomy distinct from its production or consumption. And this is also essentially the view of those liberationists who defer to the autonomous integrity of information. A third position moves to consumption alone – a stance taken up by Stanley Fish, whose readers appear liberated from all constraints – and, by contrast, devolves all power to the consumer.

By amalgamating the last two positions, supersessionists and liberationists have been able to create an idealized picture of new technologies that makes these appear as complete departures from the book's determined assaults on both texts and readers. But this conclusion is achieved only through incompatible forms of analysis. Furthermore, as we saw, it also leads to the tangle between the two alternative positions, one of which sees the text as becoming independent of technology, while the other sees consumers as becoming independent through technology. Looking at communication technologies in the round, by contrast, circumvents these partial, isolated, and antagonistic accounts. For the book at least, cultural theorists, contemporary bibliographic critics, and literary sociologists have recently begun to do this. It still needs to be done for alternative information technologies.

The attention to the book as a material object involved in a social circuit helps in particular to explain some problems with evolutionary accounts like Sterling's, which view information technologies as progressively removing material encumbrances from the "true" information assumed to lie beneath them.[42] In Sterling's view, the printed codex can be no more than a material burden on the information "inside," which technology now permits us to remove. This approach, the essence of what I have called "liberation technology," discounts the substantial role the book plays in coordinating consumption and production, and so maintaining the social system of information. In so doing, such an approach renders the process of publication particularly absurd, for instead of removing material constraints, publishing appears to add them. The manuscript appears as the more authentic form from which the various stages of book production retreat into artificiality and imprisonment.

Considered as part of a larger social system, however, publication is not so easily portrayed as an act of incarceration. It is rather, as McGann describes it, an act of socialization. The production of a book is a shaping of an artifact capable of traveling a public circuit and coordinating production and distal consumption. On their own, manuscripts have a very limited reach and are essentially private documents for local circuits, lacking the forms and warrants that make them more generally consumable. Publication is then very much a process of producing a public artifact and inserting it in a particular social circuit. Indeed, what general intelligibility manuscripts have is due not to the autonomy of information, but to a reader's understanding of the broader literary system. Manuscripts are read not as a purer form of the book, but as incomplete versions, rapid prototypings of the artifact they are intended to become. To turn them into public forms requires more productive work. Consequently, what from the liberationist point of view are looked upon as material constraints, from which text should be "freed," are more often social resources that, if removed, need to be reconstituted or invoked in some other way if the status of the text is to be maintained to any degree.

Newspapers, more easily thought of as purveyors of information than producers, in fact provide another example of the production process. Certainly newspapers convey information as news. But before they convey news, newspapers make it. News is not simply made elsewhere and then put onto paper, affirming the simple, dualistic separation of information and technology. News is made in the process of editing the paper, which determines not so much what news is "fit to print," but that what fits and gets printed is news. Editing and copyfitting are not mere "mechanical" tasks, but social processes of abstraction through which events become stories that become or fail to become news.[43] The ensuing circulation of the printed paper through a society (ensuring that the "same" news is available to everyone at roughly the same time) then warrants the selected items as "social facts".[44]

This process is also quite distinct from the related liberationist vision of people individually gathering sui generis news out of a vast database. Without constraints, data so stored lack both the shape of news (when should a correspondent stop writing, taping, filming?) and its social status (can an item I download be "news" for me but not for anyone else?). News is, rather, a shaped product, and the shaping contribution of technologies is implicitly recognized in the way news databases rely on newspapers of record to warrant what the database carries as news. Radio and television programs similarly report the content of the front page of the major daily papers. But radio and television have proved themselves capable of producing news themselves as well as carrying news produced elsewhere. I don't want to stumble into demonization, here. New technologies are not incapable of producing news, but at present they primarily reproduce it, deferring in the process to older, more established, public forms. This ready and often unnoticed deferral has important implications for the design of information technology. If designers assume that this technology is merely a conduit for freestanding information, new technologies are more likely to remain subordinate to residual technologies than to offer creative alternatives, let alone supersede them.

The implication that technologies are just conduits for information produced elsewhere both denies the material role technologies play in producing information and, as I noted at the end of the previous section, assumes that information has an inherent shape and integrity independent of the system in which it is produced and consumed. Information is taken to be self-sufficient, self-explanatory, and self-legitimating. Yet, as Lyotard (1979: 8) notes, legitimation is always a central problem for information. Liberationists give information the burden of guaranteeing its own legitimacy, putting it in the position of Epimendes asserting (or even denying) the Cretan paradox.[45] But information cannot so validate itself. Merely writing "Legal Tender" on the face of a bank note is not proof against forgery. Rather, it is the record of the material process that provides collateral for writing: the material difficulty of producing the inscription warrants the banknote. This is not to argue, of course, that the material warrant guarantees legitimacy or determines consumption. But it does represent an attempt to coordinate production and consumption through a mediating artifact. And even acts of transgression, poaching, or deconstruction acknowledge the attempt.[46]

Acknowledging the coordinating role books play doesn't entail accepting a rigid correspondence between what we think of as "form" and "content." Chartier is right to note that "meaning changes when form changes" (consequently, irony, the trope of self-denial, travels particularly badly). But within a robust system such as the modern system of lapidary publishing, many changes can be easily negotiated. Despite new forms for old words, it's often possible to recognize a putative form (much as we recognize putative narrators and putative audiences) despite the changes in the actual material. Nevertheless, the changes we are contemplating at the moment concern more than particular inscriptions and may involve the system itself. Faced with the changes at this level, it becomes important to think not idealistically about information, but materially, in terms of what Genette calls the "ensemble heteroclite" or McGann the "laced network of linguistic and bibliographic codes." Systemic changes reach beyond particular semiotic effects, altering our understanding of not just what things might mean, but also why they matter.[47]

5. Future concerns

As I noted at the close of the previous section, the advent of multiple new technologies is probably changing not only particular works, but also the social system in relation to which the works were written and read. It will take care and thought to negotiate these changes, and the task will inevitably become more difficult if changes are made in material processes without regard to the social practices they underwrite. Information is taken to be a natural category and its material substrate ultimately immaterial or if supersession is assumed to be inevitably beneficial, the problems will remain invisible, though their effects may be increasingly felt. So, contrary to the convention of ending with solutions, I end by trying to raise two related concerns that seem to me hidden to optimistic eyes (the pessimists, of course, see nothing but problems). I do not pretend that a nondualistic, social-material approach automatically resolves these problems, only that it makes them visible and so open to attention.

Borrowing a portmanteau word coined by Toffler and packing a little more into it, I call the first problem the paradox of demassification. *Demassification* refers to the increasing ease with which socially complex technologies can be made not just for broad masses of people, but for small groups and individuals. Economies of scale, necessary for material-intensive and labor-intensive products, once guaranteed common artifacts. Flexible production of post-Fordism has made this increasingly less important. Less generically Taylored production can be more easily individually tailored. This sort of social demassification or individualization is, to a significant degree, the result of material demassification, which might, indeed, more strictly be called *dematerialization*. As technology is transformed from mechanical to digital-informational, machines shed mass dramatically. Huge mainframes, for instance, have been reduced to individual laptop computers which people can work on alone and, more significantly, separately.

Individuation and separation, two effects of the two kinds of demassification, in the end pull against one another. With large machines, from production lines to time-sharing computers, activities were implicitly coordinated because people worked together in the same place, on the same machine. With dematerialized, portable objects, people no longer need to congregate in single buildings or communicate through central, unifying machines in order to work together. Nonetheless, while they remained uniform, mass-produced artifacts (and books offer one of the earlier examples) continued to support social coordination despite prompting separation. With faithful duplication, people had access to what was, for all intents and purposes, the "same" object, and so, though physically separated, could easily negotiate among themselves coordinated interactions. The more artifacts are tailored to individual users, however, the more such separation becomes problematic. It's hard to share and coordinate practice if you don't share the same physical space. It's much more difficult if you also don't share common artifacts. In brief, centrifugal forces of individualization and separation are coming into conflict with centripetal social needs, which were met previously and unproblematically through shared or common material objects.[48]

Certainly, no one wants to throw away their laptops and move back into the world of time-sharing. But having blown apart the mainframe with personal computers, we have spent a decade or more valiantly struggling to recoordinate or "network" computational practice. (It's interesting to note that MOOs, which return users to shared space, virtual though it may be, have been compared to time-sharing machines.) To prevent similar problems with other artifacts, it may be more prudent to attend from the first both to material and social needs and the way in which these have been met by the circulation of public forms and to avoid succumbing to ideas of information in the abstract or of consumption as an individual and unfettered practice.

Yet one response to this paradox may be the increasing individuation and personalization of the production of information. Using new technologies, people seem to be trying to produce and consume information with less reliance on impersonal forms and more on personal warrants for legitimation. In this context, it is interesting to consider the coming of hypertext systems, which often seek to replace public, general forms with particularized, individual links. Hypertext also offers to replace linearity with random access, narrative structure with *lexias*, distinctions between reader and writer with an elision of consumption and production. This type of electronic text has been greeted, as I noted earlier, with some extravagant claims, and in keeping with these, hypertext is sometimes portrayed as the means to achieve the triumphant deconstruction of old institutions and forms of authority, in particular those Marinetti attacked, the academy and the library, and with these the publishing houses and the news media. It sometimes appears possible to think of hypertext only in terms of supersession and liberation.[49]

To understand hypertext and its implications, however, we should look back as well as forward. Hypertext is not unprecedented. Hypertext theorists themselves often cite the footnote as a shadowy predecessor, but there is a less obscure and more important one, overlooked not only as a consequence of the forward-looking ideology of supersession, but also as a result of the narrowness of the sociology of literacy and information. If I am right and hypertext has a significant precedent, then of course it may lack the novelty to offer either supersession or liberation; on the other hand, precedent may offer us some way to understand the social implications of the technological shift to hypertext forms.

For a precedent, we should look beyond the newspaper and related pamphlet and journal forms and beyond the book and its related forms to the robust and enduring forms of "the books." For half a millennium, bookkeeping, a system of individual blocks or *lexias* interconnected by multiple links, created and maintained networks of information, "books mutually dependent on each other" as the *Catechism of Trade and Commerce* called them.[50] A conventional set of account books comprised several generically quite different types of document: the waste book, the journal, the ledger (with its distinct types of account), the letter book (with its many authors), the bill book, the cash book, the sales book, inventories, and so on.[51] The accounting system also embraced several media, including physical objects (goods, merchandise) and complex intermediate representations (tags, tallies, chits, receipts, bills of lading, and the like). Items, books, and sets of books were elaborately linked in ways that connected items not only to those in the other types of book within a single business but to other books in other businesses (for of course every credit in one "real" account is a debit in someone else's; every bill receivable represents a bill payable elsewhere). With the spread of merchant capital, these links in effect produced a global network with several of the characteristics of hypertext. It was an endless, unfinished, nonsequential, transnational, and highly practical web of circulating information. As with hypertext, there was no single or sequential route through these entries, but only ever-new and perpetually unfinished pathways created by each new reticulating reader-writer. And, as with information technology, the system was triumphantly described by great and sober minds as the ultimate rational technology of an ultimately rational society.[52]

Far from an obscure or reserved practice, this system was both geographically and socially widely dispersed. As Braudel shows, from the thirteenth century, the travels of merchants quickly spread the complex form of the *partita doppia* with its necessary accoutrements from the Mediterranean around the world. At its height in the nineteenth century it had in one form or another penetrated (and interconnected) almost all societies at a variety of levels, crossing class, race, and gender boundaries. Household and petty-commodity accounting, for instance, required accounts, and this was done predominantly by women. Consequently, the fishwives who surround Peter Simple's ship in foreign ports and the bourgeois English wife of Pendennis's publisher are bound together by the books they wave. The wealthy of both sexes in both capitalist and feudal societies also kept their books, so we find Colonel Newcome and Anna Karenina (and others that had neither a wife nor servant to do it for them) engaged in the same practice. The countinghouse stool provided early education for many with insufficient social connections (among them Hume and Dickens). Meanwhile poor men long provided the bulk of clerks of one sort or another and probably had more to do with accounting books than discursive ones. Many of the hanged apprentices described in Linbaugh's *London Hanged* appear to have been united not only in death but in the skill of "casting accompts."[53]

The history of accounting as a cultural rather than just a business practice is, as yet, too-little explored to read too much into the effects of accounting on other types of literacy. But accounting may help explain the diffusion of the common conceptions of "information" as the content of rational technology. Bookkeeping is a process for producing apparently robust individual items or *lexias* and a social practice that helped naturalize a misleading concept of information as seemingly autonomous items, put into, rather than developed out of, books.

The idea of information as a product of certain forms of literacy has been traced back to the emergence of the newspaper and the journal.[54] It is both possible and productive, however, to push this history back a little further. Habermas, for instance, traces related ideas back to the commercial precursors of newspapers such as *Lloyds' Register*, in which information from business letters was progressively commodified. The daily abstraction of items from the flow of practice and their coding into a particular "universal" form was the work of the countinghouse "traffic in commodities and news." Gradually, news itself became commodified as "useful truths" were transformed into the content of newspapers. As with the serendipitous entries in a waste book, but now in increasingly public ways, items from different sources were given force and unity through being translated into a particular, socially acknowledged form. Under the warranting masthead of a newspaper, these were then circulated and sold. As Kronick and Shaffner both show, a somewhat similar process went on with scientific periodicals. It is not then surprising that the *journal*, the refined form of the waste book, gave its name to both newspapers and scholarly publications. Other forms of standardization (indexing, alphabetization, page numbers) were probably also refined first in the countinghouse before appearing in print.[55]

To take anything from this genealogy, we should note immediately a central difference between the account book and the newspaper, journal, or periodical. Unlike the last three, account books are primarily the forms of civil society, not the public sphere. The *lexias* of account books relied for warrants on the personal authority and private warrant of the countinghouse and family firm to which they belonged. At least until the nineteenth century and the development of the public limited liability company, any account or entry was an entirely private affair with no autonomous or public standing. Indeed, private accounts were incapable of achieving the disinterested status required for the public sphere. The sphere of business is always the sphere of private interests.

In Habermas's account, the contrasting public sphere developed out of the agonistic contest between state regulation and the bourgeois merchants of the private sphere to whom these regulations applied. For support, both state and merchants appealed to a public sense of disinterested argument. The development of pamphlets, newspapers, and other public forms of information and debate must be seen as a part of this social struggle involving the attempt to transform the particularity of personalized links, private testimony, and individual power into public, impartial, and disinterested forms. Public forms and institutions were developed to be independent of the personal privilege of the individual bourgeois merchant, the aristocracy, or the monarch. And for this to happen, personal links had to be replaced by impersonal warrants. Ideas of news, information, science, and public opinion developed as part of this process. In conclusion, then, this history is not, as pastoral views would have it, ignorant of *lexias*, links, and webs, but one that developed very much in direct opposition to their limitations.

Undoubtedly, hypertext is clearly distinct from the old technologies of the public sphere. It remains to be shown, however, how distinct it is from the preceding private forms and, in consequence, how much genuine liberation it can really achieve. Undoubtedly, as a concept and a social context, the public sphere and its forms and institutions are not without serious problems. Nevertheless, a retreat into civil society (glimpsed in some of the more Hobbesian enclosures of cyberspace), if that's what hypertext presages, seems a far more problematic development. It would, for instance, be foolish to believe, as some seem to, that putting warranting back on an individual, personal basis makes everybody equal. This may remove the trappings of power, but, unlike the move to the public sphere, it leaves the sources and structures of power unaffected.

Of course, my own argument insists that technology alone cannot drive us into this privatized corner and that it is particularly important to look beyond the rhetoric of determinism, supersession, and liberation to the actual social-material practices that are developing. Here, to some extent, a more sanguine picture emerges. The popularity of hypermedia on the World Wide Web shows that much of the rhetoric of hypertext is quite inaccurate and ineffectual. Text is not being decomposed into Barthean *lexias*; rather very conventional whole documents, with much of their authority and their material origins putatively ascertainable, are being linked. Divisions between author and reader, producer and consumer are being technologically enforced.

On the other hand, as these features indicate, much of the Web is being used as a conduit for old institutional forms (the careful scrutiny of institutional authority thinly inscribed in domain and site addresses of Internet URLs suggests this) and so instead of being an alternative it is probably more dependent on older forms than it need be. It will take, I suspect, more serious analysis than has yet been undertaken and a clearer recognition of the productive interdependence of technology and information to avoid either regression to private forms or dependence on older institutional ones. My own goal is not to demonize the new, but to suggest that the facile demonization of the old, and the book in particular, allows aspects of the new to slip by unexamined, to the ultimate detriment of both old and new.

6. Conclusion

The debate about the book is caught between two voices a little like those heard at the opening of *A Tale of Two Cities*, one proclaiming the best of times and the other the worst, one proclaiming the future is our salvation and another pointing back to a lost Eden. I have tried to argue that, with regard to the book, both of these positions too easily separate the past from the future, the simple from the complex, technology from society, and information from technology. To escape both utopian and dystopian oversimplifications, we need first to question such ready separations.

We should, for example, look not at technology in isolation but within its social-material and historical context. Enlarging our viewpoint in this way sets aside ideas of simple supersession (the separation of the past from the future) or liberation (the separation of information from technology) and avoids quasi-Weberian dichotomies between, for instance, progressive technological logic and regressive social illogic or between technologically tractable constraints and socially useful resources. Instead, we discover that the technological and the cultural, constraint and resource are finely and inextricably interwoven. If we consider the book in this light, we should discover that despite its apparent simplicity, it has a great deal to teli us and will, for some time yet, be both a useful, practical tool and a resourceful precedent for designers of alternative technologies to go by.

So if Victor Hugo is to remain our guide in these matters, to the Archdeacon's fatalist prediction of supersession, I prefer a scene from another work – that claustrophobic moment in *Les Miserables* where Valjean lies alive in his coffin and, having expected liberation, hears the unexpected and terrifying clods of earth dropping slowly into the grave. His life, the words on the page seem to say, is over; but, of course, the seven hundred odd pages remaining in our right hand materially insist, to the contrary, that Valjean is quite unlikely to die soon. Nonetheless, as if to caution the overly sanguine, Hugo called this section "Cemeteries Take What They Are Given." If nothing else, this offers a useful caution not to permit the burial of what yet has useful life.

Acknowledgments

Thanks to Laura Hartman, Jean Lave, Geoff Nunberg, and Shawn Parkhurst for patiently reading earlier drafts of this paper.

Notes

[1] The "coming of the book" was famously mapped in Febvre and Martin (1984; first published 1958). Its elegy was read just four years later by McLuhan (1962). McLuhan, less a technological determinist than some allow, did not make the "going" as brief as more contemporary accounts, for he backdates the beginning of the "going" some 150 years (see McLuhan 1962: 3). Nonetheless, the transition from coming to going remains brief, for this dates the "going" barely a decade after Febvre and Martin close the "coming."

[2] For a recent example of the gloomy, see Birkerts (1994); for the triumphant, see Lanham (1994).

[3] Butler's Erewhonians destroyed all machines; books then became the only way future generations knew about these malign objects (Butler 1970: chapters 23, 24).

[4] The problem with predictions about the demise of older artifacts such as the book, I suspect, is that they actually harm the old less than the new. Underestimating what replacement really involves and overselling what technology can currently achieve too easily combine to give new technologies an unfortunately bathetic launch into the world. In the case of the book, in exchange for some of the elaborate social-material processes that Jerome McGann has suitably embraced with the term "textual intercourse," we have been proudly offered technologies with all the clinical charm and less of the physical versatility of a three-by-five index card or a seamless roll of paper (McGann 1991: 3). Faced with these, the book's polymorphous appeal remains relatively undisturbed. (Indeed, many who proclaim its end most loudly choose the book itself to make their case, which has much of the logic of making yourself executor of your own will.) On the other hand, vaunting predictions coupled with limited utility have already diminished enthusiasm for potential hypertext and multimedia alternatives.

[5] Of course, the hinge also survives because it is technologically simple.

[6] It's unwise to be too complacent about the resilience of the book. It may well survive, but librarians who have had their acquisitions budgets cut and colleges that have had whole libraries cut in the name of alternatives that still don't exist are unlikely to have those funds restored. The proclamation that the "library without walls" exists strikes me as an opportunistic move by budget cutters rather than a reasonable, if mistaken, prediction.

[7] Erewhonians lived by a similar image: "Man is drawn through life with his face to the past instead of the future" (Butler 1970: 181).

[8] See, for example, Lanham (1994: 23), who talks of "this remarkable convergence of social, technological, and theoretical pressures," or Landow (1992); Jameson (1994: xi), McLuhan (1962).

[9] Landow (this volume) rightly points out that bibliophiles will fetishize the book and argue as though all books were incunabula if it helps their argument. This image of Mitchell's makes it clear that technophiles do the very same thing when it suits them. This convergence endorses my central point that in many ways the bibliophiles and the technophiles are more alike than different.

[10] Negroponte's idea of a "new culture" looks modest beside his dominant assumption of the "new ontology" of "digital being."

[11] See Toffler (1971: 12), Lanham (1994: 23), and Feigenbaum and McCorduck (1983).

[12] See, for example, Eisenstein (1979; 1983). The degree of determinism embraced by Eisenstein's argument has been much debated (see McNally 1987).

[13] See, for example, Baudrillard (1981: e.g., 2ff), where the count is particularly high. Baudrillard has perhaps amassed more cultural capital than Toffler and given postmodernism a grander status than futurology, but his views of simulacra often appear as little more than a frenzied extension of Toffler's early assumption that "simulated and non-simulated experiences will also become combined in ways that will sharply challenge man's grasp of reality" (Toffler 1971: 213). Baudrillard's trick has been to say this state is here, now, while Toffler, no doubt as a wise professional speculation, set it off in the future.

[14] For the close link between development and marketing, see J. Seely Brown, "Changing the Game," in preparation.

[15] See, for example, Niethammer (1992), Anderson (1992: 279-376).

[16] See also Roberts (1994).

[17] F.T. Marinetti, "Premier Manifeste du Futurisme," in Ballo, Cachin-Nora, Leymarie, and Russoli (1973). While much of Marinetti's Manifesto sounds quite familiar to postmodern ears, there is one noticeable difference. Where the Manifesto set goals to pursue, more recent supersessive claims often replace iron resolve with digital determinism. Certainly, *The Postmodern Condition* presents not an option but a fait accompli.

[18] As Williams makes clear, a focus on the differences between generations tends to obscure differences of class. So Negroponte (1995) claims there's no need to worry

about social divisions between "information rich" and "information poor"; the only significant division, as he sees it, is between the generation of analog adults and digital kids. This, his extrapolative mind tells him in an argument common among the digerati, time will erase. Yet Stuart (1995: 73) points out that in 1989 nearly half of households with an income of $75,000 or more owned computers while under 5 percent of households with an income of under $15,000 had them.

[19] The strategy of pastoralization is extremely complex. It plays with both time and space, calling to mind L.P. Hartley's resonant phrase, "The past is another country." The postmodern condition, according to Lyotard, is a property of the "highly developed" alone. So like the past, other countries take on the primitive, pastoral mantle and are subject to similar dismissive judgments. Edward Said's concept of "orientalism" (Said 1978) elaborates the effects of this elision between the past and the primitive.

[20] Quotations from Lanham (1994: 9 and 4) and Landow (1992: 11).

[21] The "coming of the book" involved almost from the start books that made fun of naive and gullible readers.

[22] Cf. Rothenberg (1995) and Cook (1995).

[23] I discuss some of these issues in section 4 below.

[24] See, for example, Williams (1961).

[25] Toulmin (1972: 65), who analyzes claims of supersession in science and history, in particular in the works of Kuhn and Collingwood, is strong in his condemnation of extreme versions of this strategy: "the absolutist reaction... emancipates itself from the complexities of history and anthropology only at the price of irrelevance."

[26] Marx (1994: 237-258). Even the dystopic cyberfiction of Gibson and others presents both sides. On one are the corporate empires, and on the other the hacker resistance. This conveniently allows all programmers, however large the corporation they work for, to identify with the forces of liberation.

[27] The aphorism "information wants to be free," often quoted, is attributed to Brand in Barlow (1995); Bolter (1991: 21); Nelson quoted in Davis (1993: 613). See Sterling (1995).

[28] The influential Vannevar Bush spotted the ideological potential in such rhetoric when he wrote the promotional report *Science. The Endless Frontier* at the request of the president in 1945, about the time he was pondering the possibilities of his influential memex. Cf. Bush (1945b). The report was requested by Roosevelt. See White and Limerick (1994).

[29] Futurologists, particularly when they take a flight from simple technological extrapolation, often show dualistic leanings. Thus, for example, Kahn and Weiner break from sensible projections about automatic teller machines and on-line libraries to more exotic ideas about personal flying platforms, changeable sex, and controllable diets and body shapes. All reflect a spiritual yearning to escape the material inertia of the human body. See Kahn and Weiner (1968).

[30] J. Milton, *Paradise Lost and Selected Poetry and Prose*, Northrop Frye (ed.) (New York: Reinhart and Co., 1951: 464); Barlow (1995). Barlow's image is more apt

for his central issue, the relationship between music and discs and tapes. The relationship between a song and a disc is not the same as that between text and book. The latter relation is more akin to the relation of music to instrument or song to voice. Barlow perhaps also overlooks the point that while good wine can be poured out of bottles, it attains its maturity in them. The quality of wine in the glass is not indifferent to its career in the bottle.

[31] Lanham (1994: 21, 105, and 219); Landow (1992: 10-11); Morgan in Landow (1992: 10); Bolter (1991: 143).

[32] Cf. Lyotard (1979: esp. 37ff).

[33] Futurologists from the military include such highly influential figures as Herman Kahn, much admired by Daniel Bell, and Vannevar Bush, much admired by hypertext champions. The idea of the weapon to end all weapons is very old, and has probably helped to fund military procurement since procurement began. Such weapons appear in such futurological exemplars as Bulwer Lytton's *Coming Race* (New York: Hinton & Co., 1873) and Wells's film *Things to Come* (1940).

[34] Cf. Marvell (1972). The more down-to-earth Caliban was perhaps wiser than Ariel when he acknowledged his only option would be to have "a new master, get a new man." In the end, then, liberationists tend not only to choose their allies incautiously, but to ensnare themselves in a supersessive claim that relies on technology while claiming to escape it. In some cases, this has the curious effect (often signaled in requests for "transparency") of demanding of new technologies a self-effacement that insists on the indifference of what they carry to the carrier. In the nineteenth century, Leo Marx argues, Americans refused to see the machine in their ideologically pastoral garden. The trait seems to have reappeared in contemporary attempts to render the role of modern technology invisible (Marx 1964). The combination of supersession and liberation suggests that technology must simultaneously be present and wish itself absent. This view entails that the information be self-sustaining and the technology self-consuming. For thoughts on looking "at" and "through" technology, see Lanham (1994).

[35] Here I draw not only on Empson's work, in particular Empson (1947; 1950), but also De Man (1983: 235-41).

[36] The influence of dualism on technological thought is not wholly surprising. Information technology in general and artificial intelligence in particular have a long and problematic history of trying to separate mind and matter. For some helpful insight into the pervasiveness of dualistic thinking or "Cartesianism," see Gumbrecht (1995). Thanks to Shawn Parkhurst for this reference.

[37] Some of the ideas offered here are sketched more fully in Seely Brown and Duguid (1994a); (1994b).

[38] See Seely Brown and Duguid (1994a) and Landow (this volume) for further reflections on the significance of thinking of books as machines.

[39] From this point on, for ease, I refer unashamedly to the content of books as "information," though my central point is that the two are only conceptually, not materially separable.

[40] See Reddy (1979).

[41] McGann (1991), McKenzie (1986), Genette (1987), Chartier (1991); (1992) and Darnton (1979). Though these authors raise related issues, there are clear differences among them. See Sutherland (1989). For comments on the distinctive view of bibliographic criticism, see Chartier (1992).

[42] For Sterling's comments, see section 3, above.

[43] This idea that journalists make news is a development of Carr's (1964) notion that it is historians who make history.

[44] The newspaper, Huizinga argues, "fulfills in America the cultural function of the drama of Aeschylus. I mean that it is the expression through which a people – a people numbering many millions – becomes aware of its spiritual unity. The millions, as they do their careless reading every day at breakfast, in the subway, on the train and the elevated, are performing a horrendous and formless ritual" (Huizinga 1972: 243).

[45] In a discussion of Russell, Frege, and the Vienna Circle, Toulmin (1972: 59) makes a similar point: "They have not sufficiently faced the question how any abstraction can be self-validating, or can guarantee its own relevance." See also Chartier (1992).

[46] For the idea of "poaching," see de Certeau (1984: 12); for an insightful discussion of transgression, see Stallybrass and White (1986).

[47] Chartier (1992); Genette (1987: 8); McGann (1991: 13). McGann assumes that materiality only has significance for literary works, but such a view is far too narrow. Ziman, for instance, has argued that science too is a product of similar social-material processes that create "public knowledge" and insert it into the system of consumption. Latour and Woolgar's sociology of science reaches similar conclusions. See Ziman (1968), Latour and Woolgar (1986). More generally, the distinction McGann makes between "noise" and "information" assumes that constraints can always be distinguished from resources.

[48] This paradox is laid out more fully in Seely Brown and Duguid (1994a). As I read it, Derrida's distinction between speech and writing tends to suggest that all distal coordination is not merely problematic but impossible, because communicating artifacts introduce temporal deferral passing beyond immediate negotiation. I am suggesting that in fact social systems of negotiation have allowed coordination that this abstract philosophical skepticism cannot explain away. See Derrida (1977).

[49] For the characteristics of modern hypertext, see Landow (1992: 4-5), Bush (1945a), Nelson (1990), Delany and Landow (eds.) (1994). For an insightful and more moderate and practical approach, see McGann, "The rationale of hypertext" (online, available WWW: http://jefferson.village.virginia.edu/public/jjm2f/rationale.html). Landow suggests that the electronic links of modern systems provide a certain ease that supersedes earlier forms. Ease certainly seems important, but not defining. Moreover, the importance of ease is often missing from assaults on the codex book.

[50] W. Pinnock, *Catechism of Trade and Commerce: Intended to Lay the Basis of Practical Commercial Knowledge in the Youthful Mind...* London: G. & B. Whittaker, 1828: 26.

[51] There were two main types of accounting, single and double entry. Usually only large firms (and not all those, the Dutch East India Company being a classic exception) used a full set of books and double-entry accounting. Many businesses and most individuals kept single-entry accounts, but even these usually involved some sort of journal and cash book as well as the accounts themselves. Personal accounts are often an intriguing combination of all three.

[52] Weber saw "rational capital accounting" as the "most general presupposition for the existence of present-day capitalism" (M. Weber, *General Economic History*, quoted in Giddens and Held eds. 1982: 81). According to Braudel, Sombart also saw it as the essence of the rationality of capitalist practice, arguing intriguingly that capitalism and bookkeeping were as close to one another as form and content. See Braudel (1992: 573 *passim*) and Yamey (1949). As with other supersessive arguers, both Sombart and Weber have problems with their periodizing, for the technology of bookkeeping long predated the capitalist society they so closely linked to it.

[53] See Anderson (1976) and Linebaugh (1992).

[54] See, for example, Nunberg (this volume).

[55] Habermas (1989: chapter 1), Kronick (1962); Schaffner (1994). The relationship between bookkeeping and the novel's moral accounting (with *Robinson Crusoe* as an emblematic instance of the suspect practice of keeping two sets of books) deserves greater exploration. See some suggestive comments in Teichgraeber (1993).

References

ALTHUSSER, L.
1990 *For Marx*, London: Verso.

ANDERSON, G.
1976 *Victorian Clerks*, Manchester: Manchester University Press.

ANDERSON, P
1992 "The ends of history," in *A Zone of Engagement*, London: Verso.

BALLO, G., CACHIN-NORA, F., LEYMARIE, F., AND RUSSOLI, F.
1973 *Le Futurisme*, Paris: Editions des Musés Nationaux.

BANHAM, R.
1967 *Theory and Design in the First Machine Age*, New York: Praeger Publishing, second edition.

BARLOW, J.
1995 "Selling wine without bottles: The economy of wine on the global net", available FTP or Telnet: ftp.eff.org Directory: on line\Pub\Publication: John-Perry-Barlow: idea-economy-article.

BARTHES, R.
1974 *S/Z: An Essay*, New York: Hill & Wang.

1979 "From work to text," in J. Harari (ed.), *Textual Strategies: Perspectives in Post-Structuralist Criticism*, Ithaca: Cornell University Press.

BATE, W.J.
1970 *The Burden of the Past and the English Poet*, Cambridge (Mass.): Belknap Press.

BAUDRILLARD, J.
1981 *Simulacres et Simulations*, Paris: Editions Galilé.

BENJAMIN, W.
1969 "Theses on the philosophy of history," in H. Arendt (ed.), *Illuminations: Essays and Reflections*, New York: Schocken Books.

BIRKERTS, S.
1994 *The Gutenberg Elegies: The Fate of Reading in an Electronic Age*, Boston: Faber & Faber.

BLOOM, H.
1975 *The Anxiety of Influence: A Theory of Poetry*, New York: Oxford University Press.

BOLTER, J.D.
1991 *Writing Space: The Computer, Hypertext, and the History of Writing*, Hillsdale: Erlbaum Associates.

BRAUDEL, F.
1992 *Civilization and Capitalism. The Wheels of Commerce*, vol. 2, Berkeley: University of California Press.

BUSH, V.
1945a "As we may think," *Atlantic Monthly*, 176: 101-108.
1945b *Science. The Endless Frontier: A Report to the President for Postwar Scientific Research*, Washington: National Science Foundation.

BUTLER, S.
1970 *Erewhon*, Harmondsworth: Penguin Books.

CARR, E.H.
1964 *What Is History: The G.M. Trevelyan Lectures*, Harmondsworth: Penguin Books.

CHARTIER, R.
1991 *The Cultural Origins of the French Revolution*, Durham: Duke University Press.
1992 *L'Ordre des livres*, Paris: Alinea.

COOK, T.
1995 "It's 10 o'clock: Do you know where your data are?" *Technology Review*, January, on line available WWW: http://web.mit.edu/afs/athena/org/t/techreview/www/articles/dec94/cook. html.

DARNTON, R.
1979 *The Business of the Enlightenment: The Publishing History of the Encyclopédie*, Cambridge: Harvard University Press.

DAVIS, E.
1993 "Techgnosis, magic, memory, and the angels of information," in M. Derby (ed.), *Flame Wars: The Discourse of Cyberspace*, special issue of *South Atlantic Quarterly*, 92, 4: 585-616.

DE CERTEAU, M.
1984 *The Practice of Everyday Life*, Berkeley: University of California Press.

DE LANDA, M.
1993 "Virtual environments and the emergence of synthetic reasoning," in M. Derby (ed.), *Flame Wars: The Discourse of Cyberspace*, special issue of *South Atlantic Quarterly*, 92, 4: 793-815.

DELANY, P., AND LANDOW, G. (EDS.)
1994 *Hypermedia and Literary Studies*, Cambridge (Mass.): MIT Press.

DE MAN, P.
1983 *Blindness and Insight: Essays in the Rhetoric of Contemporary Criticism*, Minneapolis: University of Minnesota Press.

DERRIDA, J.
1977 *Writing and Difference*, Chicago: University of Chicago Press.

EISENSTEIN, E.
1979 *The Printing Press as an Agent of Change: Communications and Cultural Transformations in Early Modern Europe*, Cambridge: Cambridge University Press, 2 vols.
1983 *The Printing Revolution in Early Modern Europe*, Cambridge: Cambridge University Press.

EMPSON, W.
1947 *Seven Types of Ambiguity*, London: Chatto & Windus.
1950 *Some Versions of Pastoral: A Study of the Pastoral Form in Literature*, Norfolk, CT: New Directions.

FEBVRE, L., AND MARTIN, H.-J.
1984 *The Coming of the Book: The Impact of Printing, 1450-1800*, London: Verso.

FEIGENBAUM, E., AND MCCORDUCK, P.
1983 *Fifth Generation: Artificial Intelligence and Japan's Computer Challenge to the World*, Reading: Addison-Wesley.

FORD, M.
1995 "Without a city wall," *TLS*, 4798.

FOUCAULT, M.
1972 *The Archaeology of Knowledge and the Discourse on Language*, New York: Pantheon.
1977a "Nietzsche, genealogy, history," in *Language, Counter-Memory, Practice: Selected Interviews and Essays*, Ithaca: Cornell University Press.
1977b "What is an author," *Language, Counter-Memory, Practice: Selected Essays and Interviews*, Ithaca: Cornell University Press.

GENETTE, G.
1987 *Seuils*, Paris: Seuils.

GIDDENS, A., AND HELD, D. (EDS.)
1982 *Classes, Power, and Conflict: Classical and Contemporary Debates*, Berkeley: University of California Press.

GUMBRECHT, H.
1995 "A farewell to interpretation," in H. Gumbrecht and K. Pfeiffer (eds.), *Materialities of Communication*, Stanford: Stanford University Press.

HABERMAS, J.
1989 *The Structural Transformation of the Public Sphere: An Inquiry into a Category of Bourgeois Society*, Cambridge (Mass.): MIT Press.

HUGO, V.
1978 *Notre Dame of Paris*, Harmondsworth: Penguin Books.

HUIZINGA, J.
1972 *America: A Dutch Historian's Vision from Afar and Near*, New York: Harper Torchbooks.

JAMES, H.
1987 *The American Scene*, London: Granville.

JAMESON, F.
1994 *Postmodernism or the Cultural Logic of Late Capitalism*, Durham: Duke University Press.

JOHNSON, R.
1986 "The story so far and further transformations," in D. Punter (ed.), *Introduction to Contemporary Cultural Studies*, London: Longman: 277-3.

KAHN, H., AND WEINER, A.
1968 "One hundred technical innovations likely in the next 33 years," in *Toward the Year 2000: Work in Progress*, American Academy of Arts and Sciences, Boston: Beacon Press.

KRONICK, D.
1962 *A History of Scientific and Technical Periodicals: The Origins and Development of the Scientific and Technological Press, 1665-1790*, New York: Scarecrow Press.

LANDOW, G.P.
1992 *Hypertext: The Convergence of Contemporary Critical Theory and Technology*, Baltimore: Johns Hopkins University Press.

LANHAM, R.
1994 *The Electronic Word: Democracy, Technology, and the Arts*, Chicago: University of Chicago Press.

LATOUR, B., AND WOOLGAR, S.
1986 *Laboratory Life: The Construction of Scientific Facts*, Princeton: Princeton University Press.

LINEBAUGH, P.
1992 *The London Hanged: Crime and Civil Society in the Eighteenth Century*, New York: Cambridge University Press.

LYOTARD, F.
1979 *The Postmodern Condition: A Report on Knowledge*, Minneapolis: University of Minnesota Press.

MARVELL, A.
1972 "Horation ode," in E. Story Donno (ed.), *The Complete Poems*, Harmondsworth: Penguin Books.

MARX, L.
1964 *The Machine in the Garden: Technology and the Pastoral Ideal in America*, New York: Oxford University Press.
1994 "The ideology of technology and 'postmodern' pessimism," in M. Smith and L. Marx (eds.), *Does Technology Drive History? The Dilemma of Technological Determinism*, Boston: MIT Press.

MCGANN, J.
n.d. The rationale of hypertext (on line), available WWW: http://jefferson.village.virginia.edu/public/jjmaf/rationale/html.
1991 *The Textual Condition*, Princeton: Princeton University Press.

MCKENZIE, D.
1986 *Bibliography and the Sociology of the Text*, London: British Library.

MCLUHAN, H.M.
1962 *The Gutenberg Galaxy: Making of Typographic Man*, Toronto: Toronto University Press.

MCNALLY, P. (ED.)
1987 "The advent of printing: historians of science respond to Elizabeth Eisenstein's" *The Printing Press as an Agent of Change*, Occasional Paper 10, Montreal: Graduate School of Library and Information Studies, McGill University.

MITCHELL, W.
1995 *City of Bits: Space, Place, and the Infobahn*, Cambridge (Mass.): MIT Press.

NEGROPONTE, N.
1995 *Being Digital*, New York: Basic Books.

NELSON, T.
1990 *Literary Machines*, Sausalito: Mindful Press.

NIETHAMMER, L.
1992 *Posthistoire: Has History Come to an End?*, London: Verso.

OZENFANT
1952 *Foundations of Modern Art*, New York: Dover Publications.

PETROSKY, H.
1990 *The Pencil: A History of Design and Circumstance*, New York: Alfred A. Knopf.

REDDY, M.J.
1979 "The conduit metaphor," in A. Ortney (ed.), *Metaphor and Thought*, Boston: Cambridge University Press: 284-324.

RICHARDS, I.A.
1960 *Principles of Literary Criticism*, London: Routledge & Kegan Paul.

ROBERTS, J. (ED.)
1994 *Art Has No History: The Making and Unmaking of Modern Art*, London: Verso.

ROTHENBERG, J.
1995 "Ensuring the longevity of digital documents," *Scientific American*, 272, 1: 42-47.

SAID, E.
1978 *Orientalism*, London: Routledge & Kegan Paul.

SCHAFFNER, A.
1994 "The future of scientific journals: Lessons from the past," *Information Technology and Libraries*, 13, 4: 239-47.

SCHRAGE, M.
1995 "Revolutionary evolutionist," *Wired*, July: 120-124.

SEELY BROWN, J., AND DUGUID, P.
1994a "Borderline issues: Social and material aspects of design," *Human Computer Interaction,* 9, 1: 3-35.
1994b "Patrolling the border: A reply," *Human Computer Interaction*, 9, 1: 137-149.

STALLYBRASS, P., AND WHITE, A.
1986 *The Politics and Poetics of Transgression*, Ithaca: Cornell University Press.

STERLING, B.
1995 "Free as air, free as water, free as knowledge", on line available FTP or Telnet: ftp.eff.org. Directory:\Pub\Publications:Bruce_Sterling:Free_As_Air.speech.

STUART, R.
1995 "High-tech redlining," *Utne Reader*, 68.

SUTHERLAND, J.
1989 "Publishing history: a hole in the centre of literary sociology," in P. Desan et al. (eds.), *Literature and Social Practice*, Chicago: University of Chicago Press: 267-82.

TEICHGRAEBER, R.
1993 "'A Yankee Diogenes': Thoreau and the market," in T. Haskell and R. Teichgraeber (eds.), *The Culture of the Market: Historical Essays*, New York: Cambridge University Press: 293-325.

TOFFLER, A.
1971 *Future Shock*, London: Pan Books.

TOULMIN, S.
1972 *Human Understanding*: *The Collective Use and Evolution of Concepts*, Princeton: Princeton University Press.

WHITE, R., AND LIMERICK, P.
1994 *The Frontier in American Culture*, Berkeley: University of California Press.

WILLIAMS, R.
1961 *The Long Revolution: An Analysis of the Democratic, Industrial, and Cultural Changes Transforming Our Society*, London: Chatto & Windus.
1973 *The Country and the City*, Oxford: Oxford University Press.
1974 *Television*, New York: Shocken Books.

YAMEY, B.S.
1949 "Scientific bookkeeping and the rise of capitalism," *EHR* (second edition series), 1, 2 and 3: 99-113.

ZIMAN, J.
1968 *Public Knowledge: An Essay Concerning the Social Dimension of Science*, Cambridge: Cambridge University Press.

Geoffrey Nunberg

FAREWELL TO THE INFORMATION AGE

Paper is just an object that [some] information has been sprayed onto in the past... (Ted Nelson)

And one of the side effects of digital technology is that it makes those containers irrelevant. Books, CDs, filmstrips – whatever – don't need to exist anymore in order to get ideas out. So whereas we thought we had been in the wine business, suddenly we realized that all along we've been in the bottling business. (John Perry Barlow)

[In cyberspace, communication will be] redeemed from all the inefficiencies, pollutions, and corruptions attendant to the process of moving information attached to *things*. (Michael Benedikt)

1. Introduction: The word turned upside-down

Nothing betrays the spirit of an age so precisely as the way it represents the future. Take the picture that appeared in *Popular Mechanics* magazine in 1950 in an article on "The Home of the Future." It shows a woman in an apron in the middle of a living room full of furniture with the rounded "futuristic" forms of the period, which she is spraying with a garden hose. The caption reads, "Because all her furniture is waterproof, the housewife of the year 2000 can do her cleaning with a hose." Like most such representations, it gives itself away in two complementary misapprehensions. The first and most obvious comes of taking some recent innovation at the steepest point of its curve and projecting it linearly to a point where it has swept all its predecessors aside. No one makes provision for the inevitable banalization of the new, or for the reactions that it invokes – what Régis Debray describes in his essay here as "neolithic backlash" (though "neolignic backlash" might be more appropriate, if you'll excuse the etymological blend). And indeed, just twenty years later the hippies were using "plastic" as a general term of disdain for the artificiality of modern culture.

The second misapprehension is the opposite of the first. It comes from a failure to appreciate, not how durable some features of the material setting will turn out to be, but rather how contingent and mutable are some of the categories of social life. What is most telling to us now about the *Popular Mechanics* picture is its presupposition that in the year 2000 the household cleaning will still be woman's work – and indeed the function of the picture, wittingly or unwittingly, is to naturalize that assumption. This is a much harder kind of misconception to avoid, because it rests on the unspoken presuppositions of a discourse, and as such is more difficult to bring to consciousness. Or to put it another way: the first sort of error is in seeing the future as being insufficiently like the present, and that is relatively easy to correct for; you just imagine the future furnished like the room you are in, whereas the second sort of error involves seeing the future as insufficiently different from the present, and this we can correct for only by a determined act of imagination: forty-five years from now gender roles will be different... how?

Discussions of the future of the book involve both kinds of misapprehensions. For the thematization of material change, we have the picture of electronic media driving the printed book and the institutions of print culture to the margins of discourse. (To paraphrase the closing line of the mad scientist in the movie *Back to the Future*, "Books? Where we're going we don't need books.") For the present it's enough to observe that there is nothing in the economics of publishing as a whole or the body of practice surrounding the use of the printed book that militates for its disappearance, even over the long term. And while it is certain that many forms and genres will migrate in part or in whole to an electronic mode of existence over the coming years, there are numerous other printed genres that stand to benefit from the new technologies, whether in the form of electronic text preparation, demand printing, Web advertising, or, what may be most important, the computerized inventory systems that have made possible new types of retail distribution that have vastly extended general public access to texts over the past five years in ways that are arguably more significant than the effects of electronic media.[1] There will be a digital revolution, but the printed book will be an important participant in it. And by the same token, there is no reason to expect the digital library to replace the brick-and-mortar library, even less so once we can make a physical replica of any book in the collection of the Gregorian University and put it on the shelves of a university library in Iowa or Lyon at the same time we make it available over the Web in digital form. In all of this we are likely to be seriously misled by analogies to technologies like movable type, which established a privative opposition between two kinds of artifacts. There never was a technology less amenable to determinist arguments than this one.

For the indefinite future, then, there will be printed books, just as surely as there will be wooden shelves and coffee tables to put them on. But none of this should be taken as depreciating the cultural effects of electronic media. Enthusiasts of the new technologies are right to point out that the introduction of these media is bound to be accompanied by sweeping changes in all the features of the modern literary system, to use Carla Hesse's phrase, including the relation between author and reader, the nature of the public, the conception of intellectual property, and the nature of the text itself. It is true, as writers like Jay Bolter and Raffaele Simone point out here, that many of these changes have been prefigured by tendencies in modern print publications, to an extent that visionaries are slow to acknowledge. But the effects of the new media will be profound.

The difficulties, both conceptual and practical, come when we try to spell out the effects of the new technologies in detail. And here, for all the revolutionary talk of the enthusiasts, there is a persistent tendency to yield to the second kind of misapprehension that representations of the future are liable to, where we naturalize contingent features of the current order of things. Indeed, the revolutionary rhetoric of the enthusiasts makes them especially susceptible to this presupposition, because the goal of making the material advantages of the new media sound inviting and exciting requires us to assume a continuity of communicative needs and interests. It is not the brief of visionaries to make the New Jerusalem sound like an alien place (the enthusiasm of *Popular Mechanics* readers for the new chemistry might have been more tempered if the designer of that picture had had the prescience to put the hose in the hand of a man).

The tendency is pervasive. When theorists talk about the power of the new media to make everyone an author, for example, or to provide everyone with universal access to potential audiences of millions of readers, they invoke a notion of authorship and a model of access that are more appropriate to traditional print media than to electronic communication. What is an author, after all, if the new media no longer support the legal status or institutional privileges that have traditionally defined that role? And what real increase is there in the ability of the average citizen to affect public opinion if anyone who wants to gain the attention of a mass audience has to compete for attention with millions of other "authors"? There was a telling example of this sort of difficulty not long ago in a story in an academic newsletter about an assistant professor at a Southern university who had posted on a news list a bibliography of sources on the uses of virtual reality in education and was sedulously keeping a record of all the electronic queries that she had received about her work from all over the world, in the hope of being able to demonstrate to her tenure committee that her work had "an international reputation." But the assumption implicit in that phrase – that the magnitude or breadth of someone's reputation is proportional to its farthest geographic extension – has no relevance in the electronic world, where it takes no greater investment of resources to make a text available to distant readers than to local ones. Electronic publication implies a new calculus of reputation, which I think no one has yet come to grips with.

One other example. Enthusiasts of the media have sometimes said that a medium like the Web makes it possible to actualize intertextuality to the point of eradicating all of the boundaries and divisions between texts, so that we arrive, finally, at a perfect Derridean *débordement* of meaning – a text, as George Landow has put it, that cannot shut out other texts. The implication is that digital technology makes it possible for literature to do in the light of day what it has up to now been able to do only furtively. It is true that we can have something of this feeling when we are moving amongst Web documents, where there need be no material difference, say, between the link that takes us to the subsequent chapter of a text and the link that takes us to one of its predecessors or to a commentary on it, even if these are stored at different sites. But there is a difficulty even in speaking of "intertextuality" when the individuation of texts themselves becomes so problematic: what could *débordement* signify when there are no *bords* in the first place? Ultimately, this sort of argument rests on an anachronistic sense of the text that is carried over from our experience of print. Whereas what electronic media really give us, in the end, is something stranger than that: a domain where there can be intertextuality without transgression.

It's understandable, of course, that it should take a while to accommodate the conceptual consequences of any technologies whose effects are so pervasive we have to rethink not just obviously print-based categories like "publication" and "authorship," but also notions like "reputation," with all the temporal and spatial presuppositions it trails in its wake. Perhaps the most basic and least well examined of these, though, is the notion of content itself. The quotations that I began this essay with are typical of virtually all the manifestos issued on behalf of the new technologies in their assumption that content is a noble substance that is indifferent to the transformation of its vehicles. In the print world it was attached to things or contained in them, but now it can be liberated and manipulated as a kind of pure essence: we can break the bottles and have the wine. In this essay, I want to show that these metaphors play false to the truth; we are rather in the situation, as Paul Duguid puts it, of breaking the banks and hoping still to have the river.

Of course writers like these do not usually talk about content as such, of course, but rather as "information," a term that incorporates assumptions of nobility and transferability in its meaning, so that it seems foregone that content will be preserved intact when its material and social supports are stripped away. But considering how much work we ask the word "information" to do, we don't spend time thinking critically about what it means. As Philip Agre (to appear) has put the point: "... the term 'information' rarely evokes the deep and troubling questions of epistemology that are usually associated with terms like 'knowledge' and 'belief.' One can be a skeptic about knowledge but not about information. Information, in short, is a strikingly bland substance." The reason for this, Agre argues, is that information is a category shaped by professional ideologies and, like most ideological terms, is invested with a "pregiven" character that makes it impervious to interrogation. This is surely right, but it doesn't justify our discounting information as a notion whose interest is exhausted once we've dispelled the forms of semantical false consciousness that it embodies. Agre is certainly right, for example, to say that part of the work that "information" does for librarians is to flatten and obscure the subjective social topographies of content that are implicit when we speak of the holdings of a library in terms of "literatures." And from a different point of view, Dan Schiller (1994) has argued that as used by postindustrial theorists like Daniel Bell, the word "information" "... both covers and covers up much of what was referenced by the anthropological sense of 'culture.'" But even granting all this, it doesn't follow that we can simply drop the word "information" from our vocabularies in favor of "literatures," "culture," "knowledge," or whatever other items it seems to be standing in for.

One simple reason for this is that once we begin the purge we might not know where to stop. Like many of the words that do important ideological work, "information" is anchored in unexceptionable ordinary usage. It goes without saying that "information" is not simply a substitute for "culture" or the rest when we say something like "Can you give me some information about vacation rentals?" Nor for that matter do we have any right to complain about the technical uses of the word as such, for example when somebody talks about the amount of information in a particular television signal or in the genetic code. But where and how do we draw the distinction, and what kind of distinction is it? Is the suspect use of "information" merely a "loose" use of the word or a separate sense? And in either case, what is its relation to the technical and ordinary-language uses of the word? As a kind of propadeutic, then, we have to do a certain amount of philological reconstruction.

2. The philolology of "information"

The OED2 gives the word "information" only two relevant current senses.[2] The first is of these is what we can think of as the particularistic sense of the word, the sense it has in an ordinary sentence like "I'm looking for a book with information about guinea pigs," where it means, as the OED2 puts it:

> Knowledge communicated concerning some particular fact, subject, or event; that of which one is apprised or told; intelligence, news. spec. contrasted with *data*.

(This definition isn't quite as precise or as complete as we might like, but it will do for now.) The second sense given by the OED2 is what we can think of as the naturalistic sense, which arose in the twentieth century when the word was made a term of art in fields like cybernetics and information theory. The OED explains this sense as follows:

> Separated from, or without the implication of, reference to a person informed: that which inheres in one of two or more alternative sequences, arrangements, etc., that produce different responses in something, and which is capable of being stored in, transferred by, and communicated to inanimate things.[3]

The OED makes this second sense a subsense of the first, with the implication that it is really a kind of reconstruction or elaboration of the ordinary use of the word. As it happens, William Weaver explicitly rejected this interpretation of the theory that he and Shannon had developed:

> The word "information," in this theory, is used in a special sense that must not be confused with its ordinary usage. In particular, information must not be confused with meaning. In fact, two messages, one of which is heavily loaded with meaning and the other of which is pure nonsense, can be exactly equivalent, from the present viewpoint, as regards information. (Weaver 1964: 4)[4]

Weaver's reservations are warranted, though of course if he and Shannon had really wanted to avoid confusion they would have done better to refer to their enterprise as "entropy theory" or "signal theory" (both of which were seriously considered for a time), or at least as "informativeness theory," which would have more closely captured the notion of information as a property of a signal relative to an interpreter. In any case these reservations did not stop postwar social scientists from trying to put the theory to use in their accounts of human communication. More generally, people have come to assume that the "information" that figures in computer science – the stuff of bits and bandwidths – is the same use of the word that figures in its ordinary usage. As *BusinessWeek* put it in a special number on "The Information Revolution":

> We can glean it from the pages of a book or the morning newspaper and from the glowing phosphors of a video screen. Scientists find it stored in our genes and in the lush complexity of the rain forest. And it's always in the air where people come together, whether to work, play, or just gab. (*BusinessWeek*, 1994)

One effect of this is to create the retrospective anachronism that is implicit in that "contrasted with *data*" clause in the OED2 definition, which suggests that the "information" that we contrast with "data" is the same sort of stuff that Lydgate was talking about when he used the word in the fifteenth century, two hundred years before the word *data* entered the language. This trope is ubiquitous in writing about the cultural implications of the new technologies. For example the *BusinessWeek* article goes on to say: "... all technologies that 'process information' (although they were never described in those terms in the predigital era) affect deeply the societies that use them. Johannes Gutenberg's printing press eventually helped reformers to erode the Catholic Church's political power...". The trope is crucial to the claims of enthusiasts of the technology that it will usher in a new and epochal discursive order. We have to believe, that is, that the substance that computers traffic in, "information" in the technical sense of the term, is the same sort of stuff that led to the Reformation and the French Revolution, whether or not contemporaries talked about it in those terms.

But the fact is that the use of "information" that people have in mind when they talk about "the information age" or say that information brought about the Reformation is not quite what the OED is describing in its definition of the ordinary particularistic sense of the word – what we get when we call an airline to find out about flight times. They are thinking rather of what I will call the "abstract" sense of the word, where it refers not to "knowledge... concerning some particular fact, subject, or event," but rather to a kind of intentional substance that is present in the world, a sense that is no longer closely connected to the use of the verb "inform," anchored in particular speech acts. This is the sense of the word which bears the ideological burden in discussions of the new technologies.

The distinction between the particularistic and abstract senses is not immediately evident, particularly in English – after all, it escaped the attention even of the redoubtable compilers of the OED. And indeed, our first temptation is to say that "information" in this abstract sense is really the same sort of thing as "information" in the particularistic sense, only taken in the aggregate; it merely denotes the sum of all the bits of information about particulars that are at large in the world. In this way these general uses of "information" might be compared to the general uses of a word like "gossip." When we say something like "gossip is unreliable," for example, we are simply taking "gossip" as a universal that comprises all the instances of particular gossip – gossip about the Smiths, gossip about the new boss, gossip about movie stars, and so on.

It is true that the particularistic sense of "information" can have something like this aggregate use. When we say that such-and-such a book contains much useful information, for example, we mean that it has numerous bits of useful information about particular things. In the end, though, the story doesn't quite explain the use of the word we are interested in. One way of making this point is to consider how we translate these various phrases into other European languages, where the particularistic sense of "information" is rendered by count nouns, usually in the plural – French *informations* or *renseignements*, Italian *informazioni*, Modern Greek *plirofories*, and so on. (English too permitted such a usage until the mid-nineteenth century.) So we would translate a sentence like "The book contains a lot of useful information" into French as *Le livre contient beaucoup de renseignements* (or *informations*) *utiles*. But we would not use the plural to translate a sentence like "The world is overwhelmed by information," or a phrase like "the information age" – uses like these are generally translated using either a mass term (as in *l'age d'information*) or sometimes by using an unrelated word like *connaissance*. Of course the fact that French has two words where English has one does not necessarily mean that the English word is ambiguous (they have two words for "river," after all), but it does suggest that there is a principled distinction to be made.

There is another bit of circumstantial evidence that is relevant to the distinction, which may help to explain why the first edition of the OED did not record it: this abstract sense of the word did not appear in English (or in any other language) until the mid-nineteenth century. Before this period you could not really speak of information in an abstract way. There is a revealing example in *Gulliver's Travels*: "For he argued thus: that the use of speech was to make us understand one another, and to receive information of facts...". It's notable that Swift could not say simply that the use of speech was "to receive information" *tout court*, but could only refer to an aggregation of particular propositions (this sentence would be translated into French using a plural). He had no way, that is, to speak of information as a kind of abstract stuff present in the world, disconnected from the situations that it is *about*.

This "presence" of abstract information is one of the crucial properties that distinguishes it from particularistic information. This is what makes it possible to talk about it as a measurable quantity, particularly in the claims about the "information explosion" that people like to make with extravagant exactitude. For example, there is a widely repeated claim to the effect that a daily issue of the *New York Times* contains more information than the average seventeenth-century Englishman came across in a lifetime.[5] Now whatever writers have in mind when they make such claims (not a great deal, you suspect), it's clear that they are not talking simply about the sum of individual propositions that are communicated from one agent to another. That seventeenth-century Englishman was doubtless informed of any number of things over the course of his life – relatives wrote to tell him when they were coming to visit, a gardener told him that the peaches would be particularly sweet this year. But clearly these things were of no account to whoever made the estimate, since it would be absurd to suppose you could calculate their number. Nor do people who try to quantify information have in mind the naturalistic sort of information that inheres, say, in the markings on a mushroom that indicate it is poisonous or in the darkening sky that announces the imminence of a rainstorm. Clearly there is no way to estimate how much of *that* sort of information there is in the world, nor is it possible or for that matter interesting to know whether there is more of it now than there was a few centuries ago.

When people refer to the amount of information that the average seventeenth-century Englishman came across in a lifetime or say that the amount of information is doubling every five (or twenty, or fifty) years, they are talking about the information in published documents, in the broad sense of the term – documents, that is, that have been made available for unknown others to refer to, whether by circulating them or putting them in files or archives. And this way of talking rests on two assumptions. First, they assume a correlation between the size of a text (as measured in characters, bytes, column inches, or whatever) and the amount of content it conveys – a step that implies the commoditization of content that is central to the cultural role we ask information to play. And at the same time they privilege this content communicated in this way at the expense of content communicated privately or irreproducibly.

And indeed, this sense of "information" was privileged from its inception. As it happens this use of the word is probably not directly derived from the ordinary particularistic sense, but rather from the now-obsolete use of "information" to mean "formation or moulding of the mind or character, instruction," a sense that's equivalent to the German *Bildung*. The OED2 has nothing to say about this development (as we saw, it doesn't even recognize the abstract sense at all), but the point is clear enough when we look at early nineteenth-century uses of the word to mean "instruction" and note how often we are tempted to interpret it in the modern way. The misreading is particularly easy to make when the context involves talk or "having," "acquiring" or "receiving" information, or in phrases like "man of information." For example:

> "Mr. Martin, I suppose, is not a man of information beyond the line of his own business? He does not read?" (Jane Austen, *Emma*)

> Susan was growing very fond of her, and though without any of the early delight in books which had been so strong in Fanny, with a disposition much less inclined to sedentary pursuits, or to information for information's sake, she had so strong a desire of not *appearing* ignorant... (Jane Austen, *Mansfield Park*)[6]

> I would not be hurried by any love of system, by any exaggeration of instincts, to underrate the Book... [G]reat and heroic men have existed, who had almost no other information than by the printed page. I only would say, that it needs a strong head to bear that diet. One must be an inventor to read well... (Ralph Waldo Emerson, *The American Scholar*)[7]

Austen would not have considered it admirable in Fanny to have been interested in "information for information's sake" if the word for her had entailed no more than knowing the names and dates of all the kings of England. And it would be wholly alien to Emerson's thought in this passage to assume that the "information" that heroic men might derive from books was merely a matter of knowledge of facts. At the same time, though, each of the uses *could* be misread, with just the slightest change in understanding, so that "information" was taken to denote not the instruction derived from books, but the content of books from which instruction is derived – the same kind of "cause for effect" metonymy that has left us with "mystery" and "horror" as the names of genres. And this, I suggest, is exactly what contemporaries did in creating the new sense of the word.

Like most of the misreadings that underlie such shifts of meaning, this one was highly strategic. On the one hand, it resituated the agency of instruction in the text and its producers, and reduced the reader to the role of a passive consumer of content, far from Emerson's "inventor." Michel de Certeau talks about this process in *The Invention of Everyday Life* under the heading, "The Ideology of 'Information' through Books" (the title plays on a similar polysemy in the French word). He casts it as a stage in the progressive evolution of the Enlightenment belief in a society produced by a textual system [*système "scripturaire"*], which "always had as its corollary the assumption... of a public shaped by writing (verbal or iconic), but in both cases, a society that starts to resemble that which it takes in, to the point where it is, so to say, *imprinted* by and in the image of the text that is stamped upon it" (de Certeau 1990: 241).

At the same time the shift in the denotation of "information" from effect to cause facilitated another, no less strategic confusion between abstract and particularistic information, which was conflated under the assumption that the production of "informed" public consciousness was to be achieved chiefly through the production and dissemination of "objective" propositional content – the "information," that is, on whose free exchange the functioning of democratic society, the free marketplace, and the rest are routinely held to depend. And by way of response, the older, particularistic use of information came increasingly to be restricted to the sorts of things you might learn from a book or from an official or institutional source. When your six-year-old daughter tells you that she doesn't like vegetables, for example, you wouldn't ordinarily describe her as having provided you with information about her tastes (not that you'd be lying if you did, but you would open yourself to a charge of archness). We can no longer use the word the way Emily Brontë could in *Wuthering Heights*, to refer to a casual communication about immediate experience:

> "A letter from your old acquaintance, the housekeeper at the Grange," I answered... She would gladly have gathered it up at this information, but Hareton beat her.

This development has contributed to the confusion between the two senses, as particularistic information has come to be treated increasingly as a subtype of abstract information – the particles of propositional content derived from public sources that make up information in the mass.

The modern public sense of "information," then, has arisen through a conceptual creolization, first of the *Bildung* and particularistic senses, and subsequently of these two with the naturalistic sense provided by information theory. In this sort of situation, any effort to try to extract a coherent conceptual structure for the notion would be not just futile but false to its phenomenology: "information" is able to perform the work it does precisely because it fuzzes the boundaries between several genetically distinct categories of experience. Ultimately, then, the question we want to ask is phenomenological rather than lexicographical: not, What does "information" mean? but rather, How is the impression of "information" constituted out of certain practices of reading and the particular representations that support them?

3. The phenomenology of information

In "The Storyteller," Walter Benjamin described information (by which we should understand abstract information) as a "form of communication" that emerged with "the full control of the middle class, which has the press as one of its most important instruments in fully developed capitalism" (Benjamin 1936/1969a: 88). The description nicely encapsulates the two kinds of conditions that the phenomenon of information rests on. The first are social: the rise of industrial capitalism and all the apparatus that accompanies it. The second are the particular forms of expression and representation that served as what Benjamin calls the "instruments" of these social forces, what we can think of as the informational genres. Both Benjamin and Richard Terdiman (1985) lay particular emphasis on the appearance of the modern mass newspaper – ostensibly apolitical, eclectic in content, and sold to a vast readership for a low price on a copy-by-copy basis. The newspaper was, as Terdiman has observed, the first disposable consumer commodity, and it brought with it a new, commercialized conception of content. It was characterized by "journalistic" objectification and depersonalization of voice; it spoke with (literally) everyday matter-of-factness. But while the modern conception of "the news" (*les informations* in French) is in many ways the prototype for information in the large, a number of other forms of publication contributed to the same effect. The archetype of these is the modern "reference work" (a phrase first used in its modern sense in English in 1859, and in French in 1870) – the "national" dictionaries and encyclopedias of Brockhaus, Webster, and Larousse, the travel guides of Karl Baedeker and John Murray, and the census reports and other government publications that introduced into public discourse the notion of "statistics" in the original sense of the term. In the private sector, too, the growth of managerial organizations was accompanied by the emergence of printed schedules, work rules, and forms.[8] Finally, there were the genres that exploited and inverted the informational mode of reading, particularly the modern novel, which as Benjamin suggests emerged directly out of the crisis created when information confronted the epic form. It is impossible to imagine Dickens, Twain, Galdós, or Zola in a world without newspapers or newspaper readers. There is very little in modern literature that is not either parasitic on information or in violent reaction against it.

These forms were closely mirrored by a new set of institutions and structures charged with representing the modern world. There were the public libraries, great and small, card catalogs, and the "library science" (now "information science") that grew up along with them. There were the public art museums organized "thematically," by period and nation.[9] There were the museums of natural history that grew out of the eighteenth-century cabinet of curiosities, with rows of labeled exhibits that made them seem the material instantiation of the encyclopedic dictionary. There were the museums of science and industry and the international expositions that inscribed the Baedekers on urban spaces. There were department stores, which as Terdiman observes, mirrored the organization of newspapers in their deliberate scattering of "articles" and the putative universality of their offerings. There was fiat money.

4. The properties of "information"

Each after its fashion, these forms impose a particular registration on their content, with characteristic syntax and semantics, which in turn elicit a particular mode of reading from its consumers. What I want to show in this section is how all the properties we ascribe to information – its metaphysical haeceity or "thereness," its transferability, its quantized and extended substance, its interpretive transparency or autonomy – are simply the reifications of the various principles of interpretation that we bring to bear in reading these forms.

Materially, we talk about information as a uniform and morselized substance. By saying that information is uniform I mean that it is held to be indifferent not just to the medium it resides in but also to the kind of representation it embodies; for example *BusinessWeek* speaks of "the computer's ability to reduce all conventional information forms into one big digital stew," so that "a stream of digital bits can be engineered to represent a complex expression of text, calculations, sound, moving pictures, real-time simulations...". In this sense information is as I suggested a noble substance. It doesn't change its nature according either to the medium it is stored in or the way it is represented – in principle, we needn't alter the informational content of a table when we transform it to a bar graph, of a novel when we convert it to a comic book. These are all matters of information "visualization," "presentation," or "access," which stand to the right of information on the value-added chain. All of this is an important element in the commoditization of information, since it seems to allow us to establish the quantitative parities among its various manifestations that ensure its general fungibility; if we think exclusively in terms of column inches or disk space, we can set precise equivalencies among pictures and words.

The complement of the uniformity of information is its morselization or quantization, which seems to make possible its measurement. Unlike knowledge, which we often regard holistically, information is essentially corpuscular, like sand or succotash. It consists of little atoms of content – propositions, sentences, bits, infons, *morceaux* – each independently detachable, manipulable, and tabulable. These atoms are spread about in broad regions that correspond to subject-matter domains – there is medical information, sports information, information about the French Revolution, and so forth. But this is a question of geography rather than structure; we can break off pieces of information and ship them around while at the same time preserving their value. This understanding of the substance of information is implicit in all the images that people invoke nowadays when they talk about large accumulations of information. It's a cosmos punctuated by celestial bodies, an unbroken landscape crossed by highways, a vast body of water dotted with archipelagoes. Or sometimes it is several of these in a single passage:

> Cyberspace: A new universe, a parallel universe created and sustained by the world's computers and communications lines... A territory swarming with data and lies, with mind stuff and memories of nature... The realm of pure information, filling like a lake. (Benedikt 1991)

In each case information is a continuous domain in which more or less homogeneous atoms of content are dispersed. It's significant that infospace is rarely depicted by comparison to anything more structured, like a city.

These impressions grow directly out of the material organization of the informational genres. The newspaper, for example, imposes both a temporal and physical corpuscularity on its content. All historical processes have to be rendered as events of immediate daily significance, each occurring in a single place; universalities or generalities can be presented only in the context of their particular manifestations as "news." And as Terdiman observes, descriptions of these events appear on the page alongside descriptions of other, wholly unrelated events presented in exactly the same physical form, which answer only to the topographical requirements of layout – "a disposition of space whose logic, ultimately, is commercial." The effect is all the more marked because the content of the newspaper is so varied: reports of political events and natural disasters, gossip, *faits divers*, editorials, letters to the editor, stock prices, advice columns, reviews, personal announcements, and display advertising (a heterogeneity mirrored in the organization of any TV news hour). Moreover, as Habermas has pointed out, the newspaper has tended to efface the stylistic distinctions between these genres: reportage and editorial material "assumes the guise of narrative from its format down to stylistic detail" and is increasingly "dressed up with all the accouterments of entertainment literature," whereas "on the other hand the belletristic contributions aim for the strictly 'realistic' reduplication of reality 'as it is'... and thus, in turn, erase the line between fiction and report" (Habermas 1989: 150) (again, think of television, and the blurring of genres on "infotainment" shows and the like). As a result of all this, content tends to lose its individual character, even as the presentation suggests the absence of any connections among its atoms. It becomes a matter of column inches; its exchange value comes to dominate its use value.

Other forms and genres achieve the same effect through different means. As Agre (to appear) observes, the structure of a card catalog serves to "flatten" the contents of a collection and obscure the historically constituted organizations of texts that are implicit when we speak of "literatures." In one way or another, this flattening of internal structure is inherent in the principles of organization of most informational genres. Travel guides scatter observations about history, religion, art, architecture, biography, and geology according to the locations of the physical objects they are more or less accidentally associated with, just as dictionaries and most encyclopedias organize their entries according to the accidental properties of their orthographies. It isn't a particularly essential property of Raphael's "La Muta" that it is located in the Ducal Palace of Urbino, no more than it is an essential property of

Raphael that his name begins with an *r*, but in each case that's what determines where the reference is listed in the relevant reference work.

Second, for the boundedness of information. As we saw earlier, (abstract) information is not just quantized but quantifiable in the large, in the sense that people imagine they can determine just how much of it there is in the world, usually in the interest of making alarmed observations about its rate of growth. And this in turn implies that information has a public character, a determinate if fuzzy collective extension. But here again the impression is simply a reflex of the properties of the informational genres. For one thing, as published documents they have a fixed public presence that enables us to index, catalog, and count them and that reinforces the conception of them as public places or loci. (As Benedict Anderson has observed, it is in virtue of this public extension that forms like the newspaper could play a central part in delimiting "imagined communities" like the class and the nation, by offering manifest evidence of a uniform and universal national experience.) No less important, each of these forms offers itself as the exhaustive representation of its domain. The *New York Times* promises to give us "all the news that's fit to print," a claim that is credible even as hyperbole only if we take "the news" to be a circumscribed public quantity whose relevance is uniform for everyone in the community. Analogously, the dictionary is expected to give us all (and only) the words that are appropriate to the language of public discourse, whatever the demurrals of "descriptive" lexicographers. It accomplishes this through a studied spatialization of the language, a process described in a famous passage from Murray's "General Explanation" to the OED:

> That vast aggregate of words and phrases which constitutes the Vocabulary of English-speaking men presents, to the mind that endeavours to grasp it as a definite whole, the aspect of one of those nebulous masses familiar to the astronomer, in which a clear and unmistakable nucleus shades off on all sides, through zones of decreasing brightness, to a dim marginal film that seems to end nowhere, but to lose itself imperceptibly in the surrounding darkness...

The same process is recapitulated, with appropriate differences, in the travel guide that offers us an exhaustive enumeration of all the points worth visiting in a region, in the "universal" exposition, or in the national libraries charged with conserving the entirety of the literary patrimony of the nation. These claims to inclusiveness in turn permit us to attach a significance to exclusion – to an event that doesn't appear in the newspaper, a word that doesn't appear in the dictionary, a historic site or restaurant that doesn't appear in a travel guide, and so on. But of course this kind of claim is only possible when the boundaries of a document or building impose a manifest physical limit on the amount of material it can contain.

The material properties of information, then – its morselization, its uniformity, its quantifiability – are the reifications material properties of the documents that inscribe it – their layout, their boundedness, the collective presence that establishes them as fixed places. By contrast the semantic properties that we ascribe to information – its objectivity and autonomy – are the reflexes of the institutions and practices that surround the use of these documents. "Objectivity" is a complex notion here. It refers, first, to a kind of perspectival objectivity, the impression that information gives us its content in the "view from nowhere," without reference to private states or privileged points of view. This perspective neutrality is the feature of information that gives it a more or less uniform exchange value, so that a piece of information that I give you can in principle be as comprehensible or as useful to you as it is to me.

The impression of objectivity rests first on the stylistic apparatus of "journalistic objectivity": the suppression of self-reference, personal voice, and obviously subjective terms in favor of the "neutral" presentation of observable fact that represents itself as mere "reporting." Behind this there is another suppression of the point of view of the reader. Reportage doesn't simply presume a community of interest among its readers; it also presumes that the relevant interests are universal and themselves objective, or rather, that information is not an interest-relative term at all. That is, it suppresses not just the "I" but the "we." This is implicit, for example, in Murray's comparison of the lexicographer to an astronomer gazing at a distant nebula, rather than to an observer on Earth looking at the Milky Way, which would have come closer to the truth of the matter – obviously there is nothing in the structure of the language itself which implies such an organization or which commends any particular region of speech as a "clear and unmistakable nucleus."

The suppression of the subject in the language of information corresponds to the suppression of explicit authorship in the document, in both its phenomenal and institutional guises. With the emergence of the informational genres, the writer of a news story no longer appears either as one of its characters or, increasingly, in the byline; it is the institution or the form itself that speaks. Historically, this sort of shift in authority accompanied the emergence and development of the informational genres. The progression is nicely marked in the shift from Webster (Noah) to Webster's (the publishing house in Springfield, Mass.) and finally to *Webster's* as a synonym for "the dictionary," a generic name that has in fact been in the public domain for a number of years.

It is the perspectival objectivity of information and its detachment from individual speech acts, too, that establishes information as a metaphysically objective quantity, something which can be stored in a neutral medium and can exist in the absence of a subject. (As Fred Dretske has put it, "it was here before we were" Dretske 1983: §29). This is one of the important ways in which information differs from knowledge, which always requires a knowing subject – an individual, a collectivity, or at the limit a text, which serves as a proxy for its author. (The difference is particularly clear when we prefix adjectives to the two words. We speak of "human knowledge," for example, when we want to identify a certain kind of knowledge by identifying the subjects who possess it, but we don't ordinarily speak of "human information" – you don't identify information in terms of its possessors. By the same token, we use a phrase like "medical knowledge" to refer to the body of knowledge that is accumulated in the medical community, whereas "medical information" refers simply to information about medicine, wherever it happens to reside.)

From the interpretive point of view, though, the most important consequence of the objectivity of information arises when we take it together with the morselization of its substance. If bits of information are to retain their value even when they are detached from their context and moved about from one place to another, there has to be some way of ascertaining their value independent of both the context of their production and the larger textual context they are drawn from. This is the notion that Walter Benjamin (1936/1969a) was getting at in a passage in "The Storyteller" about the emergence of the popular press in the early nineteenth century, where he contrasted information with intelligence:

> The intelligence that came from afar – whether the spatial kind from foreign countries or the temporal kind of tradition – possessed an authority which gave it validity, even when it was not subject to certification. Information, however, lays claim to prompt verifiability. The prime requirement is that it appear "understandable in itself..." . It is indispensable for information to sound plausible.

"Sounding plausible" is perhaps too narrow a characterization, but it gets at the phenomenal autonomy of information in its abstract sense.

It's important to distinguish between autonomy and other notions more closely connected to truth. Philosophers often talk about information as a veridical notion, but it is not, in either of its senses.[10] When we talk about "information" particularistically – as information about such and such – we can modify it using qualifiers like "reliable" or "unreliable," "correct" or "incorrect," and so on. It's true that there is a marked statistical preference for the negative items here, which suggests that, unlike a word like "report" or "account," say, "information" carries with it a presumption of confidence.[11] When we speak of someone's giving us information about the date of the exam or the price of a stock, that is, we usually imply that the source is authoritative and reliable and represents the content as being true (for this reason we don't often modify "information" using words like "wild," the way we might describe an account or report). Indeed, "information" in the particularistic sense of the term is better thought of as an evidential as opposed to an epistemological notion.

But if particularistic information is not veridical, it is clearly propositional – its content is the sort of thing that can be true or false whereas the qualifiers that we ordinarily apply to particularistic information sit uneasily with the abstract use of the term. This may be easiest to see if we look at the French translations of the word. You can speak, for example, of *les informations correctes* or *les informations fiables*, but you can't say *l'information correcte* or *l'information fiable* (unless, in an unrelated way, you are talking about a particular definite report). And we can see the same thing in English, even if there the distinction between the two senses is not morphologically marked. Someone might say, for example, "This is not simply the age of information, but the age of reliable information," but you would have the sense that the word was being used in the second phrase in a different and more restricted way – it no longer refers to the whole ensemble of representations that computers or knowledge workers trade in, but only to propositional representations like market reports, news stories, and the like.

The characteristic semantic feature of abstract information, rather, is autonomy, by which I mean that the authorizing context is folded into the form of the document itself. It is true that autonomy often carries with it a strong presumption of veridicality. You get into a rental car in a strange city, turn on the radio, and hear an announcer saying that the Giants have been eliminated from the division race on the last day of the season; you accept what you hear without interrogating it, or without having to know anything more about the speaker, the program, or the radio station. You accept it, that is, in virtue of the form of language that expresses it and the kind of document that presents it. And it is important to bear in mind that this is a phenomenal experience that Adam Smith or Condorcet could never have had. They knew only information in its older sense – what I'll call "intelligence" from here on in – and would not have thought of accepting the truth of a text on the basis of its form alone, in the absence of any knowledge of its source.

But autonomy doesn't always imply veridicality. As sophisticated readers we are all far too intelligent to take everything we read in the paper as true; the transparency of information starts to cloud over when we move from the sports pages or the stock columns to the political news on the front page. The fact is, as everybody knows, that newspapers tell us the truth about the things that are important to us so they can get away with misrepresenting the things that are important to them. But the fundamental principle of information is not altered by observations like these. News reports are information for us skeptical readers no less than for the credible readers who take everything they read in the papers at face value (if such people exist outside of the fantasies of early critical theorists). The crucial point is that even for us, the interpretation of such documents is shaped by their syntax and their material form, rather than by any more-or-less conscious reconstruction of the relationship between ourselves and its producers. This is what I mean when I say that information is a mode of reading – or "a form of communication," as Benjamin called it, which may be pretty much the same thing.

5. The future of information

Since its inception, information has managed to colonize every new form of public representation. If you think of communication primarily in terms of its mode – via texts or via sounds and images – then you will see an abrupt break between print and the broadcast media. But the emergence of a form like television seems less consequential from the informational point of view. All the features that sustain the impression of information in print are realized here as well: the blurring of genres; the fragmentation of content into "bites," segments, programs, and regular editions; the circumscription of a public discourse; and a phenomenal autonomy even more marked than in print, in the sense that the identities of the responsible agents (stations, networks, producers, writers) are almost wholly obscure and irrelevant to the way we interpret what we see.

So it isn't surprising that electronic forms have been informationalized as well. The World Wide Web teems with particularistic information (stock prices, course schedules, the texts of nineteenth-century novels you can search for tokens of the word "information").[12] And the print and broadcast media that mediate the impression of abstract information have already established important beachheads here: you can call up *Time* magazine, *Webster's Tenth Collegiate*, university catalogs, and the *Encyclopedia Britannica*.

On the face of things, in fact, electronic documents like those on the Web seem not only to preserve the impression of information but to reinforce it. They are highly modular, amenable to extraction and reorganization, and are much easier to dislodge and decontextualize than print documents are, features that support the sense of corpuscularity and transferability. They can be reformatted and reformulated – you can change the visual presentation or cause a table to be reformulated as a bar graph – which supports the conception of their content as a kind of fungible abstract substance. And the ease with which we can move from one document to another leads to the conception of content as a kind of extended substance, the conception that underlies the metaphors of "infospace" and the rest.

But while the content of the documents we find on the Web has a lot of the syntactic and formal properties that we ascribe to information, it is less well adapted to supporting the semantic properties that the informational mode of reading requires, particularly the impressions of objectivity and autonomy. The problem, as I suggested at the outset, is that these media don't preserve the social and material boundaries that the informational mode of reading requires. On the one hand, they disrupt the constellation of properties embodied in the notion of "publishing" – the connections, that is, between accessibility, diffusion, and "publicity," in the older sense of the term. On the other, they efface the material and phenomenal boundaries of and between both documents and collections.

It's true that neither of these has much effect on the way we interpret the on-line versions of informational publications that are well established in print, which we read, essentially, as transcriptions. But it creates difficulties for the development of new, autochthonous forms of electronic communication. And for various reasons, the Web makes it more difficult to marginalize these forms than has been historically possible, say, in the world of print. Information may be able to colonize the Web, then, but I think it will not be possible for it to establish its imperium there.

6. Information on the Web

First, for the notion of "publishing." To a certain extent, the particularities of the Web in this regard are purely quantitative. A signal virtue of electronic technologies is to remove the capital and institutional impediments to the production and circulation of documents. As we're often reminded, "anyone" can produce a document and make it accessible to thousands or millions of readers.[13] And indeed, this is exactly what anyone has been doing in increasing numbers. (You think of what someone said about Greenwich Village in the 1950s, that it was home to 50,000 people who had a great letter to the editor in them.) In a certain sense, this could seem to be merely the continuation of a tendency that has been in progress for a long time. Walter Benjamin observed sixty years ago that with the extension of the press and the multiplication of organs, "an increasing number of readers became writers... Today there is hardly a gainfully employed European who could not, in principle, find an opportunity to publish somewhere or other comments on his work, grievances, documentary reports, or that sort of thing" (Benjamin 1936/1969b: 232). And we can find reports to the same effect in Carlyle in the nineteenth century and Johnson in the eighteenth. But while the absolute number of writers and documents has been steadily growing, the *proportion* of writers to readers has remained relatively constant or may even have declined over the centuries, along with the circulation of the average published document. The average first printing of a novel in 1780 was around 1,250, and is perhaps 5,000 or 7,500 today, but most or all of this increase is explained by the fact that a far larger proportion of the eighteenth-century editions would have gone to circulating libraries and book clubs, and by an increase in the number of books that individual readers buy.[14]

This still means, of course, that every generation has had a larger number of documents to cope with. But the consequences for the individual reader have not been as severe as we might be led to believe by the complaints about "information overload" that seem to come up in every age (though of course that particular way of putting things is recent). Up to now, each successive stage of increase has been met by a corresponding institutionalization and specialization of discourses, which constrain readers' expectations of themselves. A modern graduate student in physics is sure to feel overwhelmed by the volume of material she is responsible for, but not to any greater degree than her nineteenth-century predecessor did. There has always been too much to read.

But electronic discourse promises to disrupt this process. In the first place it sharply increases the proportion of writers to readers. (We might paraphrase Benjamin by saying that "today there is hardly a gainfully employed European or American who has not published somewhere or other comments on his work, grievances, documentary reports, or that sort of thing" – provided we make access to a computer and modem a precondition to "gainful employment.") The increase in the number of documents that any reader has to sort through is for this reason genuinely unprecedented. It could be argued, of course, that the difficulty is partially offset by an increased ease of access that makes it possible for readers to look at many more documents than previously. But the effect of this is chiefly to enable people to go through more documents in search of those that might be interesting or useful – and in the course of things, to waste more time checking out large numbers of documents that are neither. Ease of access tends to exacerbate the impression of overload, rather than relieving it.

The purely quantitative difficulties are exacerbated by qualitative ones. Media like the Web tend to resist attempts to impose the sort of solutions that enable us to manage (even imperfectly) the steady increase in the number of print documents – the ramification of discourses and forms of publication, the imposition of systems of screening or refereeing, the restriction of the right to speak to "qualified" participants. And at the same time the new forms of circulation can disrupt the long historical development of cataloging and classification systems that Roger Chartier describes in *The Order of Books*, through which emerged "[the] operations thanks to which it became possible to order the world of texts" (Chartier 1991: 7).

For one thing, there are almost no barriers to posting a document on the Web, not even the minimal requirements that have to be satisfied before you can publish your "comments on work, grievances, documentary reports" in some print organ or another. Many Net discussion groups have moderators, it's true, but their responsibilities are usually limited to screening out blatant incivilities. On the Net, there is no strong material or economic incentive to rule out prolixity or to winnow redundant postings, and the breadth and openness of the discussions and the interest in quick turnaround militate against screening for accuracy. The discussions are ruled by the sort of principle that Henry Oldenburg offered when he began the publication of the *Philosophical Transactions of the Royal Society* in 1665: *sit penes authorem* [sic] *fides*, "let it be on the author's head." And of course there is no need even to submit to the judgment of moderators. Any undergraduate is free to post her night thoughts on Mary Shelley or the Klingon verb to a "potential audience" of millions (a quick search of the Web turns up numerous examples of both), and there will be nothing in its mode of circulation to distinguish it from communications from better-qualified contributors. Nor, for that matter, is the material form of a document very informative here. If I am willing to make even a small investment of time, I can produce a Web home page that is every bit the graphical equal of the home pages of *Time* magazine or Sun Microsystems.

One effect of all of this is to undercut the autonomy of documents that is essential to the impression of "information" in the print world. You do a search over the Web on the words "Alfred Hitchcock," for example, and you come up with twenty or thirty hits, most of them "professional-looking" pages. Some of them announce their provenance – there is an essay by someone in the English department at the University of Maryland and an undergraduate's senior thesis (at an unnamed university) on *Rear Window*. But there are no material or external clues to help you evaluate the three filmographies, one apparently prepared by a Hitchcock buff in Poitiers, another in Cardiff, and a third, which looks on internal evidence the most authoritative, from someone's site in Mexico.

On the Web, that is, you can never have the kind of experience that you can have with the informational genres of print, the experience of interpreting a text simply *as* a newspaper or encyclopedia article without attending to its author, its publisher, or the reliability of its recommender. We read Web documents, that is, not as information but as intelligence, which requires an explicit warrant of one form or another. Sometimes this is provided by a masthead that announces that the document has been produced by a well-known organization or print publication, in which case the content of the document does indeed constitute a kind of derivative information. With primary electronic documents, though, the warrant more often comes, as with the intelligence of old, from sources whose reliability we can judge from personal experience. One of the most striking things about the Web is the secondary traffic in *trouvailles* that it encourages, either in the form of the mail messages that users exchange when they locate an interesting or useful URL (a universal resource locator, the address of a Web page) or of the active links to other sites that users embed in their own Web pages. From these in turn have sprung various electronic reviews, information services, and clearinghouses, most run by enthusiasts but with an increasing number of commercial efforts. And you can find hot tips, too, in print publications from *Wired* to the *New York Times,* and in Silicon Valley, even on highway billboards. It is a phenomenon reminiscent of the response to the multiplication of print forms in the early eighteenth century, when Pope described in the *Dunciad* the pullulation of "Miscellanies... Journals, Medleys, Merc'ries, Magazines," most of them produced by booksellers to publicize the increasing output of print titles.

Over the course of time, services like these will help to address some of the evidential problems that come up when we want to use the Web as source of reliable information in the particularistic sense. But we should bear in mind that they are not really the equivalents of the informational genres of print, which offer themselves as compendia of a circumscribed body of public knowledge – the news, the lexis, the library collection. In the electronic world, this goal of circumscription is chimerical, in the absence of phenomenal boundaries between documents, genres, and discourses. The implications are nicely summed up in an old joke about the *New York Times* to the effect that its slogan "All the news that's fit to print" would be more appropriately rephrased as "all the news that fits." But it is not a joke you could make about a truly electronic newspaper. It isn't just that there are no longer any relevant material limits to the capacity of a document – that we can "fit" into a newspaper as much content as we like – but that the boundaries of "news" fall away at the same time. There is no event so trivial or particular that someone might not find it useful, no piece of background that has to be left out for reasons of space. And in the same way there is no word so obscure or technical or slangy that some user mightn't want to find it in a dictionary. This might seem to pose intimidating challenges for the compilers, except that "compilation" is a different matter when the boundaries between documents are themselves so problematic. A dictionary can be linked to an encyclopedia, for example (the distinction between the two has always been as much a matter of two kinds of books as of two modularities of knowledge). Or an encyclopedia can take us directly into the primary literature (likewise).

At the limit we may want to think of these forms on the model of the new news services and clearinghouses: not as static compendia but rather as dynamic interfaces to an open-ended discourse. They are forms of automated intelligence, that is, rather than informational genres in themselves. So the true electronic "dictionary" (already taking shape in research projects) might be a tool that pairs a word in an on-line text with a body of citations that match and clarify the sense relevant to its context, without having to pass through the lexicographical processes of distillation and abstraction, with their attendant implication of a distinction between language and speech. And the "digital library" is analogous. Once the notion of a collection is no longer materially constrained, it tends naturally to extend indefinitely. Of course it includes a lot of what most readers will find trivial and ephemeral; when you take down the walls of the library you shouldn't be surprised to find the reading room filling up with street people. But the solution is not to try to close off the collection in some arbitrary way, but to provide benign Medeas (both automatic and flesh and blood) who can help users thread their way through the maze. The electronic news service, newspaper, dictionary, and library are still tools for "information access" in the particularistic sense of the word. But there are no longer the kinds of determinate public limits that are implicit when we talk about "information" in the abstract sense, and no way to talk about how much of it there is in a copy of the electronic *New York Times*.

7. After information

But from a cultural if not commercial point of view, the importance of the Net and the Web is not as a convenient if sometimes leaky alternative to the informational functions of print. Rather it lies in the forms of discourse that are emerging in all those Web sites and discussion groups that the electronic referral services are helping us to avoid wasting our time on. One of the most pervasive features of these media is how closely they seem to reproduce the conditions of discourse of the late seventeenth and eighteenth centuries, when the sense of the public was mediated through a series of transitive personal relationships – the friends of one's friends, and so on – and anchored in the immediate connections of clubs, coffee-houses, salons, and the rest. The social aggregations that assemble themselves on the Net may be virtual, but they are in no wise "imagined" in Benedict Anderson's sense – they aren't groups, that is, whose "fellow members... will never know most of their fellow-members, meet them, or even hear of them, yet in [whose minds] lives the image of their communion" (Anderson 1983: 15). It may be true that most participants in Net colloquy will never actually meet each other individually, or even have direct electronic contact, but unlike the members of nations, social classes, or even ethnicities, each of them is immediately and personally accessible to any other.

Perhaps not surprisingly, the forms of discourse that emerge tend to mirror those of the preinformation age. One place where this is very much in evidence is in the professional discussion groups of linguists, historians, literary historians, and the rest, which fall somewhere between the refereed electronic journals (a genre that has so far been slow to take form) and the freewheeling conversations of net news groups (which can sometimes be rebarbatively brusque). The participants are usually familiar enough with the forms of "official" communication, if not always in the field that the list is given over to. But their exchanges here don't have the character of the print journals of the modern ages.

There is, first, the opening up of the right to speak. The lists reverse the effects of nineteenth-century immurement and professionalization of the disciplines that Raymond Williams described as a transition from the republic of letters to the bureaucracy of letters, where a writer can no longer speak as himself, but "must continually declare his style and department, and submit to an examination of his purpose and credentials at the frontier to every field" (Williams 1983: 121). It's not just that the lists permit the participation of interested amateurs (the "virtuosi" of the age of Pepys and Wren). They also remove the burden of professionalism that was imposed in the nineteenth century to limit the published discourse of the sciences to descriptions of its "subject matter" and purge it of critical self-consideration. The amateur epistemologizing and sociologizing, the pedagogical and technical lore, the gossip and the professional politics, the anecdotal observations about curiosities that lie outside the realm of current theory – all these come bubbling back up into public view from the orality where they have been repressed for the past two hundred years. The effect is something like that of reading an early number of the *Philosophical Transactions*, which might mix the serious contributions of Boyle or Leeuwenhoeck with a report from a gentleman in Suffolk about a curious sand flood or the birth of a monstrous calf. (You wonder whether the more scholarly readers of the *Transactions* tended to skip over the contributions that came in from anyone with an "Esq." at the end of his name, the way some readers of scholarly lists give short shrift to postings from anyone whose E-mail address ends with "compuserve.com.")

Of course it can be a risky matter to read all this informationally. It often happens that a query will elicit several contradictory answers, leaving the person who posed it in something of a quandary, especially if he is not adept enough in the discourse to be able to sort out the dross either on internal grounds or on the basis of some knowledge of the qualifications of his respondents. (To take an extreme example, someone wrote to the Linguist List not long ago asking for the source of the quotation *Homo sum; homini nihil a me alienum puto*. The answers offered included Cicero, Horace, Plautus, and Virgil, and while Terence did get the most votes, you have the feeling that serious scholarship ought to require some standard more rigorous than mere majority rule.) Predictably, as elsewhere in the electronic sphere, there are frequent complaints about the unevenness and copiousness of the discussions, in tones reminiscent of those of the 1756 critic who taxed the editors of the *Philosophical Transactions* for publishing too many "crude essays that cannot appear with propriety among the works of the learned." And with these come attempts to restrict access or fragment the lists into new, more exclusionary discourses.[15] But while it's reasonable enough to look to these discussions to answer certain informational needs, once again it's futile to suppose they can be circumscribed and regimented in the way print discourse can. They are too porous to the personal.

Derrida (1995: 35) makes a point along these lines in *Mal d'Archive* about the effects of electronic mail (which seems to include for him the broader range of Net communication):

> ... Electronic mail is now even more than the fax in the process of transforming all the public and private space of humanity, and first of all the limit between the private, the secret (whether private or public) and the public or phenomenal.

This personalism is the feature that most sharply distinguishes Net discussions from the formal discourses of print. It is implicit in the forms of language, as people speak, not as authors to an anonymous public, but rather in the form of a colloquial conversation between participants who are copresent in the act of speaking. Contributors often address one another directly, a style alien to the letters column of a magazine journal, where antagonists always refer to each other in the third person. And the style of argument admits the personal, the anecdotal, the subjective. If you are willing to make allowances (rather a lot of them), the tone recalls the early eighteenth-century periodicals and the first stirrings of the modern critical spirit. It is a capacity, as Terry Eagleton puts it, that is "incurably amateur," which draws together "writer and reader, critic and citizen, multiple literary modes and dispersed modes of inquiry," and whose goal, as Eagleton quotes T.H. Green as saying, "consists of talking to the public about itself" (Eagleton 1984: 22).

We shouldn't try to make too much of this, as some of its enthusiasts have tried to do (one calls E-mail the "third revolution" in human communication, the first two having been writing and print). The discussion is very often banal and can on occasion be uncivil; certainly no one would be tempted to say of the language of the Net discussion groups, as Eagleton does of the language of the *Spectator*, that it is "mannerly and pellucid." Of course it could be argued that unevenness and a lowering of quality are inevitable whenever participation is so wide (and indeed, there are analogous complaints about the decline in standards whenever participation in public discourse seems to be broadened, which go back to Addision and Swift and before).[16] There is some truth to this, though claims about the increased breadth of participation on the Web are greatly exaggerated, just like Defoe's claims that London held "rarely a Victualing House but you meet with a Tinker, a Cobbler, or a Porter, Criticizing upon the Speeches of Majesty, or the writings of the most celebrated Men of the Age."[17] The Web is still the electronic equivalent of a gated suburban community, and it shouldn't be surprising that it contains a lot of suburban chatter.

Still, it is unfair to expect electronic media to be the agents of sweeping social revolution or even for that matter of a complete overturning of the present order of discourse. And from the literary point of view, it is early days yet; really the appropriate comparison here is not to the *Tatler* or the *Spectator*, but to the seventeenth-century "news letters" and the like that antedated these forms and made them possible. The chief difference is that these new forms inhabit a public space that is already highly developed and differentiated, so that like other technological innovations (plastic furniture, for example), they will wind up assuming certain specialized functions alongside the established informational genres of print and their derivative electronic representations. This is the only quibble that I have with Derrida's description of the Net as being "in the process of transforming *all* the public and private space of humanity." Rather, I think we should look to electronic discourse to provide a counter and complement to the informational forms of print – a domain that privileges the personal, the private, and the subjective against the impersonal, the public, and the objective.

Notes

[1] Cities like Brownsville, Texas, Waco, Texas, and Cheyenne, Wyoming, now boast book "superstores" of between 25,000 and 50,000 square feet, which can offer readers from 30,000 to 60,000 distinct titles; stores in larger cities may offer as many as 150,000 titles.

[2] I'm ignoring most of the obsolete and legal uses of the word "information," as well as the remnants of the use of the word as an action nominal, as in the phrase "for your information."

[3] The OED2 actually gives two senses for this naturalistic use of the word, the second of them applying to information as a mathematically defined quantity, but it indicates that the two are probably descriptions of the same thing, and for the present purposes the difference needn't concern us.

[4] Weaver also acknowledged the "semantic problem" of information ("How precisely do the transmitted symbols convey the desired meaning?") and the "effectiveness problem" ("How effectively do the transmitted symbols affect conduct in the desired way?"). Neither of these has been addressed formally in the information-theoretic framework, though something like these problems have been taken up in recent years by philsophers like Fred Dretske, David Israel, and John Perry. For the present purposes it is enough to observe that these have had virtually no effect on popular ways of talking about information, which is what I am concerned with here.

[5] A search in several databases of the Dialog Information Services turned up over eighty mentions of this claim in various magazines and newspapers, all of them uncritical.

[6] Austen sometimes plays on the ambiguity of the word, as in this conversation between Fanny and Edmund in *Mansfield Park*: "I speak what appears to me the general opinion; and where an opinion is general, it is usually correct. Though I have not seen much of the domestic lives of clergymen, it is seen by too many to leave any deficiency of information." "Where any one body of educated men, of whatever denomination, are condemned indiscriminately, there must be a deficiency of information, or (smiling) of something else...". Fanny uses the word here in its particularistic sense, to mean something like "intelligence, authoritative reports" whereas Edmund is using it to mean something more like "moral instruction."

[7] Cf also: "But though the interest of the labourer is strictly connected with that of the society, he is incapable either of comprehending that interest or of understanding its connection with his own. His condition leaves him no time to receive the necessary information..." (Adam Smith, *The Wealth of Nations*). "...It is well known that some of the most distinguished members of that Congress, who have been since tried and justly approved for patriotism and abilities, and who have grown old in acquiring political information, were also members of this convention, and carried into it their accumulated knowledge and experience" (Alexander Hamilton, *The Federalist Papers*, 14).

[8] See, on these, Yates (1989) and Beniger (1986).

[9] Jean Clair observed that the museum and the railway station were the nineteenth century's only original forms of public building, the one a representation of the colonization of time, the other of the colonization of space.

10 Dretske (1983: 57), who claims to be giving a reconstruction of "information" "as it is ordinarily understood," says: "False information, misinformation, and (grimace) disinformation are not varieties of information – any more than a decoy duck is a kind of duck." This would be simply wrong, if Dretske's account were taken as a rational reconstruction of the commonsense notion. But if we ignore Dretske's claims about the relation of his naturalistic notion and the notion that figures in ordinary discourse, I don't think the critique I've offered here offers any real philosophical challenge to his view. It does however underscore the dangers of arguing from intuitions about the "ordinary uses" of words that are so laden with cultural meaning.

11 A computer search of articles in the very large newspaper database of Dialog Information Services (if not there, where?) turned up just under 2 million instances of the word "information," of which 8,281 were prefixed by the word "false" and 9,568 by the word "incorrect." There were also 163 instances of "true information" and 1,773 of "correct information," a discrepancy that attests both to the presumption of truth and to its suspendabilty.

12 It is difficult to make any interesting generalizations about the full range of electronic media, given both the welter of emergent forms (CD-ROM, hypertext, multimedia, virtual reality, MUDs and MOOs, and so on) and the increasing difficulty of separating print and electronic documents now that "traditional" print documents can be electronically distributed and printed locally on demand. For the present purposes I will take the World Wide Web (or more broadly, the Net) as a model. For one thing the Web has already established itself as a means of distributing journalistic, scholarly, commercial, and institutional documents. As of this writing (in August of 1995) there are some 60,000 Web servers, a figure that has increased eightfold over the last year. (This figure is available at http://webcrawler.com/WebCrawler/Facts/Facts.htmlhttp://webcrawler.com/.) I will also assume only the functionalities currently available – that is, the possibility of reading, writing, and interacting in simple ways with hypertextually organized documents which may include audio or video, and which contain active links to other sites. It's clear that within a short period there will be basically nothing you can do on a workstation or local server that you can't do remotely over the Web – you will be able to edit your documents or OCR a text image using software available on a remote server, for example – but while the implications of this increased functionality are considerable, I won't discuss them here.

13 I'm going to assume here that the Web will remain resistant to the kind of monopolization that would make this sort of communication too costly for individual users. This is a big assumption, of course, but I think that even if the Web were bought by a few large commercial interests, it would be difficult or counterproductive to impose a commercial model that limited the accessibility of certain documents, or that militated against the continuing use of distribution lists and similar fora.

14 Over the past century the number of titles published has probably grown at something like two or three times the rate of growth of the reading public itself. In 1945 there were about seven thousand titles published in the US; by 1990 this figure was about fifty thousand. Over the same period the reading public probably no more than trebled (assuming a doubling of the population and an increase of 50 percent in the proportion of the population that buys books), though the difficulty of finding comparable statistics and of assessing what we mean by the "reading public" makes all

such estimates highly speculative. As vague as they are, though, the figures suggest that the proportion of writers to readers has remained constant within an order of magnitude. Figures from earlier periods conform to this principle. Richardson's best-selling novels in the 1740s achieved sales of around 6,500; seventy years later, when the reading public (as measured by newspaper sales) had increased roughly four times, Scott's *Marmion* and *Roy Roy* sold around 11,000 each (See Williams 1961).

[15] Quoted in Kronick (1991: 161).

[16] Cf. the remarks of Aldous Huxley in 1934: "... The proportion of trash in the total artistic output is greater now than at any other period. That it must be so is a matter of simple arithmetic. Process reproduction and the rotary press have made possible the indefinite multiplication of writing and pictures. Universal education and relatively high wages have created an enormous public who know how to read and can afford to buy reading and pictorial matter. A great industry has been called into existence in order to supply these commodities... The population of Western Europe has little more than doubled during the last century. But the amount of reading – and seeing – matter has increased, I should imagine, at least twenty and possibly fifty or even a hundred times." (The passage is quoted in Benjamin (1936/1969b: 248), who adds: "This mode of observation is obviously not progressive.") Of course Huxley was assuming, as Benjamin seems to do, that the proportion of writers to readers was increasing throughout this period, an impression enhanced by the fact that the ephemera of earlier ages tend to be forgotten, so that the overall quality of contemporary writing always seems infinitely more mediocre when it is compared to the works that are still available from earlier periods. Historically, as we have seen, the impression of proportionally increased participation is probably unjustified, but it could in fact be a cause of some change in the overall quality of public writing as we move from print to electronic communication.

[17] Quoted in Eagleton (1984: 14).

References

AGRE, PH.
(to appear) "Institutional circuitry: Thinking about the forms and uses of information," *Information Technology and Libraries*.

ANDERSON, B.
1983 *Imagined Communities*, London: Verso.

BENEDIKT, M.
1991 "Introduction," in M. Benedikt (ed.), *Cyberspace: First Steps*, Cambridge (Mass.): MIT Press.

BENIGER, J.R.
1986 *The Control Revolution*, Cambridge (Mass.): Harvard University Press.

BENJAMIN, W.
1936/1969a "The storyteller," in H. Arendt (ed.), *Illuminations*, New York: Schocken.

BENJAMIN, W.
1936/1969b "The work of art in the age of mechanical reproduction," in H. Arendt (ed.), *Illuminations*, New York: Schocken.

CHARTIER, R.
1992 *L'ordre de livres*, Aix-en-Provence: Alinea.

DE CERTEAU, M.
1990 *L'invention du quotidien*, vol.1, Paris: Gallimard.

DERRIDA, J.
1995 *Mal d'archive*, Paris: Galilée.

DRETSKE, F.
1983 "Précis of knowledge and the flow of information," *The Behavioral and Brain Sciences*, 6: 55-90.

EAGLETON, T.
1984 *The Function of Criticism*, London: Verso.

HABERMAS, J.
1989 *The Structural Transformation of the Public Sphere*, Cambridge (Mass.): MIT Press.
1994 "The information revolution," special number of *BusinessWeek*.

KRONICK, D.
1991 *Scientific and Technical Periodicals of the Seventeenth and Eighteenth Centuries*, Metuchen, N.J.: Scarecrow Press.

SCHILLER, D.
1994 "From culture to information and back again: Commoditization as a route to knowledge," *Critical Studies in Mass Communication*, 11, 1: 93-115.

TERDIMAN, R.
1985 *Discourse/Counter-Discourse*, Ithaca, N. Y.: Cornell University Press.

WEAVER, W.
1964 "Recent contributions to the mathematical theory of communication," in *The Mathematical Theory of Communication*, Urbana: University of Illinois.

WILLIAMS, R.
1961 "The growth of the reading public," in *The Long Revolution*, New York: Columbia.
1983 "David Hume: Reasoning and experience," in *Writing in Society*, London: Verso.

WURMAN, R.S.
1989 *Information Anxiety*, New York: Doubleday.

YATES, J.
1989 *Control through Communication*, Baltimore: Johns Hopkins.

Régis Debray

THE BOOK AS SYMBOLIC OBJECT[1]

1. An infantile neurosis, early vocation, and, late in life, the Nobel Prize for Literature: these make for one of the last biographical adventure stories that arise from the book in codex form. Jean-Paul Sartre was as thoroughly "martyrized" as saved by this particular physical means. And if we seek to learn the kind of existential involvement to which, at the start of this century, an artifact as misleadingly banal as this could lead, it is sufficient, and indeed imperative, to reread *The Words*.

This work (1964), as is well-known, retraces the steps that led a fatherless young son to become the only child of a grandfather's library. Or more exactly, it tells us how – by casting his consciousness in "printed characters of bronze," by finding shelter behind "the peremptory inertia of matter," and by replacing "the noises of life with indestructible inscriptions" – this misshapen orphan was able to give himself a glorious body by becoming himself the book, organically.

> I, twenty-five volumes, eighteen thousand pages of text, three hundred engravings, including a portrait of the author. My bones are made of leather and cardboard, my parchment-skinned flesh smells of glue and mushrooms, I sit in state through a hundred thirty pounds of paper, thoroughly at ease. I am reborn, I at last become a whole man, thinking, talking, singing, thundering, a man who asserts himself with the peremptory inertia of matter. Hands take me down, open me, spread me flat on the table, smooth me, and sometimes make me creak. I let them, and then suddenly I flash, I dazzle, I command attention from a distance, my powers shoot through time and space, they blast the wicked, protect the good. No one can forget or ignore me: I am a great fetish, tractable and terrible. (Sartre 1964: 194-95)

This suggests a Kafkaesque hallucination, or the oneiric transubstantiation of a contingency into necessity, that is, of a man's flesh into paper ("chance had made me human, generosity of spirit would make me booklike"). How was this Eucharist in reverse order made possible? How to explain the mystery of this mystical materialism? The answer is simple: because in this petit-bourgeois family – and in this it was not alone – books themselves came before reading. Just as the dwelling comes before the dweller, or the earth before the peasant.

And as the material is there before the worker, it guides him, induces or molds him. It is in this way that an allegory of the text, "the order of books," looks down upon the future intellectual in all its exaltedness. It watches out for the young catechumen from afar, a stately and reassuring shade.

> Though I did not yet know how to read, I already revered those standing stones: upright or leaning over, close together like bricks on the book-shelves or spaced out nobly in lanes of menhirs. I felt that our family's prosperity depended on them. They all looked alike. I disported myself in a tiny sanctuary, surrounded by ancient, heavy-set monuments which had seen me into the world, which would see me out of it, and whose permanence guaranteed me a future as calm as the past. (*ibid*.: 40)

Fetishism or shamanism, a mysterious twilight bathes these peaceful necropolises. The grandfather's study takes on the outlines of a "sanctuary" filled with "holy silence," and these monoliths are already, in the eyes of the yet illiterate child, cult objects – "mute relics" that call for the adults to cultivate an officiating priest's "dexterity."

If the book is here a good deal more than common utensil or everyday object, more like a holy object, host or altar of repose, there is moreover a hierarchy of liturgies according to the materials, weight, and size of the thing. The inert object is, truly, a sexed being. On the women's side, there are the *brochures* – brocaded bound volumes or opuscules set upon tables and pedestal stands, with "their soft and shimmering leaves" that figure as "the object of an exclusively female minor cult." These would be the trinkets and confectionery. On the sanctuary side, that of the grandfather's library off-limits to women, there are "imposing hard cover tomes bound in brown cloth" which stand removed from time, placed vertically on their shelves, petrified and impassive, like the mineral organ pipe-like formations of basalt columns. Let us not mistake, beneath the printed word, seriousness for lightness of touch. The weighty object ordains a weighty affectivity. The crushing, chaste, quasi-funereal stature of culture takes on earthly form in these brusque and musty, menacing, ponderous parallelepipeds. They do not melt into the decor, they *are* the decor, and one possessing the qualities of a plot from the very start. The idea of writing books germinates out of the material book and not the converse; the furniture invents for itself a character out of its own cloth.

2. We can consider this "true fiction" of *The Words* to be one last and long-sustained fantastical note in a very real period of our material culture (something that detracts in no wise from its joyful mood, its *molto vivace* tempo). It is given in cross-section, under a microscope, through the objective thick layering of a certain technology of literal memory: the codex as symbolic matrix, the affective and mental schematization in whose dependence we bind ourselves more or less unconsciously to the world of meaning. In this sarcastic but exact self-portrait, Sartre unearths what is unthinkable to "literature": the book as object (just as the film as object – reel, celluloid, and projection – is unthinkable to cinematic art). And the fantasies of little Poulou would not have proven as driving and productive a force for the adult Sartre had they not been borne along and sustained by a historically attested collective unconscious. The codex is an existential code unto itself, a unifying factor of a culture; and fifteen or sixteen centuries of the practices of the book give a firm skeletal structure to these imaginings of literary reconstitution. The masculinity of the folio edition for example allows the young Sartre to cut the umbilical cord with the gynaeceum, with the "storytelling" mother. Rare were the female monastics given the task in monasteries of producing copies; however minute and delicate the work, it was reserved for clerics bound by vows of celibacy. The printing trade remained for a long time, up through the nineteenth century, an exclusively male profession. "Morality as well as the proper work of manufacture is opposed to the employment of women as typesetters," stipulate the statutes of the French Typographical Society in 1849.

More essentially, the aura of the secular book, in our temporal culture, makes its appearance as a legacy of Christianity, and, beyond that, of the Torah.[2] The Pentateuch was surely written on scroll, but the Tables of the Law in Christian iconography have taken on retrospectively the aspect of an open book. Everyone knows that there is a close and necessary relation between the beginnings of the use of the codex and the expansion in popularity of the first Christian writings. The primitive notebook or polyptych of small rectangular wooden pieces coated in wax had until that time been considered of little value in the milieus of literate pagans. The definitive replacement of volumen by codex corresponds, around the fourth century, to the Christianization of the Roman Empire. A receptacle of the Revelation and privileged bearer of the messianic kerygma, the container benefited over the long run from the contents' sacredness, such that "to believe in the Book" and to believe in God gradually became synonymous. The religions of the Book did indeed dematerialize the divine, yet since one only destroys what one supplants, they were not able to do so without rendering divine the material tool of this dematerialization, without enthroning and ritualizing the access to the Word's sacred place: the codex as the house of God. As a kind of universal suction pump for all the pagan hierophancies that had expounded the now abandoned sacred mysteries, the Christian book underwent at this time an unforeseen animistic transference – with all its affective ambivalences of the sacred – that attracts and terrorizes, incites to the auto da fé as well as entices to the altar. The site of Knowledge has admittedly taken the place in people's minds of the site of Revelation. But this secularization, as the Sartrian confession bears witness, has not altogether destroyed the original halo of a formal medium of communication that has remained substantially unchanged. "Form is meaning," says McKenzie, and Roger Chartier has ably described the effects of meaning associated with devices and systems of writing. Chronologically upstream of these internal adaptations, religious faith recorded its expressions in, and left its mark on, the codex form itself, which continued to emit its aura of hope (toward 1914, on the rue Le Goff, in Paris) "as pools of water, at night, give back the day's heat." A relocating of material form, a relocating of sacredness, a *translatio studii et militae*: the process that leads from the Bible to the *Encyclopedia*, thence to the illustrated *Grand Larousse* (to confine ourselves only to books that say everything about everything) is not lacking in a certain mediological coherence. The Sartrian cult of the Book takes the form of one among various subcases of Christian materialism, scandalous indeed in the eyes of Greek intellectualism (for which body = tomb and matter = degeneration).

The dogma of the Incarnation and the belief in the resurrection of bodies predisposed one to consider sacred the body of the Book, Spirit made object, Word become papyrus or parchment. An author's soul made flesh. So too the anxious linearity of Christian time accords well with the austere linearity of the written page, with the educationally guided decipherment of Holy Writ. Reading in itself is always a good. To read is an act of faith (this is known all too well to Protestants, who raised up the Republican system of education in France), and the nephew and grand-nephew of a pastor like Sartre had optimal opportunities to entrust the salvation of his soul to reading, to that physical embodiment of the Holy Spirit.

3. Suppose we were to attempt a "psychoanalysis" of the primitive codex (similar to what Gaston Bachelard accomplished with his *Psychoanalysis of Fire*, *On Poetic Imagination and Reverie,* and *Water and Dreams*) by appealing to a more or less subterranean material imagination. It is likely that the symbolics of stone would be called for. Was not the baked clay tablet the first material base for cuneiform writing in Mesopotamia? An illuminated "Breviary of Belleville" from the fourteenth century, preserved in the Bibliothèque Nationale in Paris, has the purpose of "making apparent the agreement of the Old and New Testaments" by depicting a ruined synagogue, the prophet Zacharius having picked up a brick and being shown handing it under a veil to the apostle Matthew. The latter uncovers and displays the brick become codex, New Testament. "Thou art Peter, and upon this rock..." The metaphor recurs in our literature – of the menhir, the cobblestone, the pebble, the oyster, the plinth, the cornerstone. Think of Victor Hugo and his famous chapter in *The Hunchback of Notre Dame*, "This will destroy that" ("Ceci tuera cela"), pitting the book against the building, printing against architecture. The codex, or how to create the mineral out of the animal (parchment) or the vegetable (papyrus, ground fruit pip)... Something solid out of the crumbly, something substantial out of the putrescible. "Every book is a living stone..." It is that by which thought builds up itself, and out of which one can build, to last, towers, mountains, cathedrals. That which spontaneously transforms author into architect, a kind of touched-up reissue or remix of the great architect of the Universe. See the article under "Author" in the *Universal Dictionary* of Furetière (1615-1688): "One uses the term above all to refer to the First Cause that is God," and after that, in the conclusion, "a person who has composed some book that has been printed." The spatial analogy even took on a cosmic dimension, in the Middle Ages, because at the time the Earth was conceived as a rectangle, as was the Bible, with its central fold defining the terrestrial axis and its corners the four cardinal points.

The primordial book is taken to be edifying because it is an edifice. Illuminated, gilded, carved, locked shut, with its clasp, its hard back, its coppered corners, its intersecting architectonic edges – that archetype issuing from the monastic scriptoria duplicates the closure of the cloister. With its own interpreters as entryway guards, and its page laid out like the blueprint of a basilica. The oversize format, in the sixteenth and seventeenth centuries, retains its vaulting arches, its vestibule, and its frontispiece. The title page sometimes displays a portico, a triumphal arch, a "scaffold." One passes through it like a worshiper in a church or a king in his domain. And right up until the middle of the nineteenth century, the supple cover of the duodecimo or octavo commercially sold book was intended as only temporary, awaiting permanent binding.

And it is perhaps also because the text could take the rigid form of an architectural enclosure, be closed up into an ordered and clearly demarcated rectangle, because it could be held and weighed in the hand, leafed through by thumb and forefinger, be prominently displayed in its place for all to see, become a permanent fixture, be hoarded, incorruptible, spatially delimited that the order of books was able for so long to provide so much emotional security. To serve as a pledge of legitimacy and permanence, a shelter against the flight of time, degeneration, death. Fusing material firmness and symbolic value, the book linked persons together through its virtues as a concrete thing. It was (under this guise) the literate person's antidepressant, his survival insurance. It could stand in for the land no urbanite could love, a foothold for the man at sea, a church for the miscreant. Let us again read Sartre, a modern archeologist of a late modernity (as in "late classical period") from whom the computer screen could soon separate us with as much restrictive severity as the codex has separated us from the volumen of antiquity.

> As a rhetorician, I cared only for words: I would set up cathedrals of words beneath the blue eyes of the word sky. I would build for the ages. When I took up a book, I could see that though I opened it and shut it twenty times, it did not deteriorate. Gliding over that incorruptible substance, the *text*, my gaze was merely a tiny, surface accident; it did not disturb anything, did not wear anything away. I, on the other hand, passive and ephemeral, was a dazzled mosquito, pierced by the rays of a beacon. I would put out the light and leave the study: invisible in the darkness, the book kept sparkling, for itself alone. I would give my works the violence of those corrosive flashes, and later, in ruined libraries, they would outlive man." (*ibid.*: 183)

4. In the figural rhetoric of the world of substances, the numerized cybernetic transmission of texts suggests a change of element: from the earth to water, the fixed to the fluid. Note the guiding metaphors in the New World of computer screens: navigation, flow, tide or influx, flood, immersion, slippage. "The black, hard words" (Sartre) are demineralized and washed into the information stream, the "clam" melts away into the aquarium. This liquefaction of traces is of course no deliquescence. Textual dematerialization releases thought from the weight of things, increases its mobility, multiplies its possibilities. From the bookish metaphor to the computational one, the passage is not only, indeed, from heavy to lightweight, rigid to soft, rough to smooth, from argillaceous to agile – if the paronomasia can be forgiven – but from the inert to the animate. With data systems for user interactivity and geometrically variable hypertext, the reader is no longer simply spectator, one who looks at meaning through the page's window in rectangle, *from the outside*, but coauthor of what he reads, a second writer and active partner. He can enter *into* the landscape of meaning and modify its architecture as he wishes. Once monologue, the text becomes dialogue. It loses its mass, is privatized. It is no longer a static invariant, a road traveled in a given direction, recorded once and for all. Rather, it is a moving mosaic (text, image, sound), an unpredictable sequence of bifurcations, a nonhierarchical, unpredetermined crossroads where each reader can invent his own course along a network of communication nodes. With their "cosmopedia" project and "trees of knowledge" software, Pierre Lévy (1993) and Michel Authier (Authier and Lévy 1992) have splendidly described the emancipatory effects of this Copernican revolution that makes the text revolve around the reader, and knowledge around people. Geoffrey Nunberg and others have recently highlighted the types of advances that can be expected from future hypertexts: increased spaces of freedom, through the nonsequential association of elements of meaning; the dehierarchizing of reference works and authoritative corpuses by the new possibilities for interleaving and recomposing them through juggling with official classifications; going beyond the traditional effects of deferral in creating and reading works, and producing documents more instantaneously in real time, with writing and reading becoming *in situ* performances or intellectual "happenings"; the singularization of databases, individualization of files and programs in memory, the inventive and libertarian appropriation of sources, following the ideal of "to each his/her own book"; and the universal accessibility, via interconnected networks, in all time and places, of the global library to any human being (provided he or she has a PC and Net connection at his or her disposal). We see verified here yet again, as it turns out this time in the realm of documentation on computers, the providential law that has technology offering the best remedy for technology. At the very moment indeed when the new technologies of memory can make us fear an alarming glut of traces – a true change of scale in the collective accumulation of archives, at once written, audio, visual, and audiovisual – these same technologies increasingly lighten its load, at almost the same pace, by facilitating individualized retrieval.

To keep only within the last two decades of philosophical literature in the French idiom (the only ones on which I can speak somewhat knowledgeably), we have heard ample paeans to the transversal, the rhizomatic, the deterritorialized, to maps of immanence, the nomadic, the interactive, and so on. I feel, therefore, a dispensation from having to add any more. Information technology's manipulation and manipulability of traces are probably going to diminish the *auctoritas* of authors past and present, to the point, it seems, of putting into play the rather recent function of the unique author (with the legal disarray of copyright, stemming from the commercial proliferation of printed text). We are promised, on the information "library" side, less of the dogmatic and more of the ludic, less of the canonical and more of the festive. Fewer arguments from authority, through more juxtaposition *of* authorities. Perhaps in fact, the hypertext will be *the* ultrademocratic, fatherless and propertyless, borderless and customs-free text, which everyone can manipulate and which can be disseminated everywhere. But we should note in passing that this captivating novelty, like many post-modern innovations, has an air of *déjà vu* about it, in conformity with the rule of the spiraling recurrence of the most ancient in the form of the most new. Does not the fax bring us back the volumen, as the audiovisual reproduces a certain secondary orality, from before the age of printing? Does not the word-processing of text facilitate the scholastic gloss and Alexandrian erudition? The beautiful medieval codex, with its illuminations and margins open to the reader's annotation, is also in a sense making its comeback, with no one likely to raise objections. The traditional book, made of sheaves of folded papers sewn together and bound, with back and cover, once favored the attribution of works to their individual creators – a rather late development, I think, in the history of the manuscript, unknown to Antiquity and the High Middle Ages (a text = an author). The microchip is going to put back in circulation on our screens the hybrid, rhapsodic object, blending applications and authors. Will the collection of documents in the twenty-first century resemble the *potpourri* of the thirteenth?

5. My subject is here a different one. I wish to examine not as a historian of the book (which I am not), but as a simple mediologist, the possible repercussions of this novel mobility of words. This latter is prominently inscribed in a movement of the whole, through which its effects are overdetermined. The institution of writing without the book corresponds to agriculture without soil, to economy without materialities, to monetary exchanges without currencies. It makes common cause with the transition from the handmade trace to the remote-controlled trace, from writing as labor to writing as scanned spectacle, from the *pagus*, the field, to the screen, the mirror. The computer makes possible not only the delocalization of access and plasticity of uses, but the evaporation of the originating locale of inscription, along with its volume, weight, depth, and its permanence, its interiority. Written text converts the word into surface, time into space; but a single graphic space remains a planar surface. Written text, like screened text, has two dimensions; a parallelepiped has three, like the world itself. The memory of the world, materialized in the book, is itself a world. In this sense, the famous worldwide spread of codes that is a product of computerization is also a further estrangement of signs from the world. A volume of paper and cardboard is a resilient and deepening microcosm, in which the reader can move around at great length, without getting lost within its "walls." The book is protected because it is in itself protective (just as, having long ago been inspired by God, it remained a source of inspiration for little Sartres). One can take one's lodgings there so to speak, even curl up comfortably. The material *delimitedness* of the book as receptacle, whether or not finely bound, gives way to an *unlimitedness*, which puts the text closer to the indefinite than to the infinite (as Pierre Lévy correctly notes, we speak of "text" in the partitive, the way we speak of "water" and "sand"). With the loss of the page's spatiality and the palpable rigidity of the folio volume, a comforting landmark disappears, and a new era opens up that is also an area of volatility and instantaneousness which will doubtlessly not have only advantages. The social function of written text as much as the mode of reading (extensive or intensive, for example) are dependent for their proper functioning on the physical configuration of the technical support system. Electronic interfacing, it goes without saying, does not conduce to the patrimonial, diplomatic, or referential use of writing. Let us skip over the questions of viability or feasibility. Texts with no hard edges or shell, circulating in a library without shelves or walls, between readers who no longer need libraries because they are directly connected to one another (or between telestudents without schools or teachers) and dwelling, moreover, in networks of Los Angeles like urban communities without monuments or centers – this is what is properly called a utopia, an a-topia. Without asking ourselves here if it can or cannot be realized in fact, and playing the game of drastic oversimplification (since the computer will obviously not kill off pen and paper), let us briefly evoke a few implications of these schematic outlines.

6. The question of the book and its becoming cannot be isolated from the totality that gives it meaning in each era. The technological ecosystem of the textual relates back – in the same way as any microsystem – to the wider scale of our cultural ecology. I would be unable to forgive myself if I were to give in to vulgarities of prophetic vagueness in the McLuhanite mode. I would like simply to point out to the real fundamentalists of all-pervasive information literacy-numeracy, without in the same breath putting on "apocalyptic" airs (to cite the reservation voiced by Umberto Eco), something that bears a strong semblance to an anthropological constant: human communities *need* a unique, defining space to belong and refer to. To formulate it all too laconically: *no culture without closure* (and time alone as the defining medium of something) *cannot close it off*.

Greek culture got by without sacred books for a number of reasons, the not least significant of which is that it had its anchorage in holy *places* – sanctuaries, Olympuses, and acropolises – that were strictly circumscribed with great solemnity. The classical Greeks could enthusiastically place their trust in the temporal fluidity of speech because they had confidence in their civic space, the sacred perimeter of the *polis*, the guarantor of citizenship and even of humanity, a fundamental security confirming identity itself. Inscribing in their soil the order of the world (notably with their autochthony myths) the Athenians could afford to fear little from the restless wandering of a lively orality. In their scheme of things, the divine belongs to a geographical order, their theology is a topology (exile condemns the banned one to death from loss of contact with the divine). Jewish cultural tradition, on the other hand, makes written text sacred – a still point, the basis of oral instruction, always kept underneath the mantle, as the substitute for an absent place. Historians have commented that the (second) destruction of the Temple (in A.D. 70) had enhanced the symbolic weight of the Torah, written on parchment roll but stored in an Ark of the Covenant, a portable covered conveyance often represented as a miniature temple of Solomon. The book is what remains of Jerusalem while waiting for Jerusalem: the mobile center of the exile's or nomad's existence (Judaism does not call into question the principle of centrality, it "biblicizes" it). Primitive Christianity as well was u-topian or a-spatial, and the Christian, a peregrinator or wanderer, a *homo viator*, "a stranger who longs with every step" (St. Augustine). Anti-Christians like Celsius (if Origen is to be believed) found grounds in this trait for their polemic against these oriental will-o'-the-wisps: "You have neither shrine nor temple. Why do you hide yourselves in this way?" To which *The City of God* retorts, our Temple is the "House of the New Testament" (Book XVIII, ch. XLVIII). Our hearth and home, we who have none, is the books of books, the codexical Gospel, patria of expatriates (followed later by the missal and catechism). It is stable, tangible, indubitable. However much it is schematized and cavalierly theorized here (by a shameless philosopher), these historical examples suggest something like a reverse but constant relation between the symbolic valuations of *pagus* and *pagina*. The less a community's memory ends up being physical and territorial, the more it will be mental and scriptural. The weaker the local linking, the more prized the itinerant inking. Or more exactly, the doctrinal closure that is incorporated into one or several Books takes the place of the central reference and demarcation in real space.

In this respect, the postmodern navigator's dual loss of moorings – political and symbolic – causes one to wonder. A network approached from so many directions with no permanent still point for its turning, a decentered space, a temporality without telos, immersed in a shoreless sea of signs tied to neither port nor markers in space – this horizon at high sea signals for some a prodigious emancipation, through the disappearance of obsolesced transcendences. Here is where one can vaunt "the immanence of knowledge for the humanity that produces and utilizes it, the immanence of the people *vis-à-vis* the text" (Lévy 1994).

Why cast doubt on this utopia, in its very conception? For reasons of an argument that, given the confines of this presentation, I cannot attempt to demonstrate, and which may even be undemonstrable. Let's speak of a reasoned conviction: all progress *here* evokes a retrograde movement *there*. Every moment that deterritorializes provokes an opposite one that reterritorializes. There is no rationalization process that does not give rise to a return of the irrational, no globalization (economic) without Balkanization (political). Take for example the world of modernized Islam, where it is from the most advanced technological and scientific centers, and not the literary universities, that the fundamentalist managers graduate, just as the militants come not from the rural areas but from the most recently urbanized sectors. We can read into fundamentalist revolt the loss of the ancestral *pagus*, compensated for by obsessive cleaving to the Koranic *pagina*. Is it conceivable that, in the Westerner's case, he should be losing at the same time his two landscapes of reference, *pagus* and *pagina*, without unleashing a formidable and paradoxical reactive counterforce?

One cannot yet foresee the nature of this neolithic backlash. But it seems to me, in light of the aridly retrograde laws of progress, that the imminent ubiquity of the computer reserves a quite propitious future for those enclosures that are more or less petrifying, whether material or cultural. Barriers of dialect, religious borders; divisiveness based on ethnicity, nationality, regionality, category, and so on. And yet, there can be no enclosure or cohesion of the group without openness to an external or superior element; that is, without symbolic transcendence (the axiom of incompleteness). All of which has as a practical consequence: no collective without the sacred (that is, something, no matter what, that is not manipulable technologically). A common place for all, a platform for membership, a collective reference of identification. This fixed point of legend, owing precisely to its arbitrary or fiduciary character, calls for a hardened and lasting material form. Let us venture a possible mediological translation of these considerations that steps a bit outside the immediate subject (falling, as they do, more under a political anthropology if you will). The silicon chip cannot be excluded, paradoxically, from rehabilitating material burdens – as glass architecture has not ruled out opacity – nor the laptop from giving rise in the end to a partiality for the voluminous (even as a generalized nomadism is promoting just about everywhere the indigenist drive). Electronic immaterialism could then be the prelude to a kind of return to earth, wood, and stone. And it might reinstate, as we await the return of parchment, the rare book printed with lead-cast type and bound with animal skin, the manuscript and (why not?) even epigraphy – the science and paleography of inscriptions.

The old man has not said his last word, and in all likelihood the future little Sartres too, their classroom desks equipped with flexible, ultrathin and lightweight PC screens, will long for a good while yet, in the hope of saving their souls, for a skeleton "of cardboard and leather," its papery flesh smelling of "glue and mushrooms."

Notes

[1] Translation by Eric Rauth.

[2] See in particular the noteworthy Johannot (ed.) (1988).

References

AUTHIER, M., AND LÉVY, P.
1992 *Les arbres de connaissance*, Paris: La Découverte.

CHAUVET, P.
1964 *Histoire des ouvriers du livre de 1879 à 1881*, Paris: Rivière.

JOHANNOT, Y. (ED.)
1988 *Tourner la page: Livre, rites et symboles*, Grenoble: Jérôme Millon.
1994 "Nous sommes le texte," *Revue Esprit*, February.

LÉVY, P.
1993 *L'Espace du savoir, éléments de cartographie anthropologique*, International Business Park, Neuropelab.

SARTRE, J.-P.
1964 *The Words*, tr. Bernard Frechtman, New York: George Braziller.

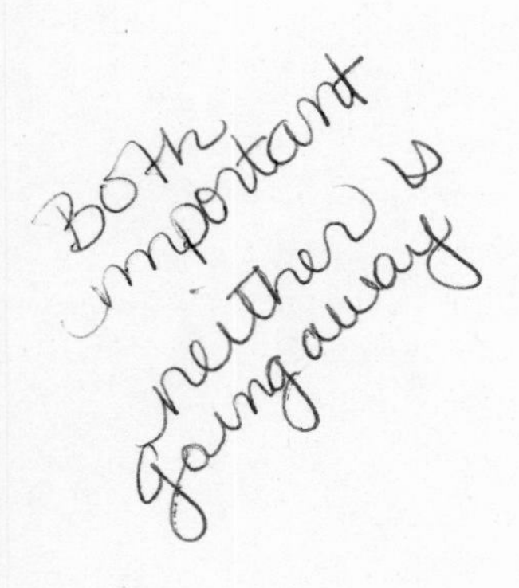

Patrick Bazin

TOWARD METAREADING[1]

In an interview given to the newspaper *Le Monde*, James Billington (1994), director of the Library of Congress, states that the new technologies of the era of multimedia should be used so as to "strengthen the culture of the book." Though my personal experience in the area of multimedia information and documentation is far more modest than that of my eminent colleague, I do not completely share this almost defensive position. It does not seem to give an adequate account of the paradoxical situation in which we find ourselves.

In one respect, the "culture of the book" – that is, a certain way of producing knowledge, meaning, and sociability – is quite definitely fading a little further from view with every passing day. From another perspective, the syndrome of textuality and its corollary, reading, is becoming omnipresent, and the myth of the universal library looks more than ever like a paradigm of knowledge. Such a paradox bears a strange likeness to what Douglas Hofstadter calls a "tangled hierarchy."[2] Books, the centuries-old foundation of textuality, can now be seen as overshadowed by a metatextuality that extends progressively to the whole complex of modes of representing the world, to all the different media, while continuing, nevertheless, to function as a referent. It is for this reason that the difficulty of perfecting and framing the methods for leafing through "pages" on screen witnesses both an effort to reconform the book as a nonbook, and at the same time the book's permanence.

Let us be clear. I am not claiming that books as concrete things are going down with all hands on deck. On the contrary, they are going to proliferate for a long while yet, and one of the major problems that the librarian has to resolve, moreover, will be how to navigate in a hybrid space of documents, at once printed and digital. But the book object *has* lost the central position it once occupied in the simultaneously cognitive, cultural, and political field which was built up around it and which we can describe using Roger Chartier's term as the "order of the book." This field is today undergoing a reconfiguration centered no longer around a founding object, but around the very process of reading.

Struggling free from the straitjacket of the book and directing its efforts toward a true polytextuality – in which diverse types of texts and images, sounds, films, data banks, mail services, interactive networks may mutually resist or interfere with one another – this process of reading generates progressively a new dimension (polymorphic, transversal, and dynamic). We might call it metareading. And the most important question in this, speaking as a professional librarian, is to discover if a new order of knowledge must emerge, and how libraries can take part in it. Of course the fundamental issues that are the transmission of corpora of knowledge, the circulation of symbols and the constitution of a community, do not change. One can even say that the capacity of the metareaderly process to take account of itself exacerbates the stakes of knowledge and power. Thus it is that, after mastering raw materials, then energy, then financial flows, mastery of the "flows of knowledge" clearly becomes the principal challenge of the next decades (Bressand and Distler 1995).

It remains, nonetheless, the case that a purely linear and cumulative vision which starts by hypothesizing a continuous reinforcement of the civilization of the book, envisaging multimedia along the ascending curve of progress, does not make possible, it seems to me, an accurate foreknowledge of the book's future.

Put summarily, my thesis is the following: the book doubtlessly still has a bright future before it, since it has sufficiently demonstrated up to now its cognitive efficacy and robustness; but it happens to have been outstripped by a process of metareading that is becoming a new driving force of culture. Let me give three illustrations derived from personal experience which may help indirectly support to my comments.

1. From incunabula to multimedia

The first illustration takes place in Lyon, one of those cities in which the future of the book was first foreseen, in a round of technological innovation, industry, monetary circulations, and social convulsions. It is at Lyon that the first book written in the French language was printed (1476) as well as the first illustrated work in France (1478). At the beginning of the sixteenth century, Lyon, along with Venice and Paris, was one of the major European centers of book distribution: the printing process was being refined, libraries were prospering, humanists like Rabelais were coming to arrange for the publication of their writings, literature flourished. Two centuries later, Jacquard anticipated computer science by using perforated cards to automate the weaving looms of Lyon's silk workers. In 1895, after having perfected the first procedures for producing color photography, the Lumière brothers invented the motion-picture camera and projector in Lyons. In 1944, lastly, Higonnet and Moiroud filed a patent there for the film-setting process, or photocomposition, which marked a definitive break with the earlier lead-based processes. It would not be far-fetched to see in the commodity of the silk itself – this semi-immaterial and "programmed" fabric, an actual material base for printing, and a possible metaphor for numerical continuum – an emblem of Lyon's passion for seeking out an evermore agile and delicate inscription of signs. In other words, through the printing trade, programming, photography, film, photocomposition, and even the textile industry, a good portion of the ingredients that will converge toward multimedia inscribe their polyphony in a city's history. This is why as a professional librarian and resident of Lyon, I find so pertinent the words with which the eminent bibliographer D.F. McKenzie defends a deliberately extensive conception of textuality:

> The very etymology of the word "text" confirms the need to extend its usual acceptation to forms other than the manuscript or printed text. The word derives of course from the Latin texere, which means to weave or plait and refers not to a particular material but to a process of manufacturing and the proper quality or texture that results from this technique... Under the label "text" I intend to include all verbal, visual, oral and numerical information,... everything ranging from epigraphy to the most advanced technologies of discography. (McKenzie 1986)

2. A library in mutation

My second illustration concerns the Bibliothèque de Lyon, of which I am the director, and its effort to adapt to the many transformations of the information and research landscape. The example of this public research library – France's second in importance after the Bibliothèque Nationale – is especially interesting because it incorporates numerous parameters whose combination translates quite dramatically the contemporary cultural givens. It renders almost palpable the necessity of new reading strategies. One finds within its walls, for instance, extremely rich holdings of many very old cataloged items that pose thorny problems of conservation and communication, but also a robust activity of circulation based on a logistics of loans and influx of titles that is almost industrial in its efficiency: manuscripts and books but also prints, photographs, films, and disks by the tens of thousands; patrons who vary from researchers to aesthetes, but also include the unemployed looking for readmittance to the work force or adolescents from the suburbs; a functioning on-line database of encyclopedic proportions but also more practical or specialized sectors of information. In short, a profusion of sources that no longer has much to do with the model of the library at Alexandria.

The situation can be summed up in terms of an explosion of documents coupled with the blurring frontiers between publics and between usages. The change is sociocultural at least as much as technological. Yet the organization and even the architecture of the Bibliothèque de Lyon still embodies the classical order of the book. For example, the hierarchizing of works and varying intensities of consultation of sources is written into a vertical stratification of user groups and functions: on the ground floor can be found the current titles, the circulation desk, the general public of readers, and the section for more popular and leisurely readings; on the top floor are the holdings of rare editions, researchers, and a characteristic silence; between the two is a subtle floor arrangement of more or less specialized sections with each stratum having its own logic, its public, and its functions. This logic of separation – independent of the *contents* of the categories of knowledge – applies also to the different material supports, and pushes nonbook holdings to the periphery.

This is why, starting from the idea that the tools of knowledge, sociological categories, and academic divisions are in a constant process of change and diversification, we are undertaking a restructuring of the library by redeploying its resources according to content. The realignment in terms of contents becomes the password of any revolution in the management of library facilities. And it is in this way that a given thematic will have to be able to mobilize around itself all the pertinent holdings, information, and tools. It will have to be undertaken from the point of view of all possible uses, whatever the level of each user. Librarians themselves will have to bring about their own Copernican revolution, rather than cling to techniques of doing things that the multimedia industry is, in any case, in the process of taking away from them. They will have to become, or rather become again, mediators of knowledge.

To be sure, the contents themselves are changing and interacting. What was once encyclopedism becomes interdisciplinarity. Like the new San Francisco Library project, our library must acquire sufficient flexibilty. It must be organized around disciplines like so many attractive pools of water whose contours fluctuate as a function of points of view and shifting usages. All in all, the library economy that was traditionally an art of classification has to become an art of passage.

3. New reading machines

My third example concerns the Bibliothèque de France and its project for a Computer Assisted Reading Environment (CARE), in which I had the opportunity to participate. It will allow me to illustrate the difficulties that are encountered in conceptualizing the new order of knowledge.

This work station, already on-line in the form of a prototype, is supposed to allow the reader to work on a corpus of digitized documents culled from the library's immense reserves. Among the diverse possibilities presented by this tool, the functions of comparison, annotation, and indexing are doubtlessly the most attractive. They make it possible, for instance, to compare on the same screen several versions of a text, or to put together a personalized document folder. The primary interest of CARE is to introduce a dynamic coupling between reading and writing. It functions as an active interface in which the reading process is immediately transformed into the writing process. It is, in a way, a tool for translating a given body of text into a new work via the user's creativity.

I will come back to the perspectives opened by this new and very powerful concept of reading-writing. But for the moment I wish to highlight the limitations of a project that is often presented as the jewel of the Bibliothèque de France when it in fact remains dependent on a conception of the book that is still relatively classical and clearly marked by academic convention. Indeed, the model to which the CARE system continues to hark back could be described as "infinite readability of a founding text." The process involves taking a given work, or a collection of well-circumscribed works, applying to it various reading grids that are more or less sophisticated, setting up comparisons with the variants, calling up a contextual documentation, and, finally, producing a new reading of the original text. The CARE model is concerned to a relatively minor degree with researching the documentary material itself, and presupposes a known point of reference.[3]

Now, the most important question that the new uses pose for librarians can indeed be located farther back upstream of the process of intensive reading, in the scanning of huge quantities of heterogeneous and decontextualized data. The true difficulty, a technical and heuristic one, resides in the interaction between the work station and its environment – with this latter being at its widest boundaries the totality of the world's reserves of information and documents which, moreover, will not for a long time yet exhibit the perfect homogeneity of the digital continuum. Once again, what we will more and more have to reckon with will be less the *appropriation* of a text or even a work than the pursuit of a carefully formulated thematic across a composite "space" of bodies of knowledge. The library of the future will have to provide the tools for this navigation. The three preceding illustrations make it apparent that a new order of knowledge is emerging through the search for a greater extensiveness of the text and its modes of reading. But before trying to comprehend the whole phenomenon it is helpful to come back to that which preceded and prepared the way for it.

4. The order of the book

The order of the book sets the stage for a trilogy – author, book, reader – based on the separation of roles and a stability: on the one hand, the author, on the other, the reader, each exchanging their singularities through the stable, reliable, and public "interface" of the book. George Landow and Paul Delany (1991: 3) are right to insist on the "three crucial attributes of book text – linearity, demarcation, and fixity – which generations of scholar-researchers and authors have internalized as rules of thought and whose social consequences have been considerable." The book thus derives its specific efficacy not so much from being a text but rather as a node of physical, economic, and legal forces that differentiate and diffuse the effect of the text.

There are, first of all, the constraining physical circumstances of the book-object that limit and give particular emphases to the text as a finite number of typographically staked-out pages. They make the book a site of memory, a "mneumonic straitjacket" in Dierk Hoffman's (1994) phrase, perfectly adapted to a global and individual grasping of meaning, in the reader's moral and psychic depths. At the same time, as Geoffrey Nunberg (1993) appropriately points out, they concretize the indefinite desire of meaning into a desire and pleasure of the object. These two properties, of cognition and affect, contribute directly to the constituting of modern individuality.

Another even more fundamental constraint structures modernity's mental space: the one which prescribes that text within the book be linear, and, especially, that it have a beginning and end. By means of this simple systematic devising, an entire logic and – one could say – epistemology of exposition and demonstration is put into effect. The signification stipulated by these is procedural – it is developed according to an order of reasons that issues ultimately in an adequate, relatively stable representation of a sequence of reality. Very unlike the digitized hypertext, which simulates the complexity of things and behaves like a game of the world, the book shrugs off all confusion between language and world, reality and representation; it intrinsically aims for effects of truth (of which literary *fiction* in particular is at bottom only the inverted double). On the whole, the book fortifies social conversation by producing arguments.

Still other constraining factors can be added, namely, those of the editorial sequence. There will never be enough to say, for example, about the importance of the "fitness to print" principle that markedly separates the act of writing – always revisable and interminable – from the finished work itself: that capsule of suspended time, padlocked into its box and given up to the plural interpretations of its readers. Identical repetition through the printing press limits the play of interpretation and, at the same time, unceasingly relaunches it with each copy, each reading, throughout the public space of its appearance. This intermeshing of interpretive loops contributes pervasively to structuring mental and cultural space, sparing it the solipsistic confinement to one unique text, to a master narrative or plot continuously taken up again, or, on the contrary, to an endless divergence toward a meaning still to come.

One can say without exaggeration that the circuit of the book, in the form it has eventually taken (that is, since the end of the eighteenth century), regulates the subtle dialectic between particular and universal, consensus and pluralism, private reader and citizen, that has been posited as the origin of the spirit of modernity. On the one hand, it spurs on the development of individual or collective singularities, on the other, it organizes a public space of circulation. As Roger Chartier and Pierre Bourdieu write, "A book changes because it does *not* change while the world changes around it" – and because its mode of being read changes. Or again: "The sharing of one single object by an entire society gives rise to the search for new-found differences suitable for highlighting that society's deviations" (Chartier and Bourdieu 1985). The library is a good illustration. Contrary to its portrayal in popular cliché, it is not only a site of meditation, of the dreary fossilization of memory or of the reactionary cross-ruled columniation of knowledge. As is proven by the constant reorganizing of spaces and catalogs or the constant redistributing of publics and uses, the library has never stopped being a dynamic interface.

Let us sum up these findings so far. The order of the book brilliantly contributed to resolving the problem of circulating knowledge and democratic sociability by instituting a total operating system of demarcations and mediations. The act and practice of reading, in its own right, was propagated (paradoxically) through an *intensive* model, materially supported by clearly delimited and stable texts. The great challenge of the new digitized order, on the contrary, will consist in getting beyond this fruitful contradiction between retention and diffusion, without, for all that, disqualifying the cognitive, cultural, and political issues at stake. The digitization of information defies at least three essential boundaries: that of the text itself, in its spatio-temporal extension; that which separates reader and author; that, finally, which distinguishes text from image – that nontext *par excellence*.

5. Exploding the text

A few of the ingredients that work together to shatter the limits of textuality are by now well-known. They include, among other things, the digitization of entire texts as opposed simply to catalogs or bibliographic references; the immense possibilities for archiving, scanning and updating in real time; the option of potentially connecting together any given string of characters with any other; the ultrarapid access, by user-friendly interfaces and Internet-type networks, to the best sources, whatever their location in the world's collections; and the rapid exchange of commentaries in electronic forums. These new possibilities favor an *extensive* reading, the comparison of diverse texts and viewpoints, multidisciplinary transversality, the "conversation" between readers. They are beginning to have a considerable impact as much on the individual mechanism of appropriation of texts as on the sociology of reading. They bring forth a new mental landscape that gives those who live there the impression of being much more immersed, collectively, in the space of a never-ending book rather than confronted, alone, with the two-dimensionality of the printed page.

This genuine hypertextuality has the effect of subverting what could be called (taking up a cognitivist metaphor borrowed from Fodor 1983) the "modularity" of document-based information space in favor of the "connectionist" model. For the hierarchized interlocking of textual capsules that characterizes the order of the book (from the form of the chapter all the way to the rational architecture of the library), hypertextuality substitutes a dynamic network. Within it, the state (the relevance) of each node depends on the other nodes and on the point of view adopted by the researcher, and what Michel Authier and Pierre Lévy call a cosmopedia can come into practice: "the fact of consulting a figural sign, a map, a relation, a text modifies the indications of centrality and stability associated with the utterance, and transforms with the same stroke the hypertextual network's topology... the cosmopedia is like a relativistic space curved by consultation and inscription" (Authier and Lévy 1992). In place of rigid interfaces that govern the passage from one hierarchical level to the other – catalog, index, table of contents, thesaurus – hypertextuality progressively substitutes procedures of self-indexing, that of the text by itself, of texts by other texts. And instead of aprioristic strategies that envisage cataloging every document under a universal classification, hypertextuality prefers a tactic of small steps, capable of binding together after the fact whole corpora generated from research and particular points of view. It wagers, in short, on the plurality of worlds of documentation. In other words, to the ideal of a coherent and convergent, unified knowledge (of which the library would be the microcosm), it opposes the heterogeneous field of shifting experience.

Clearly such a Copernican overturning gives greater prominence to the performances of the *tools* of knowledge. But it also brings with it some formidable cultural risks, closely tied to the extinction of traditional mediations and resulting from a certain difficulty in mastering the new bearings of space and time and controlling the reliability of utterance. For example, the scanning of large corpora of digitized text, combined with the intoxicating play of similarities, can lead to an absolute flattening out of the deep stratifications constituting a discipline or tradition. As Roger Chartier (1993) writes, "The now possible transference of the written patrimony of the codex onto the screen opens huge possibilities, but is also a violence done to the texts which are separated thereby from the forms that helped construct their historical meanings." Another risk, of which any Internet user is conscious, is that of a nomadic roaming or surfing that has lost its bearings – or its correlate, confining oneself around singular, self-maintained or self-sustained problematics. This doubly slippery slope *vis-à-vis* the fundamentally universalist model of the book finds an echo in postmodern relativism and can lead to a kind of cultural tribalism. A third difficulty has to do with the possible disqualification of "eyewitnessing" and its relation to reality (as distinguished from what Derrida calls proof)[4] which the book knew how to guarantee – by engaging, through the ethos of what was fit to be printed, the responsibility and so to speak the reality of the author, even if he had lied or deluded himself. On the contrary, the constant updating in real time of an electronic magazine, such as the one with which the IPSI Institute in Darmstadt is now experimenting, illustrates forcefully one of hypertextuality's paradoxes: by one reckoning, the most immediate reality bursts onto the screen; by another, it loses all its force for lack of having been truly inscribed there. At the same time that it explodes the limits of text, hypertextuality revives one of the founding questions of culture: by what mediations can private experience and collective practice enter into exchange?

6. A dynamic textuality

One area in which this mutual questioning becomes increasingly concrete today is the relation between author and reader. This relation was until recently dominated by a sharp distinction and "specular" relation between two protagonists. In reality – even though, according to Proust, every reading was at once *self*-reading, since it left consciousness free to take an inward turn – there was however nothing circular in its relationship to the book; it functioned following a universal sequence of representations: first those of consciousness writing to the "mirror" of the page, then that of the page in the mirror of the reading consciousness. The new practices of textuality would tend rather to cross the mirror. This is how, as we have already suggested, the appearance of the computer reading station (CARE) makes it possible to foresee an effective interaction developing between the reading process, translation, annotation, quotation, rewriting, and writing in the stricter sense of the word. The conditions for bringing about a CD-ROM-based multimedia, in which researchers, teachers, librarians, authors, graphic designers, artists, and so on. intervene all at once, also illustrate this general tendency toward the interpenetration of roles. So too does the possibility, from now on offered by electronic editing at a distance, of personalizing the content of a book before printing it for oneself; or even more so, the production of articles in electronic forums for which the borderline between authors and readers already no longer has much meaning. We are witnessing the appearance (following Bernard Stiegler's felicitous expression) of a "dynamic textuality" (Stiegler 1994) that by freeing itself from the straitjacket of the book is transforming not only the individual's relation to the text but also the traditional model of producing and transmitting learning and practical knowledge. In the place vacated by a linear transmission, inherited from forebears and relatively individualized, a system for the coemergence of bodies of knowledge is tending to be progressively substituted – a system in which instruction, self-apprenticing, intellectual creation, and diffusion all closely cooperate.

There is a prejudice according to which literature, unlike scientific and technical documentation, would by its very essence escape this digital mutation, inasmuch as literature depends exclusively on temporality and the sensuality of the book as object. Yet literary creation itself is already beginning to find in hypertextuality the means to get beyond linear narration or impoverished formalisms that recall the experiments of the Oulipo group associated with Perec and Queneau. The writer can, for instance, simulate several versions of one universe and make them interact; he can also introduce the reader as an actor in the game of the fiction. More prosaically, electronic diffusion allows us to imagine the day when authors short-circuit the editorial sequence to reach directly a great number of readers and dialogue with them.

We note, once again, that the digital empire puts too much emphasis on relation and circulation per se, rather than on the acquisition of content. Instead of the substantialist metaphysics of the hidden meaning which a "vertical" reading would attempt to reveal, it prefers the rhetoric of exchange and conversation.[5] It counters the aesthetics of depth with a pragmatics of interface. This shift in priority has the effect of destabilizing traditional mediations – those that are entrusted with legitimizing texts, such as publishing houses or editorial committees, and those that regulate the economy of exchanges, like author's rights and copyright. On the one hand, the instances of legitimization have a tendency to lose a portion of the legitimacy they had claim to through their position in a relatively stable hierarchy. On the other, the hard distinction that the order of the book used to establish between use-value – that infinite potential each work holds in reserve – and exchange value – the cost of the book as product – is called upon to resolve itself in the very act of reading, on a screen,... and in the billing for it. The economy of texts is akin to that of films and television.

7. The "neowriting" of images

The alliance of text and image is not, all the same, any novelty. From the fifteenth century, texts and images in printed books keep up a close dialogue and perfect one another, to such an extent that the history of the book is hard to separate from that of engraving, and then from photography. This collaboration exceeds the simple function of illustration. Frances Yates shows how with the "arts of memory" the figuration of architectural spaces stands in place for and condenses what a long discourse finds hard to immobilize (Yates 1966). And Elizabeth Eisenstein (1979) insists in her work on the role of printed text, at the dawn of modern times, in the spread of scientific images – pictures that are able to set their clear and distinct language against the circumvolutions of religious texts, newly independent of the scriptorium and still weighted with orality.

But no one more than François Dagognet has made apparent – running counter to a tenacious prejudice that would confine the image within affective experience and indexicality – the degree to which writing and iconography jointly helped along the development of an evermore operative textuality: "There is not a single discipline that does not benefit from iconicity," he writes. "... Everywhere is the presence to be felt of drawings, plotted graphs, contour lines, maps – in short, structural and geometric figuration. The mistake would be to consider them didactic substitutes or adjuncts, illustrations of convenience, when they make up a privileged heuristic instrument: ... a truly new kind of 'script,' capable by itself of transforming the universe and inventing it" (Dagognet 1973: 11 and 86). Consider for example the case of medical imagery (x-rays, isotope-enhanced radiography, tomography, magnetic resonance imaging). Its plotted grids of "reading" display behind the body's opacity (propitious, however, for an aesthetics of the inutterable) a planar multitude, a vocabulary, and a syntax. Yet multimedia goes even further. Cutting texts and images from the same digitized cloth, it achieves a qualitative leap and transforms what was until now only a text-image complementarity into a true hybridization. In fact, whereas the text is losing further its linearity and is explored like a map, the virtual image is gaining in temporality, exhibits processes, and is becoming discourse. By making itself into a simulation, the computer image rejoins, reinforces, and diversifies textual dynamics.

8. For a politics of the text

Discussing the three preceding approaches, I hope to have shed light on my opening proposition that the reading process – and no longer the book-object – is becoming central, even as its complexity grows and it combines numerous forms or levels of reading. I have described this process as metareading, first of all because it encompasses as a particular case the linear reading of a finite text, then, and especially, because it is largely self-referential; it draws, indeed, a good share of its efficiency from the play into which it brings its variables and from its capacity to experiment with its own limits.

The content of a book gives the illusion of being relatively independent of the mode in which it is read, because this mode stays quite stable and stereotyped, after the image of the text's structure. This illusion reinforces the specular ideology of knowledge, one of whose preferred metaphors is precisely that of the great book of nature ripe for deciphering. Conversely, digital technologies allow us to multiply around a given content the different angles of approach, to make the parameters vary, to process the textual material, and finally to reconstruct it. The supposed content comes to be of less account than the operations capable of displaying its potentialities and prolonging its effects. One retort to this might be that every book reader, deep inside, processes information, sets up relations, and "rewrites" his book (self-reading). That would surely be to minimize the impact of cognitive prostheses that modify the compass of certain mental mechanisms by externalizing, instrumentalizing, and socializing them. And it would be, above all, to not understand that every mode of reading carries with it and legitimates a cultural model, and that consequently the methods and devices of metareading can only call into question book culture, or at the very least traumatize it.

As a professional librarian in the service of a community, I tend to conceive the crisis of the book in politicocultural terms. Several questions have been raised using these terms in the course of our discussion. They concern the constitution and appropriation of a collective memory, the role of believable accounts or evidence, the reliability of information, the decontextualization of knowledge. They all converge finally toward the question of "meaning," that is what gives coherence to the fact of communal life. And certainly the growing sophistication of methods for processing information appears to be accompanied by an evanescence of stable referents, clearly identifiable and transmittable ones, that the order of the book used to provide.

New measures taken, particularly in the area of author's rights and copyrights, are of course going to attempt to order the new landscape of information and to provide it with reference points. But one must not lose sight of the fact that the issues at stake will be defined from now on much more on the reading processes side than on the fixed content side. In other words, we will have to see to it that all citizens have the adequate tools at their disposal and can master the new techniques for reading. More important still, it will be necessary to promote the equal sharing of the same practices.

Libraries will continue, as a result, to play a most important role, one that will far surpass the simple conservation of a patrimony. They will have to become sites of education and training, so as to avoid a widening of the gap between those who master the refinements of metareading and the others. They will above all offer citizens the chance to reinvent together, in the context of relativism and virtuality, the public space of knowledge, without which acquired knowledge is not culture.

Notes

[1] Translation by Eric Rauth.

[2] "The 'Strange Loop' phenomenon occurs whenever, by moving upwards (or downwards) through the levels of some hierarchical system, we unexpectedly find ourselves right back where we started... Sometimes I use the term 'tangled hierarchy' to describe a system in which a 'Strange Loop' occurs" (Hofstadter 1979: 10).

[3] This concern is from now on in the agenda of the project called MEMORIA, which the Bibliothèque Nationale de France is directing together with several European partners.

[4] Conversation with Jacques Derrida, *Dossiers de l'Audiovisuel*, n. 54 (1994).

[5] I follow the example here of the work of Rorty (1979).

References

AUTHIER, M,. AND LÉVY, P.
1992 "La Cosmopédie: Une utopie hypervisuelle," *Culture technique*, 24.

BILLINGTON, J.
1994 "Un chartiste de l'hypertexte," *Le Monde*, January 1.

BRESSAND, A., AND DISTLER, C.
1995 *Sous le signe d'Hermès: La vie quotidienne à l'ère des machines relationnelles*, Paris: Flammarion.

CHARTIER, R,. AND BOURDIEU, P.
1985 "Comprendre les pratiques culturelles," in Roger Chartier (ed.), *Pratiques de la lecture*, Paris: Editions Rivages.
1993 "Le message écrit et ses réceptions. Du codex à l'écran," *Revue des Sciences morales et politiques*, 2.

DAGOGNET, F.
1973 *Ecriture et iconographie*, Paris: Vrin.

EISENSTEIN, E.L.
1979 *The Printing Press as an Agent of Change. Communications and Cultural Transformations in Early-Modern Europe*, Cambridge: Cambridge University Press.

FODOR, J.A.
1983 *The Modularity of Mind*, Cambridge (Mass.): MIT Press.

HOFFMANN, D.
1994 "Edition-rhizome," *Genesis*, 5, Paris: Jean-Michel Place.

HOFSTADTER, D.R.
1979 *Gödel, Escher, Bach: An Eternal Golden Braid*, New York: Basic Books.

LANDOW, G.P., AND DELANY, P.
1991 "Hypertext, hypermedia, and literary studies: The state of the art," in *Hypermedia and Literary Studies*, Cambridge (Mass.): MIT Press.

MCKENZIE, D.F.
1986 *Bibliography and the Sociology of Texts, The Panizzi Lectures, 1985*, London: The British Library.

NUNBERG, G.
1993 "The places of books in the age of electronic reproduction," *Representations*, n° 45, (spring).

RORTY, R.
1979 *Philosophy and the Mirror of Nature*, Princeton: Princeton University Press.

STIEGLER, B.
1994 "Machines à écrire et machines à penser," *Genesis,* 5.

YATES, F.
1966 *The Art of Memory*, Chicago: University of Chicago Press.

Luca Toschi

HYPERTEXT AND AUTHORSHIP[1]

1. Background noise past and present[2]

Despite the extensive body of international research demonstrating the interdependence of the message and the medium, the conviction that a literary text is a creative entity which will remain substantially the same, no matter what physical or paratextual form it is given, remains solidly fixed.[3] This idea is so deeply rooted that editors and publishers often feel no compunction in altering the alphabetic code, establishing within this supposed hierarchies of importance in which they judge one text to be a main text, flanked by other secondary texts comprising dedications, forewords, afterwords, titles, notes, and so on. The example of Vittorio Alfieri, a classic Italian playwright – and drama is a genre particularly prone to this kind of treatment – is revealing in this respect. Alfieri in fact has been prone to notable misuse. His tragedies are usually reprinted without the important critical texts which he himself felt to be an integral part of his dramatic works (which he intended to be read carefully, until such a time was reached when they could be performed in the way in which they deserved). These texts now, if printed at all, are relegated to an Appendix in blatant contradiction of their author's fundamental conviction that a reader should be offered a work made up of a combination of fact and invention.

In the same way, the topographical identity an author wished to confer on a work by giving it a precise position within a system, be that system represented by a single volume (this kind of positioning can even operate in medieval manuscripts), or several volumes, is continually underappreciated or not taken into account by editors or publishers. Once again with reference to the example of Alfieri, the order in which he wished his tragedies to be published represents an important key to the understanding of those tragedies, for it is an important contextualizing element.

Alfieri was not alone in this wish to organize the reception of his own works, for, in the period in which he was writing, many authors began to demonstrate a new editorial sensitivity which became more and more pronounced as time went on. In 1855, Merimée published, in a collection of Stendhal's (as yet unpublished) letters, a letter (dated 18 October-3 November 1832) which offers us an insight into important details of the relationship which existed in France at that period between literature and the reading public. Having given a depressing picture of women's lives in the provinces, a restricted world he saw as being governed by *pruderie*, gossip, and loneliness, where the men "ont pris le goût de la chasse et de l'agriculture, et leurs pauvres moitiés, ne pouvant faire des romans, se consolent en en lisant," he gives an analysis of the reasons for this widespread appetite for novels. Even in a village of very modest dimensions it was easy to find two or three "cabinets de lecture," thanks to which the average monthly consumption of novels for an individual woman might easily exceed twenty volumes. Price seemed to be no object, for it seemed that women were ready to pay two or even three times the normal borrowing fee in order to secure a famous book, especially "s'il y a des gravures de Tony Johannot, le dessinateur à la mode... et si le roman est bien prôné dans les journaux." Should this be the case, the "maître du cabinet littéraire" might even cut the book in half and ask three times the normal fee for each half.

At the beginning of the nineteenth century, therefore, illustrations and advertising already wielded considerable influence and editorial choices were equally influential for the success of a work. In the letter cited above, we can find an explanation of how the format of a book was decisive in determining its success or otherwise. On the basis of the fortunes of different formats is supplied a penetrating analysis of the reading public. Beginning with the obvious observation that not all women have the same degree of education, a distinction could be made between novels intended for "femmes de chambres" and novels "des salons." The former, for which Stendhal has little patience, reigned supreme in the provinces, were usually published by Pigoreau (who before the 1831 crisis had made "un demi-million à faire pleurer les beaux yeux"), in *dodicesimo*, and usually had an extremely weak plot structure which revolved invariably around the figure of a perfect hero who was exceedingly handsome; the latter, which were mainly published by Lavavasseur or Gosselin, were in *ottavo* and had some claim to literary merit.

Here we have a material distinction which corresponds to precise difference, in content and intended readership. The in *dodicesimo* female characters, constantly distressed, innocent, and persecuted, were intolerable for the women in Paris who became utterly bored by "des détails trop circonstanciés et trop peu animés." This sociological awareness prompted Stendhal to summarize the reading attitudes of his subjects as follows: the in *dodicesimo femmes de chambre* do not mind the improbability of the plot which is put together simply to show off the exceptional qualities of the hero, because the *petit-bourgeois* crave extraordinary scenes which will move them; the in *ottavo* women in Paris, on the other hand, will have nothing to do with extraordinary people or events. This is why it is difficult to write a novel which will be well-received both in the provinces and in the city – the only exceptions seeming to be Scott and Manzoni who were read just as much in the provinces as in Paris.[4]

If a writer at the beginning of the nineteenth century could display such an awareness and sensitivity towards the public dimension of his own and others' work, then what can we expect in our present situation when, with all the developments in the means of communication and the huge steps forward which have been made by the publishing industry in particular and by the world of communications in general, publishers are very careful to take control of the paratext which they see as representing one of the principal elements of their profit? It is only natural for an author to pay evermore attention to the alchemy which is achieved by the meeting of his or her text with a printed text, which represents the first opportunity for a writer to explain him or herself outside the confines of the familiar, appropriate, expressive parameters. Pirandello, for example, was a very attentive promoter of himself and was concerned that his collection of stories, *Novelle per un anno*, when published by Bemporad should have a cover illustration which was appropriate to it. The same writer insisted that for his novel *Il fu Mattia Pascal* (1921) there be inserted at the beginning of the book, before the frontispiece, on an odd-numbered page, a photograph of himself (taken by Luigi Capuana when he was about the same age as the protagonist of the novel, Mattia), which he intended to be "un ritratto per prefazione" ("a portrait as a preface"), as though he were saying "Mattia Pascal c'est moi," leaving open an ambiguous identification between the author and the character.[5]

Pirandello's attitude reflects a tendency of contemporary writers in general, who, with the increasing weight and importance attached to literary criticism, have increasingly dedicated considerable time and space to explaining themselves, seeking to shore up their creativity with a whole series of material interventions: from prefaces to manifestoes, from replies to interviews to private letters to the extent of more or less inventing the character of themselves.

Over the last ten or twenty years, the phenomenon has taken on certain characteristics which have ended up by creating symptomatic cases of infuriating perversion of the natural order of things whereby discussion created around very minor, sometimes insignificant, works which, in the best hypothesis, have very little effect on the text itself (since quite often, on a purely statistical basis, a reader is led to believe that these "portraits" are more interesting than the original), and sometimes have the effect of totally obscuring the literary text. This has created a revolution in both reading and writing. The mass media both anticipate and accompany the publishing of a new novel. Even before they begin to encourage sales of a novel, they guide its reception, by creating around it a "noise" (in the computer science sense of the word too, that is, data not relevant and potentially damaging to the operation in progress) which is not as materially solid as paper, which after all will continue to talk to us for many years in the future (while the row dies down fairly swiftly), but which has considerable weight at the level of the text's reception.[6]

This mechanism influences a text well beyond the normal limits of the traditional paratext; rather than simply affecting the physical nature of the book (one kind of cover rather than another), it takes over the possibility of intervention or control on the part of the author. It does this to such an extent that it gives rise to a system of meanings which collides with that of the original author. Anyone who comments on or promotes a text rewrites that text, this we have known for a long time. What is new now is that the means of rewriting available to promotion or criticism of a book, be the criticism favorable, unfavorable, or backhanded, have by now become very powerful and they dominate the expressive universe of paper. The only hope for paper is that it has some concrete possibility of fighting back with the passage of time. Only with time will paper be able to demonstrate the advantages of the nature of its physical support, which is, at least for now, more durable than the other, more immediately appealing, means of communication.

From the critical-historical point of view, anyone who in the future wishes, for example, to put together a scientifically documented edition in order to understand the meaning assumed, in international intellectual society in the mid-nineties, of Umberto Eco (1994) would have to realize that they were dealing with a writing system which is considerably different from the traditional one. For this is a text which was written using a word processor and its dynamics of composition thus display the characteristics belonging to a memory made up of paper, magnetic bodies, and laser. The study of literary texts will have to equip itself accordingly, and this will be far from simple, since even those in the literary-critical community who are interested in computers often continue to see and use them with a paper-based mentality.

However, it is not merely a problem of the narrator's writing desk, be it electronic or not. Eco's undoubtedly paper-based novel not only has been produced by a world of the imagination but at the same time proposes a world of the imagination in which paper is a means of communication for the future, not the present. The human individual drifting through the space of information is a fundamental theme of the novel, which also represents the (also rhetorical) universe in which it was written. Virtuality and the combinatory logic of the text are an integral part of this writing, at all levels. Although set in a period when the computer as we know it is still far ahead in the future, the plot of the novel is governed by rhythms created by a disturbing absence of reliable, clearly defined parameters and of definitive space and time coordinates. Absolutely everything in this novel is defined not in terms of itself, but in relation to the system of which, from time to time, it forms a part.

The main character's experience of utter isolation, in which what happens takes place in a time and space constantly seen from a distance (not only in the memory), stands as a disturbing metaphor for human existence, for the individual as a powerless spectator, and this is indeed the other story of this text. Indeed, it is "the other text" which is only in very small part paper-based and over which even someone like Eco, himself an expert in mass media, is able to exercise only partial control.

Without going any further into this complex yet fascinating topic, we can conclude by repeating that the information campaign which is undertaken at the publication of a new work puts into circulation a new and very powerful secondary text which often overwhelms the original text.

Once the dialogue between author and reader returns to the silence of a meeting which, if it occurs, and of course it might not, has to be private, what will be the weight of those paratextual reasons which prompted the purchaser of the book to seek this personal encounter with Eco? It is only now that the narrative power of the book will be put to the text. Here will begin a no-holds-barred struggle on the part of the text which will now find its rightful voice and will be anxious to reclaim its own legitimate independence both from the row which has forcibly accompanied and "assisted" its launch and from its own creator who, like an overprotective parent, often harms rather than helps it (all too often we are deeply disappointed after hearing or merely seeing the author of a book we were interested in).

This is hardly a new phenomenon. All written works, once they leave the sanctuary of their creator's study, have to find their place within a tradition with which they have to set up a confrontation, and with which they have to struggle in order to gain their own, original, autonomous space. We may once again take the example of Alfieri, a writer who stood in opposition to the dominant languages of his time. Alfieri was wont to leap onto the stage denouncing the actors who had transformed his somber tragedy into comedy complete with happy ending. We may think here also of Manzoni, an author who creatively and blatantly used the mechanisms of the publishing market, which he felt offered the potential for literary renewal, and who had to start off from the inherent public condemnation and disapproval at having chosen to write in the form of the novel. Both these authors could have argued as much as they liked, claiming their right to adopt new forms, to follow a new, original path, but if their texts had not had the power to shatter the coordinates of expectations and the parameters of reception, such bold, insistent declarations would have remained simply as ephemeral paratext.

So, there is nothing new under the literary sun, then? Quite the contrary. There is much which is very new indeed. What is new is the language of this paratext as we may perceive it today in 1995. Which is to say that today the paratext has at its disposition instruments which are enormously more efficient and far-reaching than in the past. Our present society is a society based on information (leaving aside, for the moment, the quality of this information), and within this society the relationship between data and the communication of this data has become increasingly troubled. Even the encounter between author and reader now has different characteristics from in the past. Unless we can leave the reassuring (if it really is reassuring) lapse of time between these two in the hope that ideas will thus become free of so many spurious and misleading suggestions and invitations, a literary text today has to face a body of criticism (though the present situation casts doubts on the very appropriateness of the term) which seems to be increasingly prone to take the place of the text itself. At the same time, on what should be the more friendly side of the publisher, promotional techniques are often used which seem more apt to provoke indifference and concern than enthusiasm or interest.

2. An illustrated edition of *The Betrothed*? No, just *The Betrothed*

In order to explore the implications of this new scenario, in which the book, notwithstanding the apparent physical continuity of its nature, has undergone a significant change, and to decodify the text in the full range of its associations and meanings, we must perforce begin by trying to come to terms with the paratext, to come to grips with languages of a nonpaper-based nature, especially those used by television (interviews, reports, debates, adverts, etc.).

From the 50s onward, the language of television has played an ever-increasing role in our life and society, following a path first laid out by lithography, then photography, then cinema, then radio, to such a point that today the literary system, from poetry to novels, to nonfiction works, to the simple illustrated book for leisure-time reading, is inconceivable outside of the bounds of this wider system of communication. We thus have a situation which, as we are all aware, has fairly complex ethical and institutional implications.

The meeting of writing and other languages has occurred many times in the past. A writer's words have never existed in an exclusively alphabetic dimension, both from the point of view of their coming into being and their critical and popular success. Rather than look at the very obvious case of a poetic text written to be set to music, or indeed the lyrics of a song or even a dramatic text for which very often the performance represents an essential experiment undertaken in order to reach the final version, we can examine here the case of a novel, and in particular the best-known novel in the Italian language: *The Betrothed* by Alessandro Manzoni.

As is well-known, during the course of its composition, before the novel was offered for publication, Manzoni had the habit of reading aloud sections of it to members of his family and friends in the red room on the first floor of his house in Milan. It is also well-known that Manzoni attributed great importance to these meetings for indicating how much work yet remained to be done on the novel. Orality was here completely functional to written composition. We also know that Manzoni used sketches he made himself to help organize the plot (a plan of the leper house has survived, as has an "ideal" path for Renzo), whilst when he had almost finished the work he insisted on undertaking a reconnaissance expedition of the actual "text" of the places he had written about in order to make the final checks and corrections.

Even though this was nothing in comparison to the aggressive promotion which today takes control of a text as soon as it enters the best-sellers list, even Manzoni, as the time of publication approached, expressed his anxiety about the effects which "too much waiting" ("troppa aspettazione"), "which really was not my fault" ("della quale, a dir vero, non è mia la colpa") might have on the novel itself.[7]

When today we come to reconstruct the critical and popular success of *The Betrothed*, we have to think about the way in which it has been "read." We have to give the verb "to read" here the sense which, in contrast to the sense it had in previous centuries, it began to have from the beginning of the nineteenth century, when novel and illustration produced a collaboration which was to have, in later years, further developments in the discovery of other languages. There is no doubt that, from this point of view, the alphabetic text has been overwhelmingly directed toward interpretations which are quite distant from those intended for it by its author. There have been many and varied interpretations of the novel, beginning with the numerous illustrated editions produced immediately after its publication in 1827, and successively, melodramas, picture sequences, then, a little later, films, right up to photo-versions (*foto-romanzi*) and television versions (including both classic serial versions and satires or parodies).

Leaving aside for the moment a detailed excursus through the readings and rewritings of *The Betrothed* up to and including the present time, we can find a considerable chunk of this history without leaving the setting of Manzoni's literary workshop, written by the author himself with regard to the relationship between images and the alphabetic text. Within the context of the great success that romantic illustration was having in Europe at the time, as, aided by the discovery of new and more effective forms of production, it invaded works of fiction, poetry, travel writings, art and history books, Manzoni was interested in offering his novel in a new form, not only with respect to language, but also to pictures. He therefore proposed the experiment of inserting into the revised edition of the novel that appeared in 1840 hundreds of illustrations drawn by Francesco Gonin.[8]

The experiment required a huge amount of work and involved the whole of Manzoni's family, especially with respect to the notable financial investment it required. Recent studies have attempted to demonstrate that the figurative structure of the work was intended to create a parallel, double-stranded method of reading, the alphabetic strand and the illustration strand. This certainly was in keeping with an attempt to devote more attention to the vast illiterate audience for the novel, who would thus be able to follow on the illustrated page what they were listening to in the reading aloud. But there was more to it than this: the combination of the text and the illustrations in fact set up a tight interweaving of word and picture (even when the picture was very small) working from a system of mutual echoes and support.

In order to obtain the result he wanted, Manzoni was careful to establish a direction which took into consideration the tiniest details, working to produce what was almost a complete screenplay, in which he began by indicating precisely to the illustrator not only the subjects but also the very point and the very way in which the illustrations were to be inserted.

We have much surviving evidence to show how Manzoni was conscious of the requirements of the printing process, to such an extent, indeed, that he was ready to modify the written text in order to accommodate the demands of the placing of the pictures. This shows how for Manzoni pictorial language was felt to be an integral part of the alphabetic language. He applied the same methodological criteria to the illustrated text that he had followed in the initial writing of his novel; documentary precision was a fundamental element for both (his friend, the famous numismatist Gaetano Cattaneo, continued to provide him, as he had done in the past, with the necessary specialist expertise).

In April 1842, Manzoni wrote to Francesco Gonin about the illustrations for *Colonna infame* and reminded him that they should be done in Milan (rather than in Turin where Gonin has just concluded a series of frescoes in readiness for the marriage of Vittorio Emanuele) because while for inside scenes this was not so important, for the outside scenes, "I do not say that they should be drawn in exact reproduction of the real places, which in part is no longer as it was, but that they should not be any further from this than should be the ideal."[9] For the preparation of the new edition of *The Betrothed*, Manzoni set up a working group (designers, block cutters, a printer, consultants of various kinds) which recalled the happy years of the original writing of *Fermo e Lucia* and of its rewriting as part of *The Betrothed*. This was for Manzoni a period marked by the desire to start over, to start doing things again after the crisis of the 1830s, a desire stimulated in great part by his marriage to Teresa Borri Stampa.

The 1840 edition thus represents an indivisible text, a complex system in which each individual component forms part of an organic project. The fact that this project took shape within the period when illustrated works were becoming widely appreciated by no means detracts from its originality. If we continue, as is currently the case, to amputate a large portion of the work, by printing *The Betrothed* without the illustrations, it is within the persistent prejudiced perspective which sees illustrations as being either only fit for children or else as secondary to the written word. Within this perspective, illustrations are considered to provide a merely ornamental service to the written word, or else to represent a reduction or a simplification of the written text which is the price we have to pay for the desire to satisfy the needs of a poorly educated public.

However, this is certainly not the case with *The Betrothed*, in which the relationship between the alphabetic text and the illustrated elements is so close that removing the pictures means modifying a very complex structure.

Our present research is trying, with the help of multimedia support, to make a more thorough investigation of exactly this particular narrative syntax at work in the 1840 edition of *The Betrothed*. I shall here discuss only a selection of its basic features, and I shall begin by drawing attention to the tendency within the work to set up a synchronic correspondence between the verbal text and the iconic text, whereby the illustration is always placed immediately after the words to which it refers.

We can take the example of the bread riots in chapter 12, when the captain of the halberdiers who has hastened to the scene to restore order leans out of the window of the bakery in an attempt to persuade the crowd of insurgents to return home and is hit on the forehead by a stone. The placing of the picture here is in accordance with a strict synchronism: the captain is telling the crowd that they have always been reasonable people ("buoni fi..."), but the term *figliuoli* (people) already used a couple of lines earlier in an attempt to convince them to desist by appealing to their better nature here is interrupted and is immediately followed by a notably less diplomatic "Ah canaglia!" ("Ah Bastards!")[10] and by the illustration which shows the stone which hits the captain's head. The captain's hand is already drawn up to his forehead, his mouth is open ready to shout the "Ah!" and all the other "a"'s of the next word, his head is, vainly, drawn back inside the window, his right hand still leaning on the windowsill (his next move will be to close the window); the stone is already falling outside of the scene; these are all details which fix the image precisely in the about to happen of the narrative time, all these details have been given the task of visually developing the final words of the scene and of anticipating the narrator's comment from outside the moment of narration: "Questa rapida mutazione di stile fu cagionata da una pietra che..." ("The sudden change in his style was caused by a stone which...").

We may take another example from page 337. Renzo has landed at San Marco and is thinking about having something to eat before going to find his cousin Bortolo and "Si levò di tasca tutte le sue ricchezze, le fece scorrere sur una mano, tirò la [here appears the illustration of Renzo using his index finger to count his coins] somma."

Manzoni's decision to give a precise placement to the illustrations, in addition to the great number of illustrations he chose to include in the novel, enables the reader to feel at once that the illustrations are part of the text itself and form part of a system of reevocations, anticipations, and integrations which is predictable and expected. However, the narrative syntax of this remarkable novel goes well beyond this, admittedly extremely important, network of relations between words and pictures. For the sum of these two functions brings into being something which spans the specific characteristics and features of these two languages and gives rise to a completely new form of expression.

To give another partial sample of what is in effect a very large field of examples, we can look at the well-known picture of Don Abbondio walking up towards the two bravos in chapter 1. This appears on page 16, whereas the narrative passage to which this scene refers is on page 12. Between these two poles there is the lengthy historical dissertation on edicts. There is only one difference between the narrative and the pictorial representation of this scene: the right leg of the bravo sitting on the left, because it has been pulled in from the outside, "con una gamba spenzolata al di fuori" (p. 12), onto the inside of the wall gives the impression of a movement which occurred as a reaction to the sight of Don Abbondio. The placing of the illustration after the words to which it refers serves more than simply to remind the reader of what was going on prior to the insertion of the discourse on edicts. We can understand the narrative system which is being offered here if we notice that Don Abbondio is seen from behind in the picture. This is very important, not just because we very rarely see characters from behind in the novel but also because here we are dealing with the first entrance of Don Abbondio, who is one of the main characters of the novel, which thus serves as a kind of official presentation of him to the reader. There is no intention of suspense in this view of the figure, for on the facing page, and thus simultaneously, we can clearly see Don Abbondio's face as it appears during the meeting with the bravos, seen in three-quarters and with a distinct grimace: "torcendo insieme la bocca, e guardando con la coda dell'occhio, fin dove poteva, se qualcheduno arrivasse; ma non vide [the picture is placed here] nessuno" ("he turned his head and looked behind him out of the corner of his eye, as far into the distance as he could, twisting his lips at the same time, to see if anyone was coming along from that direction. But there was no one there"). This is an appearance marked by unease and fear, which shows Don Abbondio just as we shall see him for the whole of the novel. In just the same way that here he is pretending to set his collar straight in order to see if he can catch sight of anyone nearby who might be able to come to his aid, so he will continue to pretend to doubts or worries rather than admit to his real ones. This kind of behavior makes Don Abbondio a solitary man, permanently in flight even from those who are well disposed toward him.

The following page has another illustration. In this, Don Abbondio is faced by the two bravos who are holding up their index fingers in the classic gesture for imposing silence. The words preceding and following the illustration here do not seem to be directly related to the scene presented; only at page 19 do we find a phrase in which one of the bravos forbids Don Abbondio to go and deliver the order he has been given, with the words: "Signor curato, l'illustrissimo signor don Rodrigo nostro padrone la riverisce caramente" ("Your Reverence, the most noble lord Don Rodrigo, whom we serve, sends you his very best regards"). Immediately underneath this phrase is to be seen, rather than a portrait, a kind of ghostly premonition of Don Rodrigo, which, while certainly anticipating the portrait gallery of his forebears which appears in chapter 7, first of all gives form to Don Abbondio's mental reaction on hearing the name of Don Rodrigo. This iconic sequence is given a further installment a few pages further on (p. 26) when Don Abbondio appears in an illustration bowing in the street to a Don Rodrigo who, in his bearing and apparel, recalls very closely the earlier apparition.

Yet another installment comes on page 32, in the illustration of Don Abbondio's nightmares. At the top right of the picture, as befits the instigator of the scene, with his index finger raised in warning and threat, is to be seen the arrogant Don Rodrigo. The bravos are attacking Don Abbondio's bed, and Renzo is holding him still, threatening him with a dagger, a diluted premonition of the gesture (which Renzo performs the next day) of putting his hand "sul manico del coltello che gli usciva dal taschino" (p. 39) ("to the handle of his dagger, which stuck out of his pocket," p. 52).

Thus, in the case of the meeting between Don Abbondio and the bravos, the picture is used to enrich the alphabetic text, helping the reader to apprehend the underlying meaning of the episode. For, as is demonstrated further on in the novel, this is one of the most significant episodes in the whole work. Rather than what is said aloud in this episode, what counts is what is said to oneself, without speaking, not publicly, not officially, what amounts to the unsaid. The complexity of the seventeenth-century language and the details of the ceremonies of the time tend to hide the elementary reality of the right of the strongest which is reproduced continually along the whole social scale. A complex mechanism indeed, springing from a few basic terrible elements.

Before going too deeply into the interpretation which could be given to this part of the novel, it is important first of all to emphasize that the words and the pictures, thanks to their powerful interdependence, work together to create an extremely rich semantic structure in which each individual element assumes its identity at different times on the basis of the function which it is called upon to perform in different systems of relations. As a result, we have the enormously more powerful possibility of reading a text from different perspectives. In order to achieve such a result, Manzoni undertook an innovative literary experiment which effectively threw down the traditional divisions between the iconic sign and the alphabetic sign.

This powerful interdependence between words and pictures in

Manzoni's work has only just begun to be explored in what has been discovered to be an impressive number of cases, due to a methodological slowness which exists not merely among Manzoni scholars. It is to be hoped that this critical gap can now be filled with the help of the development and experimentation of new computer languages.[11]

An interesting phenomenon to note in the examination of the relationship between words and pictures is the use of punctuation. The 1840 edition of *The Betrothed* presents many examples of changes in punctuation which have been brought about by the insertion of the illustrations in such a way as practically to absorb the illustrations into the very syntactical structure of the novel. In the same way, we may note the use of interrupted lines within a sentence, especially when there is a desire to collocate the image in the gravitational field of the paragraph which precedes it rather than in that which follows it, thus indicating a breaking off which has an intentional narrative value. There are also numerous cases in which the alphabetic text has undergone changes owing to the presence of the illustration. Among these we can find examples of "index finger," suggesting a recommendation to silence, which undergo adjustments thanks to the arrival of an illustration and give way to more generic "fingers" (if such is the sense shown in the picture), and in the 1840 edition it becomes enough for Ferrer, when placating the crowd from his carriage, to put his hand to his chest ("la mano al petto") rather than the 1827 version of "his right hand to his heart" ("la destra sul cuore").

The rewriting of *Storia della colonna infame* represents a case apart, but for our present purposes it presents one particularly interesting use of an illustration, at the beginning of the story. *The Betrothed* finishes at page 746 (even though the word *Fine* [The End] appears only after the story of the trial of the anointers, for which reason recent initiatives such as that undertaken by the publisher Mondadori in reprinting the illustrated volume without including the *Storia* seem questionable), and on the right-hand page there is a full-page illustration. It shows the scene of the site where once stood the house of Mora (one of the two supposed anointers who were tortured to death), with, to mark its former position, the notorious column, *la colonna infame*. The picture contains no human figures. At the bottom of the picture, heavily overgrown by grass and weeds, appear three stones bearing the legend *Storia della colonna infame*. It is a reconstructed scene, for the whole area had been transformed at the beginning of the nineteenth century as the old buildings were demolished and new ones built in their stead. The return to the past continues on the following page.

Here the "Introduction" begins, preceded by an illustration which shows, from the same perspective though on a smaller scale, the same area of the city. In this picture we can see the day on which, following the terrible sentence, Mora's house is being razed to the ground, watched by a large group of curious onlookers. This movement back through time implied in the narration is effectively substantiated through the physical movement of turning the page which achieves the transfiguration of the reconstruction into the original seventeenth-century scene. The result would be already both extremely original and remarkable if it stopped at this, but the effect in fact goes even further. It moves on into a long-range dialogue with another illustration which appears at the beginning of the actual story of the *Colonna infame*, where readers of *The Betrothed* living in, or familiar with, the city of Milan are invited to recognize the same view of the city as it appeared at the time of writing the novel (p. 756). All this may be considered also against a – perhaps hypothetical – background of another echo achieved by the preceding page, where the "Introduction" concludes with a small drawing of sheep, which if these link back to the vigorous plant growth noted on the stones of the title, according to a very widely used tradition of landscape scenes showing ancient ruins, represent Manzoni's chosen vehicle for his irony at the expense of the writers whom he compared to "Dante's sheep" (*Purgatory*, III), who, Verri apart, had dealt with this sordid story before him.

However, the conscious use of the effect created by turning the page, whereby one image is substituted by another which shows the same subject with different features, had already been used in the first three pages of the opening chapter of the novel. The illustration at the very beginning of the chapter shows the bridge at Lecco, Azzone Visconti, at the point at which Lake Como becomes (almost) a river, seen from more or less a point at the level of the water, with hazy outlines of mountains in the background and a boat in the foreground. The illustrator's position here seems to be in harmony with the voice of the narrator, for we read precisely what we have just seen in the picture. Two pages further on, the bridge appears again, but this time seen from a distance, and from above, giving a wider panorama of the surrounding countryside, dominated by the huge mass of Saint Martin's Mount. What we have here is a long-distance dialogue, once again, between the illustrations, mediated by the capital Q (for the opening word "Quel") which is shown in the form of an arch. The reader is immediately drawn into this dialogue, working from the general to the particular and from the particular to the general, which moves in parallel and develops what is happening in the alphabetic text. We should not ignore, either, the symmetry created by the placing of these two images at the beginning and at the end of the long scene-setting passage. The second illustration in fact also serves as a connection to the beginning of the private story which the novel recounts. The reader's eye is drawn down the part of the illustration showing a road, down which a man and a beast of burden are moving, toward Lecco, to reach the level of the water and in the same way the eye is drawn by this road up to the edge of the picture to find the words "Per una di queste stradicciole, tornava bel bello dalla passeggiata verso casa, sulla sera..." ("Along one of these tracks, returning home from a walk on the evening of...").

This tight interweaving of the pictorial and alphabetic text gives rise to another text. In the present example the narrator's words at first seem to be describing the landscape from a position located to the north, since the right bank "a promontory" ("un promontorio") and the left bank ("un'ampia costiera") are described.[12] After this, the narrator's point of view moves to the left bank "la costiera, formata dal deposito di tre grossi torrenti, scende appoggiata a due monti contigui, l'uno detto di San Martino, l'altro, con voce lombarda, il Resegone" ("the stretch of shore we mentioned is formed by the silt from three considerable streams, and is backed by two contiguous mountains, one known as Saint Martin's Mount, and the other by the Lombard-sounding name of Resegone"). The narrator then moves into the zone just described, along one of those "strade e stradette, più o men ripide, o piane" ("roads and tracks, some steep and some gently sloping"), commenting that from there "la vista spazia per prospetti più o meno estesi" ("the eye can wander over landscapes of varying extent"). There then follows a rapid succession of glimpses of the landscape moving from north ("lago, chiuso all'estremità o piuttosto smarrito in un gruppo, in un andirivieni di montagne" ["a lake cut off at the end by mountains, or rather lost in a cluster, a maze of foothills"]) to south ("braccio di fiume, poi lago, poi fiume ancora" ["a stretch of river, that widens out into a lake and narrows into a river again"]). The illustrations, in contrast, seem to have been drawn standing on the right bank, below Mount Baro, with a perspective always from the north, thus creating a new perspective with respect to that which comes out of the alphabetic text. As a consequence, going beyond mere similarities or ideas, the road we have seen in the illustrations leading down to the bridge at Lecco has nothing whatsoever to do with the road Don Abbondio is coming along, which we can only imagine, somewhere on the opposite shore of the lake. It is precisely in this way that the iconic plot helps to set up a narrative stereography which otherwise would be impossible.

Manzoni's extreme care in the organization of his story and his illustrations obviously complicates any kind of editorial choice in the prospect of publishing an edition of the novel, and focuses attention on certain elements which have not previously been encountered in publishing. It is hardly surprising, therefore, that the history of this iconic writing is still to be written. And, as we have seen already from a first examination of it, this kind of iconic writing is itself far from being homogeneous. Yet again we discover that Manzoni's creativity in all its forms is inseparably bound to his own history. The final version of the novel reveals many glaring cases of dissonance, or examples which may be perceived as such. We can see, for example in chapter 35, that on page 686 an illustration shows Father Cristoforo holding Renzo by the hand, looking at him "con un misto di gravità e di tenerezza" ("with a look of grave tenderness") before taking him into the hut where Don Rodrigo is lying. On page 687, an illustration shows Father Cristoforo pointing to the dying man on the bed. The two illustrations are next to each other, and the iconic syntax is clearly discernible, but precisely because of this the differences in the way of presenting the characters in the two pictures are even more striking. For there are differences which go well beyond the minor differences due to two different artists. Renzo appears to be a completely different person, with completely different clothes; so, too, does Father Cristoforo. Even worse, Renzo has long hair tied back in a ponytail in the second picture. This is an etching made by Louis Boulanger, an important *peintre-graveur* of the time (who among his other works also illustrated the works of Victor Hugo), which he had sent to Manzoni in the autumn of 1837, in the period in which Manzoni was attempting to form the group of collaborators to produce the illustrations for *The Betrothed*. Manzoni obviously decided to include this etching, despite the glaring differences between it and Gonin's illustration. Why?

While waiting for further research to clarify the compositional dynamics of this and other episodes, I think we can define the pictures as "author-approved illustrations," planned and executed under his direct, continuous control – and we have many records to attest to this control – with the final result of standing in parallel to and increasing the effect of the traditional narrative sequentiality, supplying it with a thick web of references, anticipations, reminders, suggestions, evocations, and sometimes even hallucinations which give rise to a reading of the novel which is absolutely different from the reading possible in 1827.

It is important to remember that this kind of writing using words and pictures comes into being in the context of a wider and more radical linguistic reworking, according to a perspective which intended to invent a new type of text and narrative writing.

Having condemned the novel as being a genre incompatible with historical accuracy, and trying to compensate for the hopeless cause of reconciling history and fiction through the use of a language which was closer to that of speech, Manzoni ended up by endowing the novel with an expressive potentiality which up until then had been very little explored. His attempt to go beyond strictly linguistic boundaries and to show what words alone are unable, or unwilling, to communicate, represents an extremely important and far-reaching achievement. Not for the use of illustrations alone, for he had no wish to delegate the iconic narration to anyone or anything else, but because he realized from the very beginning of his plans that if he could move out of the traditional logic of languages in juxtaposition and try to take on the task of an overall reorganization of words and pictures, he would be able to offer an important contribution to the definition of a new typology of storytelling.

This was an important achievement also at the European level. Not only did Manzoni pay particular attention to the question of language and how this should be dealt with according to the political and social situation of Italy at that time, when rewriting *The Betrothed*, but he also paid considerable attention to the experimentation which was being carried out in France with respect to illustrated novels. The layout, the kind of pictures, the entire graphic conception of the novel is modeled on successful French examples of the time such as *Gil Blas* and *Don Chisciotte*. There is also evidence of a certain neomedievalism in applying elements from illuminated manuscripts to printed works. However, this does not in any way detract from the great novelty of Manzoni's illustrated *The Betrothed*, for by deciding to write and also tell a story by means of pictures and by inventing for himself a morphology and a syntax through which he might do so, Manzoni stands as a precursor of future storytelling methods which have yet today still to be fully accepted as may be seen from the fact that many people are unwilling to accept that the novel should be read as Manzoni intended it to be read.

We can see to what level of misunderstanding this refusal to pay heed to Manzoni's intended reading of the novel may lead by looking closely at one particular case, which, though it may at first glance appear marginal, is in reality emblematic of many others.

At the end of chapter 32, we come to the end of the long section of the novel dedicated to a general view of the plague. The phenomenon of "anointing," the despicable superstition which also forms the basis for the episode of the *Colonna infame*, is mentioned. At this point, referring to the existence of a work (*De Pestilentia*) written by Cardinal Borromeo in the Biblioteca Ambrosiana in Milan, Manzoni gives a free translation of a passage from this which reveals how the cardinal too had been guilty of the same superstitious error. Preceded by the phrase "Ecco le sue parole" ("Here are his exact words"), there follows a picture of the original Latin manuscript which occupies half of the space on the page, placed there by montage. Are we dealing here with an illustration or part of the text? Syntactically as well as conceptually, this phrase is linked to the context in which it appears, being preceded by the phrase quoted above ("Ecco le sue parole"), followed by a colon which graphically signals the beginning of a quotation or citation. Nonetheless, editors of *The Betrothed*, even editors who in every other respect show themselves to be alert and conscientious, seem to have had considerable difficulty in admitting these words to the dignity of rank as part of the text of the novel. In some cases, only too rare, unfortunately, the words have been normalized by being made uniform with the form of characters used in the rest of the text, and the bibliographical reference which is in fact an integral part of this quotation, has been omitted. In many editions, the whole passage has been put into a note (as indeed it is in the English translation, cf. p. 602), which has the additional effect of confusing the numbering of the notes which Manzoni himself appended to his novels. Where the phrase has been given as a note, the editors have obviously decided that since it is a note, it might as well be a *full* note, and bibliographical references not included in the original have been added. The exception to this is in the special schools editions where, since Manzoni's notes are not included, in order to assist the reception of the text by less skilled readers, the question does not arise.

Barbi, a highly regarded critic, understands the methodological implications of these lines, as he displays in his *Adagio col testo dei "Promessi sposi."* However, he considers the words "Ecco le sue parole" as an "appiccagnolo" ("a cavil"), and he considers the quotation from Borromeo given in "facsimile" to be a "repetition" of what has already been communicated in the preceding sentence, and therefore justified only in an illustrated edition of the novel.[13] In support of his opinion, he refers to Manzoni's own treatment of this passage in the 1827 edition of the novel, where the passage appeared as a note. He feels that the fact that the image includes, in the same manuscript form as the quotation, the title of the work from which it is taken as well as some bibliographical details ("De pestilentia quae Mediolani anno 1630 magnam stragem edidit") which are not directly connected to the text of the novel is evidence that it is an illustration and not integral to the narrative thread of the novel.

Thus, Barbi, in the light of a reprinting of the 1840 edition omitting the illustrations, suggested a solution for this passage which is slightly different from most of the nineteenth-century printings which leave it within the text itself and put the title of Borromeo's work as a note. Barbi proposed the reestablishing of the sequence of the 1827 first edition, putting the passage into a note from *Ecco* to the end of the Latin quotation. This is in fact what happens in the Mondadori Chiavi and Ghisalberti edition,[14] adding to Manzoni's note the indication of the chapter of *De Pestilentia* from which the quotation comes. Barbi's position is typical of the regard in which the illustrations have been held and the treatment meted out to them since their first appearance. The word "repetition" used here by Barbi is particularly revealing and significant.

The original illustrated edition confirms that Manzoni decided to insert the historical document, in its graphic integrity, in such a way that it would be absorbed by the normal narrative text. A historical document was admitted into the body of the novel, if only for an instant, and as a tiny sample, to draw attention to the problem which for Manzoni was becoming more and more complicated, the problem of the relationship between history and invention. Was the use of the historical document an extreme attempt by the author to transmit to invention the trappings of truth, or, vice versa, the confirmation of how easily a historical document could be engulfed and manipulated by the literary text?

Until further research throws more light on the interaction of printed text and image, we can meanwhile turn our attention to another case of mechanical reproduction of a manuscript document. A few pages before the example dealt with above (p. 604), Manzoni, after giving a summary of a letter sent by the governor in response to urgent requests for help received from the plague-infested city of Milan, confirms the shallow pomposity and inconclusiveness of the letter by explaining that it was rounded off by a "girigogolo... che voleva dire Ambrogio Spinola, chiaro come le sue promesse" ("a hieroglyph, as clear as his promises, which evidently stood for "Ambrogio Spinola"). As proof of a true correspondence between content and graphic form, Manzoni followed the word *girigogolo* ("hieroglyph") with the reproduction of the (illegible) signature of the governor. This seems to be another small sign in the same direction, the direction which confirms Manzoni's strategy of using illustrations for a much more than merely decorative function. Here there is no doubt that the few strokes of image succeed in communicating far more than any further explanation could.

We can find a further example of the kind of observations we have been making so far in *Storia della colonna infame*. At the end of chapter 3, Manzoni inserts an illustration representing a note made by Pietro Verri on the confession dragged out of Piazza, on the margin of an extract from the trial of the anointers concerning the part of Paidilla (an aristocrat caught up in a trial of humble people). At the umpteenth extremely impossible or extremely unlikely event related in Piazza's confession, Verri had written "Ma perché il Barbiere senza arrischiare non ungeva da sé di notte!" ("But why on earth did not the Barber anoint alone by night in order to avoid suspicion!"). These words are included by Manzoni in the manuscript form, in a narrow column as is fitting for notes in the margin. The printed text then continues "postilla qui, stavo per dire esclama, il Verri" (p. 798) ("notes here, I was about to say exclaims, Verri"). The continuation of the nonimage text, especially with the lowercase initial letter for the first word, here accentuates enormously the assimilation of the image word into the plot of the printed word. By now, we should hardly be surprised by the fact that almost all editions of the story render the manuscript text uniform with the printed text, without giving any kind of indication that they are doing so, or that Manzoni intended that the text should be otherwise. It is even more significant that this has happened even in illustrated editions which reproduce all the illustrations intended by Manzoni, except this one. Why bother to put the manuscript in form if it can simply be transmitted in printed characters? So this is what has been done, thereby depriving the passage of its meaning which is not simply alphabetic, losing any other, even emotional, connotation, that is, as though the phrase had been forced from Verri's pen in an outrage of intolerable disgust at the blindness and bad faith of judges. These manuscript lines, as Manzoni explains, demonstrate the feelings of someone who is not content merely to "note" but intends to "exclaim." When the image of these words is removed, they become weakened, more like all the other words.

Up until now, no attempt has been made to come to terms with the mechanisms underlying the choices made by Manzoni which prompted him to illustrate one passage rather than another. This is in itself an extremely important interpretative thread which it is impossible to follow adequately within the bounds of the present brief notes. One small point may be made here, however, as a means of revealing the complexity of the problem. Manzoni, for example, gave a lot of space to representations of the several but various nightmares which afflicted his characters: those of Don Abbondio, of the Unnamed, of the anonymous sick person tempted by the forces of evil, later obsessed in his sleep by three huge cats and a wolf, and of Don Rodrigo. It seems quite clear here that this attention given to nightmares can be related to Manzoni's own well-known experience of troubled dreams and indeed Don Rodrigo's nightmare of being squeezed by a crowd of plague sufferers seems to point to Manzoni's own agoraphobia. It is worth noting how, in the illustration of Don Rodrigo's dream, Manzoni does not miss the opportunity of setting up internal cross references within the novel, insisting that the illustrators make these clear. Father Cristoforo's raised hand is not sufficient to act as a quotation reminder of the episode which had occurred several months earlier at Don Rodrigo's palace, and Manzoni decided to present the friar wearing the same cloak and Don Rodrigo wearing the same clothes as they wore in that episode in order to strengthen and support the evocative intention of the words.

There is no space here to go any further in an examination of the relationship between manuscript words and printed words in Manzoni's work; we can simply conclude by saying that should there be a wish to reprint the 1840 edition, the problem of the illustrations would become urgent. Any intention to exclude these or to transcribe what is transcribable into printed characters, as has always been done up until now, seems not a little debatable, for by doing so a great deal of meaning would be lost. Manzoni built up a structure which we have no right to dismember. An electronic text, however, could make an as-yet-untried contribution to a way of understanding Manzoni's as-then-untried way of writing. The problem seems to stem from the lasting counteropposition between alphabetic text and images, since these are seen as two alternative languages (except in the case of the complex world of children's literature, where, nonetheless, many works have yet to find an appropriate classification). This is an attitude shared by writers both opposed to any form of visual translation (Flaubert, for example, who also viewed the reverse operation with hostility) and pessimistic about the possibilities of any dialogue between the two terms (Henry James). Nonetheless, more recently this kind of position seems to have been called into discussion. We can think about Italo Calvino, for example, who was significantly aware of the combinatory logic of storytelling and more generally of information, or of narrative proposals such as that offered by Lalla Romano who in 1975 published with Einaudi *Lettura di un'immagine*, which consisted of photographs from her father's album, an early nineteenth-century artist and photographer, inserted into a narrative structure in which, as she explains at the beginning of the work "le immagini sono il testo e lo scritto un'illustrazione" ("the images are the text and the writing is an illustration").

The history of writing serves to remind us that language continually strives to find diverse material representations (the illuminating reflections on this theme by Armando Petrucci are extremely valuable here),[15] and tries to give new forms to space in order to extend its expressive potentialities. Illuminated manuscripts stand to warn us how risky it is to look at pictures out of their context, enlarging them or reproducing them in various forms which can only confuse a reader as to their true nature. Is it wise to disembody or reduce to simple letters of the alphabet the illuminated capitals when these served as an interpretative thread of the text they introduced?[16] The history of printing is itself marked, at turns, by similar discoveries. We can find frontispieces which serve as thematic indexes. A well-known example is the opening illustration to Vico's *Scientia nova* which was intended to serve "the reader as a way of conceiving the idea of this work prior to reading it and to make it more easily memorable" ("al leggitore per concepire l'idea di quest'opera avanti di leggerla, e per ridurla più facilmente a memoria"). The volume then opens with "The idea of the work. Explanation of the picture given as a Frontispiece which serves as an introduction to the work" ("Idea dell'opera. Spiegazione della dipintura proposta al frontispizio che serve per l'introduzione dell'opera").

Halfway through a century which has often been described as the branches which led to the flowering of illustrated books, when Goldoni decided to publish the definitive edition of his dramatic works and poetic compositions with Pasquali in Venice, he decided to open each volume with autobiographical prefaces and by engravings which narrate important moments of his life: these branches tell just as much as do the written words. With respect to the eighteenth-century novel, which was extremely rich in illustrations, Rousseau showed how important illustrations could be for an author when he decided to publish the illustrations for *Julie ou la Nouvelle Héloise* separately from the text, providing them with the extensive explanations which he had given to Gravelot prior to their execution.

Lawrence Sterne's typographical experimentation in *Tristram Shandy* is worth noting here. In Sterne's novel we find a very particular use of layout and printing devices; we can find a black page, a marbled page, squiggly lines used to express ideas and feelings. Sterne seems to have wanted to make people think about the expressive capacity of words and of the ways of representing these through this eccentric use of printing and the reflections he initiated have had a lasting effect and have been further developed in later literary works.

Only a little later than *Tristram Shandy*, the invention of new techniques enabled a large number of high-quality illustrations to be printed in one book. From the early nineteenth century onward, pictures appeared increasingly often in books. Thanks to lithography, the cost of producing these pictures could be reduced and thus the quality and the quantity of illustrations increased accordingly. It was in this climate of technical advancement that William Blake's mystic experimentation could take place. Blake was, emblematically, poet, engraver, and painter, and his use of "illuminated printing" stands as a mark of his genius.[17] A little later we find further experimentation in Stendhal's *La Vie de Henry Brulard*.

The novel, the literary genre of large numbers by definition, and illustrated magazines played leading roles in this change in taste which by the second half of the nineteenth century had become universal. Futurism, an artistic phenomenon which seemed so disruptive at its time, used experimental techniques between words and images which have in fact since been used, methodologically, throughout twentieth-century culture in one way or another (advertising, for example, though this does not necessarily represent the highest peak of quality attained in this sense). However, on a closer analysis, even Futurism was not so very far distant from the compositional logic of many illuminated manuscripts.

The true novelty which lies at the base of modern developments seems to be the enormously enhanced technical ability of the printing industry. Just how much the new languages now available from this enhanced technology have turned upside down the expressive parameters of even the most sensitive writers can be revealed by reflecting on the emblematic case of the two Italian authors who are crucial to an understanding of the passage from the nineteenth to the twentieth century: Verga and Pirandello. The former at first absolutely refused to accept photography only to then abandon writing to become a photographer, while the latter proclaimed the negative value of images and then in his last months celebrated the cinema as the most appropriate means for representing reality. This process of conversion is an ongoing one.

Alongside the development of a syntax of typographical characters is the increasing development of another syntax which covers both words and pictures. This is possibly detrimental to the alphabetic text which has been experiencing an increasingly lean period aggravated by the advances in photocomposition. Sound too has been granted several new and more effective forms of registration. However, within the bounds of the present study we should content ourselves with noting the fundamental stages which have characterized the transformation of writing in developments during the present century up until the computer which represents another revolution in this transformation.

3. Aiming for the third dimension: The electronic text

The nub of the matter here is represented by the binary logic on which computers are based. For the computer it does not matter if we write the word "mountain," or if we say it aloud or draw a picture of a mountain; these three different ways of indicating the same thing are memorized in the same way, by means of a complex combination of

computer does not discriminate

electronic devices which are characterized by the property of taking on one of only two conditions, hence the definition "binary" (these two conditions are conventionally represented as 1/0). Dante's *Divine Comedy* typed up from Petrocchi's standard edition, an illuminated manuscript of the *Divine Comedy*, a film made of it at the beginning of this century, or Vittorio Gassman's classic television reading aloud of the text are all fixed in the computer memory according to the same binary logic. This has never before occurred in the whole history of writing and thus gives an unusual perspective. With respect to a means of expression, a writer is now in the position of being able to "write" a text on one platform which can make use contemporaneously of three of the traditional artistic languages. As a consequence we have an inevitable overturning of the conventional artistic situation from the point of view of invention, historical-critical expectations, didactic possibilities, potential audiences, and so on.

we have the power to destroy the world

With respect to the analysis of the past and ways in which we can recount it, today the computer enables us to go back to study the past using new techniques and tools which can only enrich, and possibly even call into discussion, our usual ways of considering the past. We have in fact, at the present time, reached an important anthropological turning point. We are now, with the technological tools at our disposition, capable of bringing about the destruction of the race, both physically, for example, with atomic energy, chemical or bacteriological warfare, genetic manipulation, and so on, and mentally or spiritually, with the new tools of information technology. This turning point has forced humankind to reflect deeply on the forms and motives of living together and about the value of differences. There is an increasing gulf between rich and poor nations and a pressure which as yet has shown itself only in the first wave of a massive exodus building up from the tension of the suffering nations toward the areas of greater wealth and higher standards of living, which are creating a world situation in which the urgent need for a new culture of peace can be ignored only at the peril of reaching total self-destruction. This new culture of peace has as its motivating force the growing awareness that difference lies in each one of us and that aggression toward others has its roots in the violence which, prompted by untrustworthy urgings of fear, we turn on ourselves in our own everyday life. All this is an insuperable obstacle between our well-being, be it real or apparent, and the well-being of others.

We find ourselves, therefore, in the situation where the new, which affects even those who do not wish to have anything to do with it, and which reaches deep into the furthest areas where least you might expect it, is forcing humankind to reexamine its own identity and to reread its own history. Information science is not immune from this logic. Any progress which can be made in its application (notwithstanding the persistent crisis in this economic sector) will depend strictly on our ability to understand our own brains and to know how to dismantle and reconstruct our way of operating.

The language of computer use, even when applied to the study of artistic creativity, is subject to the forces at work in this anthropological situation.[18]

Binary writing stands as an emblematic case of how the future we have yet to construct must needs have a mind and conscience which reflect ancient models. If it is a time when everything is changing, it is equally a time when in order to build the new, and to defend it from the neobarbarianism which every generation inevitably and invariably has to come to terms with, it is essential to have a clear idea of what has happened in the last centuries. This is why electronic writing needs, among other things, sound critical and philological knowledge, a knowledge of rhetoric, of aesthetics, and of the history of writing in all its different forms. Thus it needs the culture of the printed book in order to come to an understanding of how this can be freed from all its unnecessary ballast and transformed. The very physical nature of the book, the way it communicates, is still essential.

From this point of view, it might be useful to recall some of the characteristic features of the relationship between creativity and criticism.

An author's highly-developed self-awareness which takes the form of autocriticism, that is, his or her choice of leaving a trace (however vain, but still a trace) of himself or herself in the form of a becoming, a progressive transformation, the desire to give back to the fixity of the printed page and to its *ne varietur* the dynamic activity which went before it, the long, intricate history of which the printed page is the final, even though often only very provisional, form represents a keystone of the culture in which and by which we live. When Alfieri was correcting the printer's proofs of his works he claimed it was as though he was reading them for the first time, since he noticed things which he had not seen in them before; he was not simply acknowledging the fact that when words change their physical state they reveal meanings which are otherwise difficult to identify (even though he was happy to find this, for it gave him a further opportunity to correct himself). He was in fact showing the anxiety of the writer who realizes when faced with the rise of big-numbers publishing and the first faint but undeniable signs of the developing mass society, that the literary or artistic product in general is moving away and will continue to move away from authorial control. The text which will go off to be circulated outside of the restricted community of intellectuals and aristocrats is no longer the same text. Writers, when faced with the evaporation of the automatic codes of understanding with their readers as a result of any audience being admitted to culture for the first time, want to make sure that they will not be misunderstood and thus want to provide notes and glosses, endless explanations, and thus to guide the text through that social and economic fabric which will remain extraneous to them.

As is well-known, the author's control over the process of composition had already, by Alfieri's time, slipped, starting in the period when printing had physically appropriated the manuscript, to the gross advantage of the printers who, thanks to their technical interventions, had become in many ways coauthors. However, it was the entry into the historical field of vast numbers, emblematically represented by the American and the French Revolutions, which signaled the start of an entirely new and different epoch in the history of communication. Literature was immediately involved. The doubts and unease felt by so many eighteenth-century writers (as well as a previously never before experienced sense of liberty which the market offered them) are a symptom of a radical change of direction which asserted itself with the further opening out toward a new audience, an opening out which was sustained and reinforced by the development of the new technical discoveries which we have already mentioned. When Manzoni, a poet of Europewide fame and esteem, ventured into the dangerous waters of the novel, a genre generally considered in Italy to be of slight literary value, he caused a scandal and his choice was considered to be profoundly mistaken by educated society. Nonetheless, behind Manzoni's choice and in his obsessive seeking for alternative languages (from the alphabetic to the pictorial), there lay a profound historical awareness and sensitivity. It is enough here to consider his way of working which took root at his home in Milan, with important offshoots in Paris, which was both highly individual yet at the same time had great need of a group of people to support him. It was a redefinition, at the level of creativity, of the private/public balance which caused, among many other things, considerable difficulty and painful misunderstandings even at the personal level. His was a choice which found, on the literary level, in the form of the historical novel the fulfillment of this desire to communicate as widely as possible, and because of this he found it imperative to turn his back on the neoclassical conventional code.

It is difficult not to notice in this context the wave of great insecurity which seems to invest contemporary writers (only minimally compensated by the certainly justified battle for copyright). This is a form of suffering which seems to have lasted through many decades and could even have involved those writers who saw the new publishing industry as a powerful means for self-affirmation. Gabriele D'Annunzio, for example, even while urging Treves to publish *Il Piacere*, was worried about a slight delay and declared that he felt that then (the spring of 1889) was "the 'right moment'" for the work to come out. He also had the idea, as a means of assisting the launch of his work, of publishing two (later one) etchings described in the novel as being the work of the main character ("We shall print a limited number of copies and sell them with a certain air of mystery. The publicity for the novel will benefit from this, for the superb etcher is the hero of the novel" ("ne tireremo un numero limitato di copie e le venderemo con un certo mistero. Ne guadagnerà la réclame del romanzo; poiché l'acquafortista raro è appunto l'eroe del romanzo"). In the same letter D'Annunzio declares, "The manuscript is linked, I would almost say has an umbilical link, to the being of the writer. The printing press cuts this beloved terrible link" ("Il manoscritto è legato, quasi direi da un legame ombelicale, all'essere dello scrittore. I torchi recidono quel legame caro e terrible").[19]

The realization that texts are written for a much wider world than that which existed prior to the major political upheavals of the late eighteenth century and that they must journey through universes of a communication the mechanisms of which cannot be foreseen creates almost by backlash the need for writers to safeguard their personal history, the history of their writing desk, of their own creative workshop. Since it is not possible to control the users of the text, writers seem to feel a pressing need, perhaps as a form of compensation, to leave behind them an archive, orderly or chaotic, perhaps to entrust it to friends or to some institution or simply to the vagaries of fortune.

Caution has rightly been urged with respect to the mine of information represented by material ranging from manuscripts of works to materials used in planning, composing, and correcting them, letters, notes, diaries, photographs, drawings, tape recordings, video recordings, computer disks, the writer's personal bookshelf and its contents, the infinite notes and postscripts to various volumes. There is always the suspicion of a prepackaged impression, an intended vision consciously created by the writer. However, it might be more fruitful to consider all this material as a macrotext, with all the traps and problems typical of such, which the writer has consigned to material which is different from the traditional kind. In Manzoni's case, this macrotext was written even in fire, in the sense that he had the habit of burning certain strategic papers in his fireplace in front of a select audience.[20] It is a macrotext which is made up by all the data which gravitate around the various published or unpublished works of a writer but which overall seem to be attributable to an attempt on the part of the writer to tell the story of his or her workshop (with respect to publishers' marketing strategy, this could be linked to works like Edgar Allan Poe's *The Philosophy of Composition*). This is such a new subject that as yet we have no language to use for it, and despite museums of this, that, or the other writer, university and other funding, exhibitions, and so on, we not only have been reluctant to grant this material the dignity of a text but it has also been difficult to allow it to exercise any role in critical considerations.

As we come closer to the modern age, the manuscript has been experiencing a new spring. Writing has become more and more to be used as a means for self-analysis, for progressive clarification on the part of the writer. The various papers which have accompanied a writer on the journey toward a final version contain a personal experience of which it is very difficult for a writer to let go. These papers contain another story, only the eventual fruits and conclusions of which reach publication. All the rest goes to make up a writer's archive, along with all kinds of other materials which have accompanied him or her through life.

This phenomenon has by now reached such large proportions that it is extremely difficult to reconstruct the history of components which, in some cases, continued to be elaborated up until the writer's death. Many literary works, in the form we know them, are merely the tip of an iceberg, the end point of a seething mass of versions which were corrected and altered. It is even sometimes difficult, as a consequence of the pressure of the late eighteenth-century and early nineteenth-century industrialization of culture, which has placed many writers on the horns of a dilemma between highquality literature and highquality earnings, to isolate the boundaries of a world of literature and thus of its identity. We may consider here the case of Pirandello, who often, in order to earn more money, published a short story in a magazine and then again within a structured collection of short stories and even turned it into a play, which was then sometimes modified in the wake of particular productions and could then even form the material for a film script. Paul Valéry's position in this respect is well-known; he hypothesized that a literary work could never be finished (unless someone, possibly the editor of a magazine, tore it from the hands of its author). Another famous case in Italy is that of Fernando Pessoa, who decided not to publish his works at all. Pessoa has left us a vast and amazingly complex archive which reflects different phases of his literary and individual research undertaken under different names, each of which could be taken to represent a convincing real-life identity.

If we wish to print Gramsci's notebooks, which have reached us certainly not in the form their author would have wished for publication, we have to make a careful distinction between the physical continuity of his notes, which are contained in twenty-one or twenty-two line school exercise books of various colors (red, yellow, beige, black, violet, green, brown, produced mostly by the company G. Laterza e figli), and the sequentiality of their composition. We cannot resolve the problem simply by publishing them in chronological order. A space-time matching cannot refer to the material structure represented by the exercise books, for this is not a sequential compositional unit. Within each notebook there are other units, the order of which does not match the order of the pages, which have been carefully numbered by prison staff in order to keep check on what Prisoner Gramsci was doing with his notebooks. Thus it can happen that the period of writing for a section of notes which appears at the beginning of the notebook is later than another section which, even though it immediately follows it physically, in the same notebook, is in fact chronologically of earlier composition. This is an extreme example of the mismatching between physical sequence and temporal sequence which is to be found in almost any newly finished manuscript.

The task of making a text public is entrusted to the conventional nature of the printed page, while private papers retain the function of being the language of research. Printed words are granted the special nature of being definite, of being unchangeable, whereas private words are imbued with the special charm which is associated with creativity in action, in its coming into being, from ideas seeking things and which, because these things are provisional, draw from things the energy needed to renew themselves and further knowledge. The last traces of a culture unwilling to grant full literary status to the "becoming" of a text (things are different in the figurative arts and in theater, where the dress rehearsal and the preliminary sketch are by no means regarded as peripheral to the final work) have made general the use of expressions such as "rough copy," "draft," "jottings" which clearly indicate just how far we still have to go.

Nonetheless, the present century has discovered the importance of reconstructing the making of a literary work. From the end of the eighteenth century, when some critics fell back in horror at the sight of others beginning to pay attention to writers' notes and jottings, criticism has moved resolutely forward in its attempts to trace the links between the final text of a work and its creative building site. Already in France the expression "genetic criticism" has been in use for some years now within the larger area of theory of creativity.[21]

The true task, apart from the not inconsiderable theoretical and operational differences, is to return to the fixity of a written text a third dimension, of movement and of transformation.

We are met with an immediate problem in this respect, which is material rather than cultural and which is linked to the static nature of written words and of the space in which they are positioned and thus of the system of expression to which they refer. The usual method for dealing with this problem is to divide the page conceptually and, according to different forms, physically, giving the two divisions different forms: text and notes. A reader already knows that (with or without the signal of a special reference character, in smaller print, in italics, or whatever) a note offers extra possibilities. The system works in a very similar way to the electronic buttons system; the two parts of the page are in constant communication. There can be numbers which refer to lines or sections of the text in view, and these set up an interchange of references equivalent to what happens when the screen has areas (called buttons) which when activated by the mouse or other systems enable the passage to another screen which in turn contains information linked to the preceding screen or to others, according to a network of relationships which can be structured however you like.

The apparatus should allow the reader to retrace the path taken by the writer prior to reaching the final form of the work which is shown in the upper part of the screen or, alternatively, to see what features the text might potentially have had if other projects had influenced it.

In operational terms, the note should contain instructions needed to isolate in the current text the part to be substituted by the corresponding portion shown in the note, following a conventional "cut-and-paste" procedure.

Such an operation can reach considerable levels of complexity and, notwithstanding the amount of confidence an operator might have with diacritical signals, the text which can be reconstructed in this way nonetheless remains penalized with respect to the current text, which physically dominates the upper part of the page. The situation becomes difficult to manipulate and requires a considerable cognitive effort when the cross-references become numerous or when the references are not only to different compositional levels of a single version, but to different versions. Even if we group the variants together and mark them in some way, as to be immediately recognizable as such from the graphic point of view, the problem is not entirely solved.

No matter how competent the working memory of an operator, there are always physiological limits to the mental reconstruction of a text according to a large number of identify-cut-substitute operations. After a few substitutions, the new textual reality begins to vacillate, not because there are critical or philological uncertainties about it, a hypothesis which the present discussion does not consider, but rather because the identification-substitution mechanism which belongs to printing is something very different from reading an actual text. And this is the dimension to which all texts, including critically reconstructed texts, should belong. Not even a synoptic edition appears to be very useful here, that is, an edition in which different versions of a work are printed next to each other so as to enable a reader to appreciate the integrity of each. The compositional dynamics, with its continual macro and microstructural adjustment, cannot be regenerated in its full complexity.

The problem seems to revolve around the noncoincidence of the time and space of composition with the time and space of narration. In our paper-based system, the ordering element is the current text which scans the underlying story suggested in the apparatus. It thus comes about that variants, which might have been separated by days or months while the writer perhaps made significant changes to the structure of the novel in preparation, are all placed indistinctly at the foot of the page of a text the macrosystem of which is quite foreign to them. It is one thing to warn whomever consults a critical edition of the complex system of the literary workshop in question so that they can organize their own mental reconstruction and another to put these consultants into the condition of being able to read the intermediary stages of the text's composition.

Without going any further into the problems at this stage, we can stop to consider the extraordinary usefulness of an instrument which can provide us with not only different readings of a text, but also with the possibility of being able to grasp the progressive coming into being of a text, considering all the aspects it contains and implies, an instrument which can equip the reconstructed text, as far as possible, with its various layers, each one worthy of being read. This is by no means a simple operation, given the often insurmountable difficulty of identifying the precise moments and chronology of corrective interventions on the part of an author, but one which can certainly be realized at the level of the macrostructure, and this itself can facilitate the successive work of sectional restoration.

The electronic text is extremely useful for this kind of activity. It is finally possible, through the means of hypertextual language, to make material what in practice we have always done, that is, create systems of relationships in which the links that paper is only able to suggest to our mind, with all the associated above-mentioned cognitive limits, can be physically brought into being and experimented with. It is very common today to talk of virtuality, but in this present case, by no means a unique one, it is actually the computer which is attempting, and succeeding, in a way which simply has not been possible with the tools at our disposal until today, to reproduce physically the virtuality of the human mind. The computer can therefore (in the sense of the self-awareness we mentioned earlier) force us to materialize the network of relationships that we are accustomed to holding in the privacy of our imaginations. To make explicit, through simulation, a possible text, without necessarily eliminating the possibility of the survival of large areas which for the moment we do not feel it is correct to restore, and which therefore can in the future perhaps be dealt with differently, and to read this simulation without starting each time from scratch, will provide a new and valuable way of analyzing a text.

Normally, when an edition of a literary text is being prepared, decisions have to be made about the ordering element, which can be one and one only, and, once selected, because of the fixity of printing, cannot be changed. Reorganizing all the material according to a different point of view is therefore inconceivable. That is, it can be done, but only mentally and at the cost of considerable effort, by using certain indications given in the critical apparatus. This is because every single word is given a physical position which it retains permanently. However, for the electronic text this is not a problem. A single word can take part in many different systems without being printed in full each time, an expressive element can take part in many different structures without having to be reproduced each time. This is what text virtuality is, the possibility of taking apart and putting back together again a text according to whatever point of view you wish to use. This is what hypertextuality is all about.

The electronic text, far from signaling the end of sequentiality, as many people seem to think or fear, rather represents the possibility of creating numerous sequentialities, according to multiple associations. The identity of a piece of information varies according to the function it is called upon to perform in different systems of signification. Its meaning is to be seen in its belonging to a certain system at a certain moment.

The visibility, and thus the readability, of the electronic text is dynamically redefined on the basis of the perspective that the reader wishes to adopt, in order to assist the kind of analysis felt to be most useful or appropriate for the research in progress. The important thing is to have the text prepared for this kind of analysis, having set up the networks of connections which are necessary in order to move about in this multicentered system.[22]

Moving from paper-based virtuality to hypertext means taking critical experimentation to new and as yet untried levels with the consequent possibility of being able to make apparent and understandable much more than what paper-based language has so far allowed us to do. Even if the computer could only enable us to see and to read things which otherwise we would have only been able to imagine in our head, this would still be a great step forward.

Thus in the electronic environment outlined above, the text operates as a territory for experimentation at the center of which stand revolutionary ways of writing and reading. In addition to the situations described above, it is worth pointing out that it would still be possible to have on-line, ready to be recalled at any given moment, the original text (printed or in manuscript) of which the hypertext version is an interpretation, as well as critical commentaries, and so forth of these.[23]

It is to be hoped that applications of the method outlined above will will thus enable the improvement and extension of the necessarily rather sketchy reflections given here. Nonetheless, we must be certain to keep one point clearly in mind in such reflections and with respect to such applications. Even though this is a new and revolutionary situation for most of us, we must not forget that the electronic text must be thought of and treated as an original text, written by an author. It is for this reason that the logic implicit in the general nonprofessional discussion of data banks ("We'll put everything in and then I'll see what I can do with it") is wrong. The computer follows the commands that we the operators give it, and it therefore gives back to us the paths that we put into it. There can be no data without the memory, and therefore the critical approach, of the person who has chosen and structured that data.

Notes

[1] Translation by Christine Richardson.

[2] The present study does not provide any definite conclusions but rather represents the partial and continually evolving results of an investigation being carried out at the Centro Ricerche e Applicazioni dell'Informatica all'Analisi dei Testi (C.R.A.I.A.T.: email: CRAIAT@CESIT1.UNIFI.IT), of the University of Florence, on the relationship, in the literary environment, between the alphabetic text, images, and sounds. I have already presented and offered for debate these results in several seminars of which the acts are currently in the process of being prepared for publication. I would therefore like to apologize for any overlapping between these present observations and in particular my comments and observations contained in Leonardi, Morelli, and Santi (1995). The difference in intended readers of the two articles may justify any repetitions.

[3] Genette (1987).

[4] Paris, Calmann-Lévy, 1885, vol. 2: 172-77. The letter in question was longer than the version given by Merimée and was addressed to Vincenzo Salvagnoli, who was intending to write an article on *Le Rouge et le Noir* for Vieusseux's *Antologia*; cf. the edition of Merimée's collection edited by Henry Matineau, Paris, Gallimard, 1952.

[5] Cf. *Il fu Mattia Pascal*, Pietro Gibellini (ed.), Florence, Giunti, 1994: ix-x.

[6] Cf. Holub (1984).

[7] Cf. Niccolò Tommaseo and Giovan Pietro Vieusseux, *Carteggio inedito*, Raffaele Ciampini and Petre Ciureanu (eds.), vol. 1 (1825-1834), Rome, Edizioni di Storia e Letteratura, 1956: 68. Cf. also Toschi (1989).

[8] In this somewhat confused context, since so far there have been very few actual experiments carried out of this method, what electronic texts there are tend to be of poor quality, whereas there is a vast wealth of critical material on the subject. C.R.A.I.A.T. is undertaking a series of research projects which radiate out from the possible ancient roots of this language, with particular reference to the use of pictures in literary texts. The basis for this research interest is the conviction that in order for new expressive instruments to be evaluated, they must have a good historical memory, since the meeting of writing with other nonalphabetic expressive forms has existed since the far distant past, for words written by authors in their books have always existed in a not exclusively alphabetic dimension. The present study offers some of the considerations which are coming to the surface as a result of the composition of a hypertext of an illustrated edition of *The Betrothed* and the figurative history of this novel, which is proving to be a particularly interesting case for investigating certain aspects of the theory of the electronic text.

[9] "Non dico che vogliano esser presi a un puntino dal vero, che in parte non è più quello; ma non devono nemmeno esserne tanto lontani quanto può andar l'ideale," *Lettere*, in C.A. Arieti (ed.), *Tutte le opere*, vol. 7, Milan, Mondadori, 1970: 213-14.

[10]. All translations of passages from *The Betrothed* are taken from the version by Bruce Penman, published by Penguin Classics, Harmondsworth, 1972/1987.

[11] The only studies so far available of this area are the well-known study by Momigliano (1930) and the monumental Parenti (1945) which unfortunately contains many errors. See also Mazzocca (1985); Barelli (1991). Macchia makes several very acute comments in his Macchia (1989). An extremely useful and interesting volume containing many innovative interpretations and ideas is Manetti (ed.) (1989); the work contains contributions by U. Eco, G. Nencioni, M. Corti, C. Segre, F. Marsciani, G. Manetti, I. Pezzini, P. Magli, S. Agosti, P. Valesio, E. Raimondi, A. Pasqualino, R. Andò, S. Volpe, D'A.Silvio Avalle, G. Bettetini, R. Giovannoli, A. Grasso, O. Calabrese, F. Casetti, A. Nicoletti.

[12] Cf. Romagnoli (1982: 461).

[13] Cf. *Annali Manzoniani*, vol. 2, 1941: 14-15.

[14] "E' una ripetizione... ingombrante" ("It's an awkward repetition"). Cf. A. Manzoni, *Tutte le opere. op. cit.*, vol. 2 T. I, 1963: 940.

[15] Cf. Radding (ed.) (1995).

[16] Cf. Weitzmann (1970).

[17] A recent reprinting of Blake's *Jerusalem* in Italy, edited by Marcello Pagnini (Florence, Giunti, 1994), offers us a fine example of this genius.

[18] An excellent occasion for investigating in depth the terms and implications of this turning point was provided by the conference organized by the Accademia Nazionale dei Lincei and the Fondazione IBM Italia, held in Rome, October 7-8, 1991, the proceedings of which have now been published as *Calcolatori e Scienze Umane*, Milan, ETASLibri, 1992.

[19] In this way D'Annunzio encouraged a myth almost as strong as that of his own personality, the myth of a "text" over which he could maintain primary control.

[20] Cf. "La strategia del caminetto," in Toschi (1989: 34-64).

[21] The journal *Genesis*, edited by Jean-Louis Lebrave (ITEM-CRNS), provides a good general view of this area.

[22] Cf. in this respect Toschi (1991), an electronic edition of this text which was presented at the international conference on *Iconografia del teatro* held in Venice November 4-7, 1991. Cf. also with respect to this hypertext Gori and Gramigni (1994: 201-11).

[23] A hypothesis for a hypertext applied to Manzoni's novels is outlined in Toschi (1993: 219-28) and *ibid.* 2 (1993-1994: 84-93).

References

BARELLI, S.
1991 "Un romanzo per immagini," in *Archivio Storico Ticinese*.

ECO, U.
1994 *L'isola del giorno prima*, Milan: Bompiani.

GENETTE, G.
1987 *Seuils*, Paris: Editions du Seuil.

GORI, M., AND GRAMIGNI, F.
1994 "L'edizione ipertestuale della 'Famiglia dell'antiquario,'" in C. Leonardi, M. Morelli, and F. Santi (eds.), *Macchine per leggere. Tradizioni e nuove tecnologie per comprendere i testi*, Spoleto: Centro Italiano di Studi sull'Alto Medioevo.

HOLUB, R.C.
1984 *Reception Theory*, London & New York: Methuen.

LEONARDI, C., MORELLI, M., AND SANTI, F. (EDS.)
1995 *Fabula in tabula. Una storia degli indici dal manoscritto al testo elettronico*, Spoleto: Centro Italiano di Studi sull'Alto Medioevo.

MACCHIA, G.
1989 *Tra Don Giovanni e Don Rodrigo. Scenari secenteschi*, Milan: Adelphi.

MANETTI, G. (ED.)
1989 *Leggere "I promessi sposi,"* Milan: Bompiani.

MAZZOCCA, F.
1985 *Quale Manzoni? Vicende figurative dei "Promessi Sposi,"* Milan: Il Saggiatore.

MOMIGLIANO, A.
1930 "Il Manzoni illustratore dei *Promessi sposi*: da un manoscritto inedito," *Pegaso*.

PARENTI, M.
1945 *Manzoni editore. Storia di una celebre impresa manzoniana*, Bergamo: Ist. Ital. d'Arti Grafiche.

RADDING, C.C. (ED.)
1995 *Writers and Readers in Medieval Italy: Studies in the History of Written Culture*, New Haven: Yale University Press.

ROMAGNOLI, S.
1982 "Spazio pittorico e spazio letterario da Parini a Gadda," in *Storia d'Italia. Annali, 5, Il paesaggio*, Turin: Einaudi.

TOSCHI, L.
1989 *La sala rossa. Biografia dei "Promessi sposi,"* Turin: Bollati Boringhieri.
1991 *Ipertesto della "Famiglia dell'antiquario" di Carlo Goldoni*, Venice: Marsilio, in coproduction with Fondazione IBM Italia and Bassilichi Sviluppo, Florence.

TOSCHI, L.
1993-1994 "Letteratura italiana e informatica" and "Un iper-classico della letteratura italiana," in *Rassegna della letteratura italiana*, IF Fondazione IBM Italia.

WEITZMANN, K.
1970 *Illustrations in Roll and Codex. A Study of the Origin and Method of Text Illustration*, Princeton: Princeton University Press.

George P. Landow

TWENTY MINUTES INTO THE FUTURE, OR HOW ARE WE MOVING BEYOND THE BOOK?

1. Already there

Predicting how we might move beyond the book requires, first, that we recognize ways we already find ourselves there. Most readers of a phrase like "beyond the book" might assume that since books define much that seems most precious about our intellectual culture, such "beyondness" could refer only to some fearful state that lies far ahead in the future. Glancing before ourselves now, however, reveals not an impossibly distant prospect but one waiting for us – as *Max Headroom*, the science-fiction TV series, puts it – "twenty minutes into the future."

Until recently such a possibility meant exclusively moving into the analogue world of television and video and not, as it has increasingly happened, into the world of digital words and images – into, that is, an information technology comprising computerized text, images, sound, and video stored and read on geographically dispersed computers joined to form networks. In many ways, we have, for better or worse, already moved beyond the book. Even on the crudest, most materialist standard involving financial returns, we no longer find it at the center of our culture as the primary means of recording and disseminating information and entertainment. The sales of books and other printed matter, for centuries the center of our technology of cultural memory, now have fallen to fourth position behind the sales of television, cinema, and video games. Video games, that child of the digital world, only recently displaced the book in third place on this list.

Since I have raised the crude, materialist factor of economics, let me point out another material instance of the way we find ourselves already beyond the book. As I have pointed out elsewhere (Landow 1995: 3-6), when many people first encounter the notion of electronic textuality and electronic books, they point out that reading on a computer screen – itself a transitory means of reading e-text – lacks many of the pleasures offered by the printed book. Certainly, no one who has experienced the comparatively coarse resolution offered by most computer monitors would disagree with the obvious shortcomings of present-day computer technology, but many people who make this point do not stop here but proceed in such a way to make clear that their standard of comparison is not the books they actually encounter but rather some ideal utopian book, which in practice they never read and most contemporary students have never even handled.

A characteristic example of such illusions about present relation to the printed book presented itself at "Beyond Gutenberg," a conference held at Yale University in the spring of 1994. There Edward Tufte, the famous graphic and information designer, reminded his audience how many sensual pleasures books offer that computers do not. To make his point, he lovingly displayed Ben Jonson's own copy of Euclid, and his remarks made quite clear that he presented this leather-bound volume from his own collection as the standard against which reading on computer screens should be judged. Upon the briefest consideration, using this exquisite, association-laden object to represent our experience of books appears intensely problematic. First, as everyone in the audience immediately recognized, this book, unlike most we use, is a unique object, an object quite unlike almost all we encounter in our daily experience of reading.

Taking the experience of American undergraduates today, a group of readers who read surrounded by analogue and digital information technologies of radio, cinema, television, video, and computing, we have to ask, "What kind of books do they experience?" and the answer has to be not the kind of books I did when, more than three decades ago, I was an undergraduate. Going to my college bookstore, I encountered hardcover anthologies, paperbound books, and inexpensive hardbound editions, such as those issued by Modern Library, Everyman, and the Oxford Classics. Today students still encounter comparatively expensive hardcover textbooks and anthologies, to be sure, and many of these, particularly in the physical and biological sciences, seem better illustrated and designed than those of my day. Many of the texts I assign, however, are paperbounds characterized by narrow margins, typographical errors, and tiny type. Anyone who has used such paperbacks can testify to the fact that many of them begin to collapse, break apart, and drop pages during the week in which they are assigned. In ascertaining the present and future position of the book in our culture, one must recognize the way most students today actually encounter the printed book as object. For them it offers not the sensual pleasures of the well-designed, well-printed, well-bound morocco volume of our ideal. Even more important, rather than embodying the relative permanence and sheer solidity so apparent in Jonson's Euclid (or, not to reach as high for an example, in clothbound Knopf editions of Wallace Stevens), books embody ill-designed, fragile, short-lived objects.

A good bit of undergraduate reading in America, moreover, does not involve books at all. Since the invention of xerography, instructors, by necessity, have increasingly cobbled together their own anthologies of reading materials, often driven by the fact that long-used texts and anthologies have gone out of print. Ironically, at the very time that computer-based design tools have placed elegant book design within reach of the smallest publishers and book producers, the rise of these nonbooks offers ugly, undesigned, heterogeneous assemblages as a model for the reading-object. These cobbled-together nonbooks assemble collections of texts in different typefaces, design, reference conventions, and even page orientation. Such on-demand compilations play an increasingly important role in the reading experiences of many young adults today, and to them the book has lost both most of its aesthetic stature and its sense of solidity and permanence. Many of our students, in other words, have already found themselves somewhere beyond the book as solacing object and cultural paradigm. Which is not to say that they have moved beyond it to something better, to something that in any way surpasses Tufte's leather-bound volume. Instead, they have lost much of the experience of the book as we recall – and occasionally idealize – it.

We have also moved beyond the book in yet another way, for if by book we mean an object composed of printed pages of alphanumeric text between hard or soft covers, then many works until recently found only in this codex form have indeed moved "beyond" this form. Difficult as it is for those of us who professionally work with books, whether as student, teacher, researcher, or writer, a great many – perhaps most – books do not contain literature, the arts, history, or even the sciences and social sciences. An enormous number of codex publications take the form of railroad and other schedules, regulations, parts and price lists, repair manuals, and the like. Even library catalogs, which in the Bodleian and British Museum still take the form of books, in most libraries long ago metamorphosed into file drawers of written and printed cards and have now increasingly moved into the digital world. All the strengths of electronic text, including adaptability, infinite duplicability, and speed of transport, make these changes ultimately a means of saving time, energy, and other resources, particularly paper.

What implications does such a shift from physical to digital have for the culture of the book? Will it essentially leave unchanged the way readers consider novels, poetry, and nonfiction, or will the fact that such works no longer always, or most conveniently, exist in book form in some way make the book as a form, as a means of reading, and as a destination for writing seem a trifle archaic, a bit, well, self-consciously high culture? Each form of physically recording a text has its peculiar strengths and weaknesses, to be sure. What, then, are those associated with the new digital technologies of cultural memory?

An indication of some of these costs and benefits appears if we consider Tufte's warnings about the shortcomings of digitization. From his point of view, one of the chief problems in computing lies in the coarse resolution available on contemporary computer screens. Holding up an exquisitely printed map from the eighteenth or nineteenth century, he claimed that such printed sources of information have a resolution thousands of times finer than that available on standard monitors. Tufte is correct: at present inadequate screen technology means that information on computer monitors cannot come close to providing the resolution or aesthetic pleasure provided by such (albeit rare) printed documents.

Of course, this matter of resolution is not the entire story, and to Tufte's fine-grained map I would like to juxtapose an example of an electronic one that more than makes up for its comparatively poor resolution by offering interactivity, adaptability, and ease of obtaining the information required by individual users. My example comes from the Berlin U-Bahn, or subway system, which now offers travelers a touch-screen guide that exemplifies the strengths of computerized information. The traveler in need of information encounters a first screen with images of different kinds of public transportation and directions in three languages to begin. Touching the first screen produces another that permits one to choose Dutch, English, French, German, Polish, Spanish, or Turkish versions (fig. 1). At this point one can request information about U-Bahn stations, stations plus bus stops, street addresses, or special destinations. Choosing "Special Destinations", one receives a choice of embassies and consulates, museums, places of

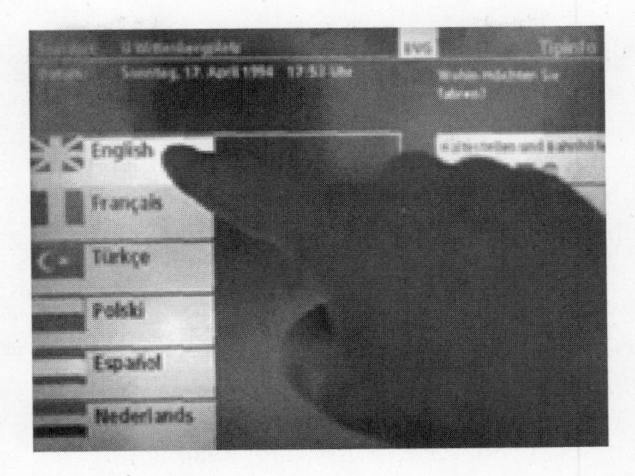

Figure 1. The adaptability of materials created with electronic media appears in this hypertext travel planner in the Berlin U-Bahn, which permits users to reconfigure the system to use one of several languages offered.

interest, theaters, concerts and events, hotels, universities, hospitals, and so on. Touching "Museums" produces a screen divided alphabetically; choosing B produces a list of which the first six entries are "Bauhaus Archiv, Berlin-Museum, Berliner Handwerkersmuseum, Berliner Kinomuseum, Berlinische Galerie," and "Bodemuseum." Pressing one's intended destination brings up a series of screens that permit one to indicate the date and time of day one wishes to travel. At this point, one receives a simple diagram indicating the station from which one departs, any necessary changes, and the scheduled times of arrival and departure of all trains involved. If dissatisfied with the resulting plan, one can request alternate routes; if satisfied, one prints out one's route and schedule (fig. 2).

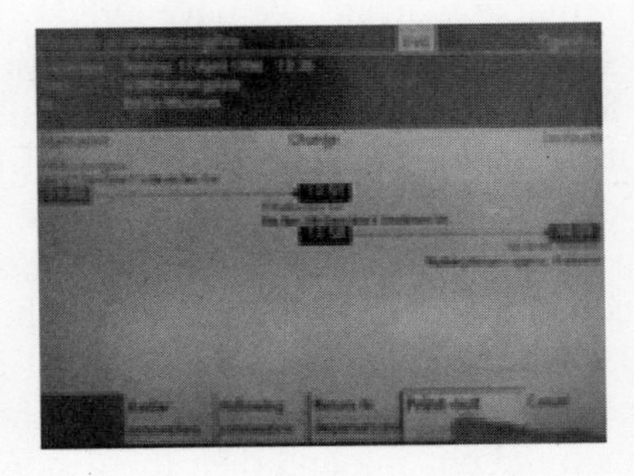

Figure 2. Combining paper and electronic media, the Berlin U-Bahn Kiosk permits the traveler to print out a paper copy of an agreed-upon route.

One can also use the U-Bahn Kiosk to plan one's travel to individual street addresses.

As this example shows, a computerized information source, which forms the digital analogue to a set of street maps, subway and bus schedules, and so forth, offers ample gains to make up for its obvious losses. Although attractively designed, it does not have, and does not need, the printed map's fine-grained detail, which it trades for vastly greater ease of use and increased information. The comparison of the printed map to the digital travel planner reminds us of several key matters, the first of which is that translating such information resources into computer form produces something quite new. The digital resource boasts speed, ease of use, and adaptability, and where these are crucial factors, they will allow it to displace the printed reference. Returning to Tufte's comparison, one also realizes that fine-grained detail does not always equate either to more information or to more easily usable information.

For the reasons displayed by the Berlin U-Bahn Kiosk, electronic text seems certain to displace certain kinds of printed matter, even that in books, though not, to be sure, those upon which most at this conference have directed their attention. Nonetheless, we must recognize the changes that take place, both because they remind us more fully what is included in the notions of "book" (and moving "beyond" it), and because they suggest the extent to which people will increasingly turn to nonbooklike objects for their textual information.

2. Printed books are technology, too

As these last remarks indicate, we have already moved far enough beyond the book that we find ourselves, for the first time in centuries, able to see the book as unnatural, as a near-miraculous technological innovation and not as something intrinsically and inevitably human. We can, to use Derridean terms, decenter the book. We find ourselves in the position, in other words, of perceiving the book *as technology*. I think it no mere coincidence that it is at precisely this period in human history that we have acquired crucial intellectual distance from the book as object and as cultural product. First came the distant hearing – the telephone – then the cinema and then the distant seeing of television. It is only with the added possibilities created by these new information media and computing that Harold Innis, Marshall McLuhan, Jack Goody, Elizabeth Eisenstein, Alvin Kernan, Roger Chartier, and the European scholars of *Lesengeschichte* could arise.

Influential as these scholars have been, not all scholars willingly recognize the power of information technologies upon culture. This resistance appears in two characteristic reactions to the proposition that information technology constitutes a crucial cultural force. First, one encounters a tendency among many humanists contemplating the possibility that information technology influences culture to assume that before now, before computing, our intellectual culture existed in some pastoral nontechnological realm. *Technology*, in the lexicon of many humanists, generally means "only that technology of which I am frightened." In fact, I have frequently heard humanists use the word technology to mean "some intrusive, alien force like computing," as if pencils, paper, typewriters, and printing presses were in some way *natural*. Digital technology may be new, but technology, particularly information technology, has permeated all known culture since the beginnings of human history. If we hope to discern the ways in which we might move beyond the book, we must not treat all previous information technologies of language, rhetoric, writing, and printing as nontechnological.

A second form of resistance to recognizing the role of information technology in culture appears in implicit claims that technology, particularly information technology, can *never* have cultural effects. Almost always presented by speakers and writers as evidence of their own sophistication and sensitivity, this strategy of denial has an unintended effect: denying that Gutenberg's invention or television can exist in a causal connection to any other aspect of culture immediately transforms technology – whatever the author means by that term – into a kind of intellectual monster, something so taboo that civilized people cannot discuss it in public. In other words, it takes technology, which is both an agent and an effect of our continually changing culture(s), and denies its existence as an element of human culture. One result appears in the strategies of historical or predictive studies that relate cultural phenomena to all sorts of economic, cultural, and ideological factors but avert their eyes from any technological causation, as if it, and only it, were in some way reductive. The effect, of course, finally is to deny that this particular form of cultural product can have any effect.

We have to remind ourselves that if, how, and whenever we move beyond the book, that movement will not embody a movement from something natural or human to something artificial – from nature to technology – since writing and printing and books are about as technological as one can be. Books, after all, are teaching and communicating machines.

3. From physical mark to code

These new digital information technologies involve fundamental changes in the way we read and write, and these radical differences, in turn, derive from a single fact, the shift from the physical to the virtual. As I have explained elsewhere:

> Text-based computing provides us with electronic rather than physical texts, and this shift from ink to electronic code – what Jean Baudrillard calls the shift from the "tactile" to the "digital" – produces an information technology that simultaneously combines fixity and flexibility, order and accessibility – but at a cost. Since electronic text-processing is a matter of manipulating computer-manipulated codes, all texts that the writer encounters on the screen are virtual texts. Using an analogy to optics, computer scientists speak of "virtual machines" created by an operating system that provides individual users with the experience of working on their own individual machines when they in fact share a system with as many as several hundred others. Similarly, all texts the reader and the writer encounter on a computer screen exist as a version created specifically for them while an electronic primary version resides in the computer's memory. One therefore works on an electronic copy until such time as both versions converge when the writer commands the computer to "save" her version of the text by placing it in memory. At this point the text on screen and in the computer's memory briefly coincide, but the reader always encounters a virtual image of the stored text and not the original version itself; in fact, when one describes electronic word processing, such terms and such distinctions no longer make much sense. (Landow 1992: xx)[1]

All such moving beyond the book derives directly from a single defining characteristic of the digital word. Unlike all previous forms of textuality, the digital word is virtual, not physical. Earlier kinds of text required physical marks on physical surfaces. The image, sign, letter, or number was scratched into a physical surface, such as stone or clay, or written upon a surface with some sort of pigment. These marks, which so obviously created a visible physical record of invisible sounds, provided a technology of cultural memory that, as Plato and many others since have pointed out, has had defining effects on human culture. However fragile the written record, it nonetheless marks a wonderful freezing of something otherwise evanescent, and from the time of the ancient Eygptians, authors have often believed that written records of speech conferred a kind of permanence and immortality upon the writer of those words.

Many other technological inventions mark the history of information technology from the development of writing to that of the printing press. These include the inventions of the alphabet, scrolls, the codex, and inexpensive writing surfaces. Printing, the appearance of which marks a great dividing line in human history, represents the next great landmark in information technology. Printing adds two major qualities to the written, physically existing text – multiplicity and fixity – that have enormous consequences for the way we conceive of ourselves and our culture. The printing press creates large numbers of copies of essentially the same text. As McLuhan, Eisenstein, and others have argued, these effects range through fundamental conceptions about education, scholarship, intellectual property, and the self. To take a simple example, the availability of many copies of the same text not only, as Benjamin realized, removed the aura of the unique object, it also fundamentally changed the way people think about preserving information. The keeper of manuscripts tries to slow their inevitable degradation (which is caused by being read) and the consequent errors introduced by copyists. The person who would preserve information in a manuscript age does so by preventing readers from having access to the text, since such readers inevitably lead to its destruction. In an age of printing, the person who would preserve a text does so, in contrast, by disseminating it as widely as possible.

Each form of physically recording a text has its peculiar qualities, qualities that often have far greater cultural effect than might at first appear. Even something as apparently trivial as the availability of relatively inexpensive writing materials can have unexpected, and unexpectedly great, effects. The great cost of writing surfaces led scribes to cram in as many letters as possible, so that written text omitted spaces between words. This economic factor made reading an act of decipherment, a craft skill generally available only to a few. The introduction of inexpensive writing surfaces led, around the year 1000, to interword spacing, and that crucial invention permitted reading silently, which, in turn, led to our modern notions of a private, interior self.

What are crucial, defining qualities, then, of the new digital technologies of cultural memory? One, above all, stands out: whereas all previous forms of writing involve physical marks on a physical surface, in digital information technology writing takes the form of a series of codes. The resulting textuality is virtual, fluid, adaptable, open, capable of being processed, capable of being infinitely duplicated, capable of being moved about rapidly, capable, finally, of being networkable – of being joined with other texts.

All fundamental characteristics of the world of digital information derive directly from this shift of modes – a shift made apparent, one realizes, by the fact that one never reads the text "itself," since that record resides invisibly in the computer's memory. Instead, one reads a virtual version of that text on a screen or other display device. By removing the text one step from its physical instantiation, a number of changes occur, the most obvious of which is that the difference between the text and object on which it appears becomes starkly clear. As literary theorists have emphasized for decades, one must distinguish between the text itself and its physical embodiment in a particular delivery vehicle, reading site, or machine. Digital information technology permits us to perceive that books, printed books, are machines just as are computers that handle or present text.

Once textuality abandons the simply physical form of earlier writing, it also abandons some of its relations to economy and scale. For example, one can reproduce a digitally stored text an indefinite number of times without in any way affecting it, lessening it, wearing away at it. Duplicating a manuscript requires that one expend an amount of time and energy similar to that expended in the creation of the text one wishes to copy. Duplicating a text by printing it with metal type or cast plates offers far greater economies of scale, but eventually the metal begins to wear – a fact readily apparent to students of engraved images. Duplicating a text stored electronically, however, has no such effect and therefore permits – and even encourages – an enormously larger number of copies.

Digital textuality also permits far greater ease of manipulatibilty and reconfigurabilty. As anyone who has used a word processor quickly perceives, one can easily search through a text or reconfigure its appearance.[2] One result of recording all text in the form of electronic codes, rather than in that of physical marks, permits the creation of so-called markup languages that permit the appearance of entire texts to

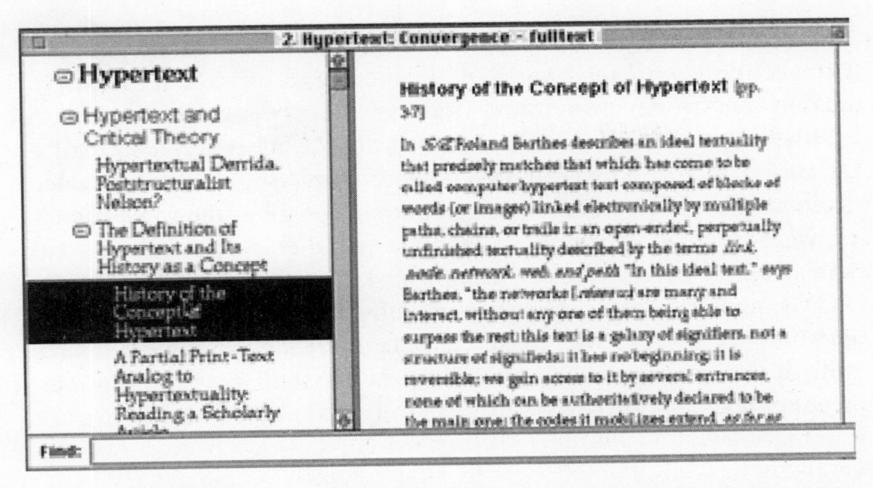

Figure 3. Dyna Text, an SGML-based electronic book system. Electronic coding permits not only near-instant full-text searches but also a dynamic table of contents in Landow (1992). Touching upon the symbol at the left of any entry in the table of contents instantly reveals the titles of subsections; touching upon any one of these brings up that section in the right window.

be reconfigured rapidly (fig. 3). Recording a text by handwriting, typewriter, or typesetting device involves performative – as opposed to descriptive – markup. In other words, when one begins a new paragraph while writing with a typewriter (or a computer used inappropriately as one), one either skips a line or indents a specific number of spaces or employs some other convention. When using a so-called markup language (or *markup* for short), one simply marks the beginning and ending of that unit of text with standard symbols, such as <p> and </p>, which permit readers and writers (depending on the system) to reconfigure the appearance of paragraphs. Such an approach to textuality allows economical reuse of texts, since one can automatically reconfigure the same text, say, for a personal printer, typesetting device, or electronic display simply by redefining the value of each symbol. Such markup, for example, also permits readers to reconfigure the appearance of a scholarly text, so that one could toggle back and forth between a modern annotated edition of a eighteenth-century text and its original appearance upon its publication, including typeface, font size, and color of paper.

Connecting computers together in networks adds another series of qualities to digital textuality. Digitizing text permits one to reproduce, manipulate, and reconfigure it with great ease and rapidity. Connecting computers together in the form of digital networks enables one to move such text from one storage and reading site to another. Until the world of networked digital information technology, disseminating a text required physically moving it from one place to another. Unnetworked digital technology still has the same limitations, and today an enormous amount of digital information is still stored and moved on tapes, floppy disks, Syquest cartridges, CD-ROMs, and so on. But as electronic bulletin boards, discussion lists, and the World Wide Web make clear, many readers and writers have already moved beyond the book into such essentially location-independent texts and text-bases.[3]

4. Moving text

One of the most interesting, as well as most daunting, ways to begin our examination of that future-text that has already begun to appear involves looking at some materials created in Macromedia Director, a widely used multimedia environment. At the Rhode Island School of Design, Professor Kryztoff Lenk's courses in digital typography have used this software to create new versions of poetry. Because Director permits one to move text within a reading area as well as to create cinematic fades and other transitions, it has produced a kind of text that calls into question some of our notions of text and interpretation.

At the beginning of Maxine Fung's adaptation or re-creation of Brecht's *My Brother Was a Pilot*, the reader encounters a white screen, shading in the lower fifth part to increasingly dark shades of gray. Moving from right to left of this screen appears in turn each line of the first stanza of Brecht's elegy for his brother who died fighting in the Spanish civil war:

> My brother was a pilot,
> He received a card one day,
> He packed his belongings in a box,
> And southward took his way.

The first three lines appear in reddish brown nonserif font, the second line a third larger than the other two. The last line, in red, emerges at screen right, and then, decreasing in size, moves toward the center, thus appearing to move away from the viewer. At this point, the screen darkens to black, returns to white, and the next stanza appears:

> My brother is a conqueror.
> Our people is short of space,
> And to conquer more territory is
> An ancient dream of the race.

This time the lines slide across the screen in opposite directions, the first, "My brother is a conqueror," appearing in reddish brown at the bottom third of the screen, moves from right to left. When half of this line has moved on screen, "Our people is short of space" appears in black at upper screen left and moves right until both are present at the same time. Above these two, the last lines of the quatrain move from left to right (fig. 4).

Figure 4. Moving text in Maxine Fung's animation of Berthold Brecht's poem *My Brother Was a Pilot.*

Next, the black at the bottom of the screen moves up until it covers the lower three-quarters of the screen, the remaining area dividing equally between shaded gray and, at the very top, white. The final stanza, now all in black letters, appears as the first line, "The space my brother conquered," moves from right to left slightly above center, and the next line – "Lies in the Guadarrama massif" – moves in smaller type from left to right. At this point, the third line appears, moving from right to left, and halts at center screen: "Its length is six feet, two inches." Then, as the first two lines recede, individual words of the final line – "Its depth four feet and a half" – appear at the bottom center of the screen, which is black, and move upward, bringing blackness with them as together with the previous line, white against black, they appear as a cruciform grave marker.

Its

depth

Its length is six feet, two inches

four

feet,

and

a half

Black then covers the entire screen, after which the cross-shaped text recedes and finally vanishes.

Almost everyone to whom I have shown Fung's work has found it an effective, moving piece, but none of us have been equally sure about how to classify it. Should we consider her version of *My Brother Was a Pilot* primarily a new form of criticism and interpretation, a performance of Brecht's poem, a new art form, or all of the preceding? Whether or not the problem of properly classifying this work intrigues one matters less than that it demonstrates with particular clarity that digital media have already created new possibilities for text, new ways of writing, new genres.

5. Simulation, visualization, and text

Another form of the new digital textuality results when one combines alphanumeric text with simulation and visualization programs. Like the Fung project with its moving images and sound, these new forms exemplify a Derridean extension of language to include a greater proportion of images and other forms of information (or forms of text) that written and printed books by their nature cannot contain. I have elsewhere described at length several projects, both experimental and commercially available, such as the electronic guide to the National Gallery of London created by Ben Rubinstein of Cognitive Resources in Brighton, England, that embody this kind of combination of simulation with text. I shall just point out that this exemplary project, which has recently been published as a CD-ROM by Microsoft, uses simple, if effective, animations to explain composition, perspective, and related issues, such as the nature of the camera obscura.

Three other texts, two already available on CD-ROM, carry this kind of extended textuality even farther. The courseware for multi-

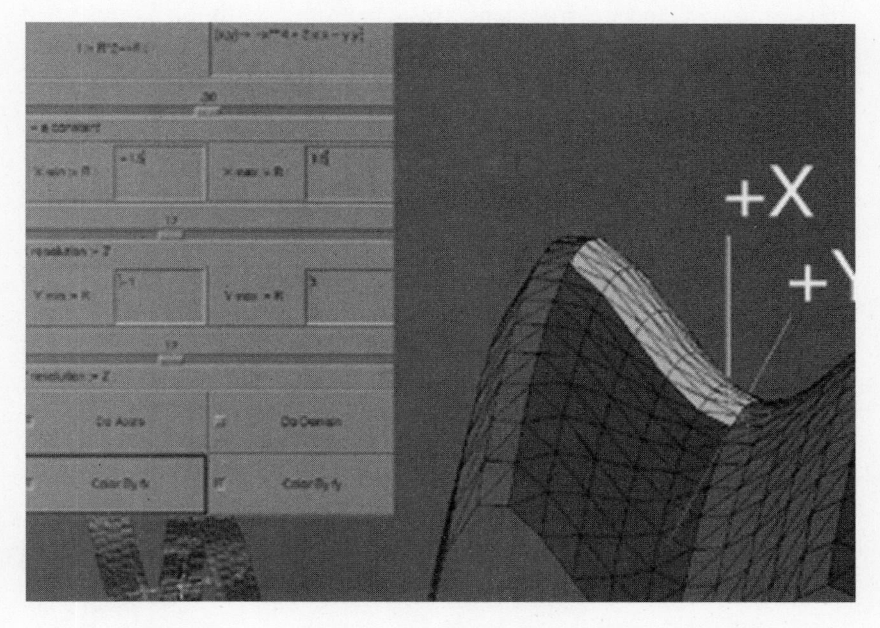

Figure 5. Visualizing mathematical data in Thomas Banchoff's multidimensional mathematics materials. In the original image (whose markers for the *x* and *y* axes I have enlarged for the sake of clarity) this interactive graphic presentation of the equation x,y → -x4 + 2xx - yy, appears in the bright blue (left center and lower right), lime green (right top and top left center), rose (left bottom and right center, bottom), and deep red (outer top left and right center, top) against a gray background. Changing elements of the equation or providing different values for *x* and *y* immediately produces changes in the graphical representation.**

dimensional mathematics that Thomas Banchoff, professor of mathematics, Brown University, has created combines simulation with the main text. While reading about certain kinds of equations, the student reader can examine the graphic presentation of them, much as one can in an ordinary printed textbook. Here, however, the student can add different values or otherwise reconfigure the variables, thus making immediately clear the effect of such action by visualizing data (fig. 5).

Electronic texts that similarly intend to develop nonverbal skills have also been created in relation to the arts. For example, Kristin Hooper Woolsey, Scott Kim, and Gayle Curtis's *VizAbility*, which MetaDesign West created for PWS Publishing, takes the form of a CD-ROM version of a textbook originally created to develop visual thinking skills. Divided into subjects, such as imagining, seeing, drawing, diagramming, and environment, this electronic textbook is designed with the expectation that its users will work both on-screen and off-screen with a pencil and sketching pad. The on-screen materials consist of introductions to a subject, such as contour drawing and perspec-

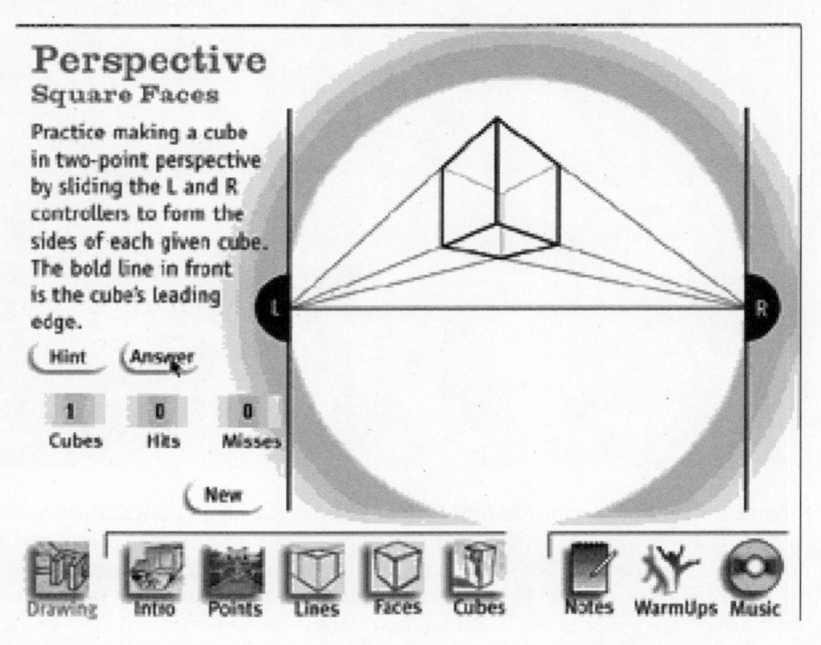

Figure 6. ***VizAbility.*** **Combining a simulation environment with text and images to develop nonverbal skills and knowledge.**

tive, demonstrations in the form of QuickTime movies that contain sound and motion, and examples that the user can consult. In addition, this amplified textbook uses animation and simulation to do things a printed text cannot. For instance, after an introduction to creating multiple-point perspective and off-screen exercises, the user can develop both seeing and drawing skills by trying to move a cube to a particular location on three perspective guidelines (fig. 6). If the reader places the cube incorrectly, it simply moves back to its starting point on the screen; if he or she places it correctly, it clicks into place and a tone sounds indicating success. Many of these exercises, like those for visualizing the hidden surfaces of various three-dimensional objects, show that the major value of such technology lies in developing skills or conveying information that the printed book cannot.

6. Linking texts

Hypertext offers another way of going beyond the book as we known it in its print form. The term, which Theodor H. Nelson introduced in the late 1960s, refers to a form of digital textuality in which electronic links join lexias, or chunks of text, which can take the form of words, images, sounds, video, and so on. The electronic link, the defining factor in this new information technology, produces multilinear or multisequential – not nonlinear – reading. By permitting readers to choose their ways through a particular set of lexias, hypertext in essence shifts some of the author's power to readers. Hypertext, which demands new forms of reading and writing, has the promise radically to reconceive our conceptions of text, author, intellectual property, and a host of other issues ranging from the nature of the self to education.

The hypertext link-in transforms the printed work, when translated into this new form, into a kind of open-ended, permeable, Velcro text in which Bakhtinian multivocality seems more appropriate than does the univocal voice characteristic of much print work. Many of these differences became apparent when I produced an electronic version of my hypertext. First, linking encouraged one not only to link together various relevant portions of the book, say, mentions of individual critical theorists or issues, but also to open up the text. The hypertext version grew to more than double the size of the print one as we added (1) texts by Derrida and Gregory L. Ulmer there discussed, (2) entries

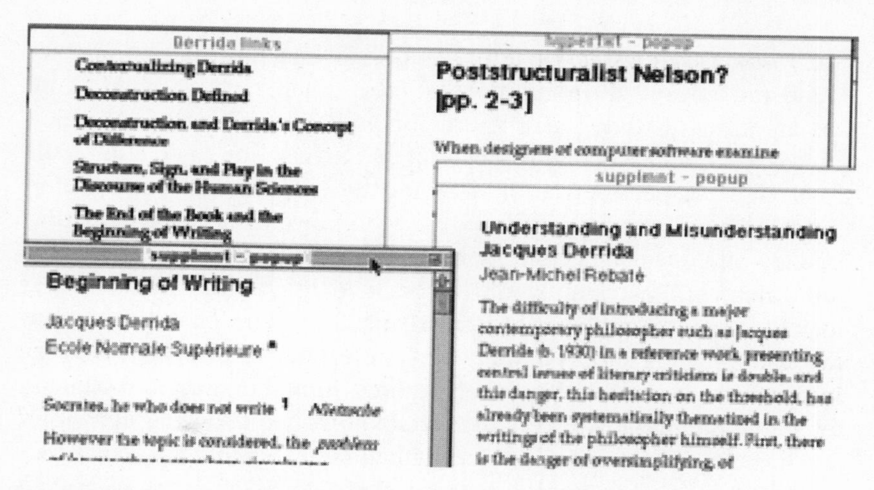

Figure 7. Linking across the borders of books produces electronic libraries, not electronic books. This example shows linked materials.

from Michael Groden and Martin Kreiswirth's *Johns Hopkins Guide to Literary Theory and Criticism* (fig. 7), (3) reviews we could locate and secure permission to include (all), (4) a few of Malcom Bradbury's parodies of literary theory, and (5) more than fifty student interventions that often carried the book in different directions than I had originally intended. For example, whereas my discussion of Barthes concentrated largely on his descriptions of a hypertext-like writerly text and his reconfigurations of what we mean by authorship, my students placed more emphasis upon his comments on narrative, particularly upon his discussions of unveiling in Balzac's *Sarrasine*, a text that some students compared to Chaucer's *Wife of Bath's Tale* and other embodiments of similar themes.

All these newly linked texts made crucial qualities of hypertext immediately obvious. First of all, hypertextualizing a work originally created for print necessarily reconfigures it by underlining relations among subsections of the text both to other portions of the "same" text and to materials originally outside its boundaries, such as the works by Derrida and Ulmer later included. Second, thus opening up the text necessarily introduces other voices, other points of view, and the entire text now embodies multiple points of view. Third, as the inclusion of reviews and student work shows, electronic linking almost inevitably tends to lead to blending and mixing of genres and modes, a fact of more importance, perhaps, in both education and fictional hypertexts. Fourth, hypertextualizing a text produces not an electronic book but a miniature electronic library.[4]

7. Linking text on the Internet: The World Wide Web

All the materials at which we have looked thus far work on separate, or so-called stand-alone, computers. But Nelson's vision of hypertext, which still inspires many workers in the field, requires something more – that all the texts in the world link into one metatext dispersed throughout a gigantic world-encompassing computer network. Some important research systems, such as Intermedia and Sepia, work over local or wide-area networks, but until the development of the World Wide Web (WWW) no system attempted so completely to fulfill this aspect of Nelson's conception of hypertext. WWW, or the Web, as it is known, is a very simple hypertext system residing on the Internet, the international network composed of interlinked computers, and it is based upon a simple markup language originally developed by high-energy physicists at CERN to enable different kind of computers to communicate with one another. Researchers at the National Supercomputing Center at the University of Illinois then created Mosaic, a viewer that transformed this hypertext markup language, html, into a hypertext system.

Html consists of a few basic formatting commands and a means of creating links between documents on different machines. For example, if I wished to link an electronic version of this document to one stored at the University of Southampton, I include a link that tells my WWW viewer program (Netscape or Mosiac) to send a command to that other location to open a specified document that resides in a specific folder on a specific machine. The resulting links produce a wonderfully free, even anarchic hypertext sprawled across the globe, as those enamored by the Web set up servers – machines on which to store and disperse html documents – in every country of the world.

The Web shares many important qualities with Hypercard. Like this Apple product, it is experienced by readers and writers as free – that is, they use it without any apparent economic cost to themselves and also like Hypercard, the Web makes reading and writing for it relatively easy. Like Hypercard, the WWW has therefore won enormous numbers of converts in an extremely short time and introduced a great number of people to ideas of hypertext and the Internet. Unfortunately,

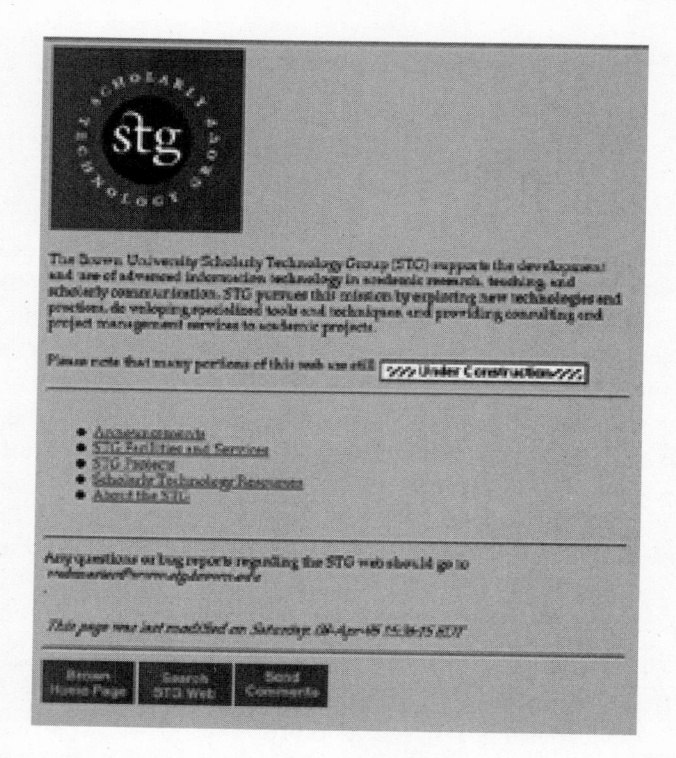

Figure 8. The Scholarly Technology Group home page as seen using Netscape.

like its predecessor, the Web represents an extremely limited, primitive form of hypertext incapable of more than simple point-to-point links. Nonetheless, despite all its limitations, it has the important effect of educating people about hypertext and whetting their appetites for better versions of it on the Internet.

And there are already a lot of wonderful things out there on the Web! As anyone who has looked at the Web or seen mentions of it in newspapers and popular magazines knows, one can obtain access on the Web to discussion groups on almost any topic, from texts of Jane Austen's novels, to all kinds of commercial and cultural announcements, to art exhibitions, to scholarly periodicals and other publications, and to countless individual directories (or home pages) added by individuals. For example, starting at Brown University's home page, I can go to those of individual departments or groups, and if we choose that, for the Scholarly Technology Group (STG) created by Geoffrey

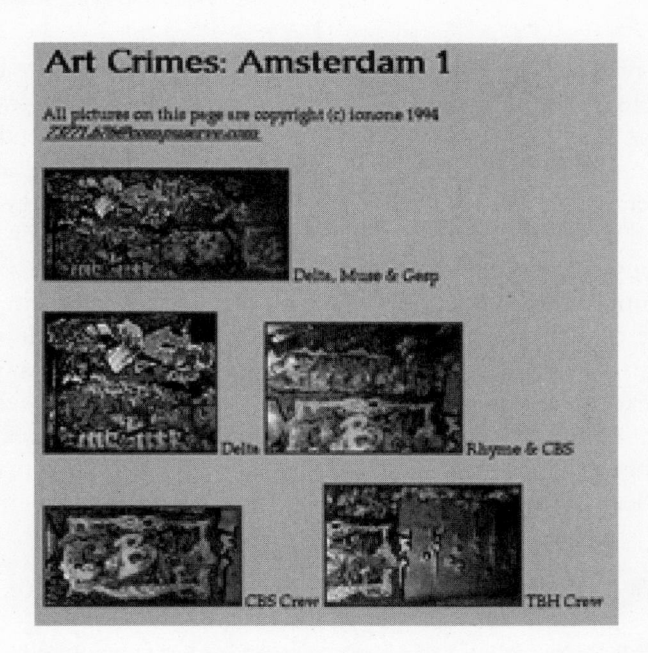

Figure 9. Graffiti in Amsterdam (from Susan Farrell's Art Crimes home page).

Bilder of Computing and Information Services, we arrive at cross-roads document (fig. 8) that directs one to information about the STG and related faculty projects. Following a link to projects produces another list, and from here one can explore materials about hypertext at Brown, including an elaborate directory of hypertext fiction and educational materials available on servers, or obtain materials about various authors and branch out from there. One can also return to the STG home page and use it to gain access to interesting WWW materials throughout the world.

The relative ease of creating WWW materials has led to new forms of scholarly discourse. At the Georgia Institute of Technology, for example, Susan Farrell has created the Art Crimes home page, which has quickly become a focus for interest in graffiti as contributors from throughout the world send photographs of materials they have recorded. Farrell has then arranged these by geographical area, so that one can obtain images of graffiti in Atlanta, Amsterdam, and so on (fig. 9). Such a collection provides an electronic archive of materials that anyone with a specialized interest can consult and to which they can contribute. If graffiti does not interest one, one can consult collections of materials on high-energy physics, literary theory, declassified CIA photographs, or meteorological data and satellite photographs.

These examples suggest that, in an amazingly short time, the Web has prompted the development of new forms of intellectual and cultural interchange. For those of us concerned about moving beyond the book, the truly interesting fact about this latest intonation of writing technology lies not in the large amount of poorly conceived, egotistical, or simply boring materials created by all these people with access to a form of instant publication but, instead, the way so much interesting material has appeared so quickly and the way new forms of intellectual exchange come about as a result. Of course the Web often looks crude. But when one recalls that it took hundred years after the appearance of the printed book to invent the title page, one realizes it doesn't seem that bad.

8. Hypertext fiction, or patching together narrative

Since I have discussed elsewhere at length some of the educational and political implications of this new information technology, I would like to close my brief discussion of it by looking at a recent work of hypertext fiction, Shelley Jackson's *Patchwork Girl*. Opening this Web, the reader encounters a drawing of a nude woman whose body is traversed by fine lines; the next screen produces a mock phrenological diagram, and the third a drawing of a chimera – an appropriate image or icon of a work whose subject and occasional protagonist is the female monster whom Victor Frankenstein assembled for his creation in Mary Shelley's novel. In the original version, the scientist destroys her out of his disgust; in this version, she survives. Moving to the fourth screen, one comes upon the Web's equivalent of a title page, which tells us that we have come to *Patchwork Girl. or, a Modern Monster, by Mary/Shelley, and Herself.*

At this point, one can choose one of the three paths reentitled, respectively, "graveyard," "journal," and "broken accents." Following the path to the graveyard produces a rearranged version of the first screen to which fragments of text have been attached, and from there one obtains the following instructions:

> I am buried here. You can resurrect me, but only piecemeal. If you want to see the whole, you will have to sew me together yourself. (In time, you may find appended a pattern and instructions – for now, you will have to put it together any which

> way, as the scientist Frankenstein was forced to do.) Like him, you will make use of a machine of mysterious complexity to animate these parts. (You may want to keep your windows open when working in the graveyard.)

Eventually one reaches "The Headstone," which indicates the sources and identities of each of the Patchwork Girl's body parts. Most come from women, a few from men, and one from a cow. Here, for example, we learn about her left leg, which

> belonged to Jane, a nanny who harbored under her durable grey dresses and sensible undergarments a remembrance of a less sensible time: a tattoo of a ship and the legend, Come Back To Me. Nanny knew some stories that astonished her charges, and though the ship on her thigh blurred and grew faint and blue with distance, until it seemed that the currents must have long ago finished their work, undoing its planks one by one with unfailing patience, she always took the children to the wharf when word came that a ship was docking, and many a sailor greeted her by name.
> My leg is always twitching, jumping, joggling. It wants to go places. It has had enough of waiting.

As we trace the history of the Patchwork Girl in the stories told by these characters, each of whom has a distinctive voice, we gradually piece together not only the girl herself but also a picture of women's lives at the beginning of the nineteenth century.

If at any point one returns to the title screen, we can choose to read through the journal instead. On this path, or set of reading paths, the multivocality changes, for rather than encountering a congeries of clearly identified and individuated speakers, one encounters lexias in which the speaker might be Mary Shelley, Shelley Jackson, Victor Frankenstein, the Monster Herself, or, in certain lexias, her lover (of indeterminable gender). Making their ways through this fascinating Web, readers encounter a rich assemblage of stories, discussions of narrative, drawings, electronic collage, and scholarly analyses until one realizes that Jackson is showing us the way we always thus stitch together narrative, notions of gender, and the identities of ourselves and others. In the light cast by this hyperfiction, we all turn out to be assembled monsters, Patchwork Girls.

9. Inside the text – cyberspace and virtual reality

As my discussion of *Patchwork Girl* should suggest, I do not think that reading and writing fiction in this new environment in any way represent the death of fiction. In fact, just as the cinema and television, which to some extent have displaced print-based fiction, both draw from it and influence it in turn, so, too, one can expect that e-fiction, particularly hypertext fiction, will exist in such a rich relationship with that created for the print world.

In contrast, Virtual Reality (or VR), which relies on nonverbal text, represents a far more radical movement away from the written word and hence a far greater challenge to the culture of the book than do the other forms of digital information we have examined. As Michael A. Gigante explains, virtual reality is characterized by

> the illusion of participation in a synthetic environment rather than external observation of such an environment. VR relies on three-dimensional (3D) stereoscopic, head-tracked displays, hand/body tracking and binaural sound. VR is an immersive, multisensory experience. (Gigante 1993: 3)

Michael Benedikt, who prefers the term cyberspace, explains:

> Cyberspace is a globally networked, computer-sustained, computer-accessed, and computer-generated, multidimensional, artificial, or "virtual" reality. In this reality, to which every computer is a window, seen or heard objects are neither physical nor, necessarily, representations of physical objects but are, rather, in form character, and action, made up of data, of pure information. (Benedikt 1991: 122-23)

Like both the digital word and hypertext, VR derives from the fundamentally semiotic nature of electronic information technology, which allows it to manipulate and reconfigure text. From one point of view, it takes its place at the extreme end of digital reconceptions of textuality, which extend it from alphanumeric text to include visual materials, sound, and movement. Even VR's fundamental, characteristic, defining quality – the user's experience of being inside the data rather than standing apart from it and looking at it on a page or screen – turns out to be an extension of the way that all computing creates a surrogate on-screen representation of the user in the form of the cursor that indicates his or her presence amid the text.

VR, which permits the simulation of dangerous, difficult activities, such as flying planes and performing trauma surgery, has obvious practical applications in education, and Fung's examples of moving text and Banchoff's simulations are steps toward VR. Its advocates, however, find its broader cultural implications even more interesting.

Figure 10. Miller (1993) popular CD-ROM adventure game.

Benedikt, for example, argues that "cyberspace can be seen as an extension, some might say, an inevitable extension, of our age-old capacity and need to dwell in fiction, to dwell enlightened and empowered on other, mythic planes" (Benedikt 1991: 6). Others, like Marcos Novak, see VR as essentially poetic ("Liquid Architectures in Cyberspace," in Benedikt 1991: 225-54).

At the moment, this developing technology, which is fundamentally "just" a means of visually representing information, is even farther from anything like full realization than is hypertext, yet at least some of its cultural implications seem clear. Already new kinds of immersive narrative have begun to appear in which the "reader" interacts in new ways with a fictional environment. Michael Nash, the president of Inscape, a company that develops multimedia CD-ROMs, calls this new narrative form that combines exploratory games and interactive narrative *storyworlds*. Successful examples include *Myst* (fig. 10) and Voyager's *Freak Show*, which Nash helped produce. These CD-ROMs contain narrative worlds whose stories unfold only to an active, even aggressively intrusive reader willing to explore independently, solve problems, and even, in the case of *Freak Show*, disobey instructions.

Although one can envisage narratives that demand the kind of activity of the professional, skeptical reader of print, one has to recognize that such a shift from alphanumeric text has as many costs as benefits. The risks are obvious, since any representation necessarily omits something, and that which is omitted always bears the marks of someone's conception of reality – someone *else's* ideology. Less obvious risks also appear inevitable: since the great strength of language, after all, lies in its abstractness, its ability economically to stand in for something else, our notions of education, good writing, and even intelligence itself relate closely to an ability to formulate and manipulate such counters. What will happen, then, when children (and adults) find introducing a three-dimensional video with the sound of, say, a rhinoceros, into a discussion so easy that they increasingly lose the ability to formulate abstract or physical descriptions? McLuhan has persuasively argued that written language had to exist before logical, causal thinking could become widespread. If so, what will happen when we increasingly abandon alphanumeric text, if that ever happens, when we would truly find ourselves beyond the book?

Notes

[1] See Baudrillard (1983: 115).

[2] Heim (1987) and Lanham (1993) both eloquently describe the nature and implications of word-processing.

[3] For the notion of location-independent text-bases, see Christinger Tomer, "Emerging electronic library services and the idea of location independence" in Delany and Landow (1994: 139-62).

[4] See Nichole Yankelovich, "From electronic books to electronic libraries" in Delany and Landow (1991: 133-42).

References

BAUDRILLARD, J.
1983 *Simulation*, New York: Semiotext.

BENEDIKT, M. (ED.)
1991 *Cyberspace: First Steps*, Cambridge (Mass.): MIT Press.

BOLTER, J.D.
1984 *Turing's Man: Western Culture in the Computer Age*, Chapel Hill, N.C.
1990 *Space: The Computer in the History of Literacy*, Hillsdale: Lawrence Erlbaum.

BUSH, V.
1945 "As we may think," *Atlantic Monthly* 176: 101-8.
1967 "Memex revisited," *Science Is Not Enough*, New York: William Morrow: 75-101.

CHARTIER, R.
1987 *The Cultural Uses of Print in Early Modern France*, Princeton: Princeton University Press.
1987 *The Culture of Print: Power and the Uses of Print in Early Modern Europe*, Princeton: Princeton University Press.

COOVER, R.
1992 "The end of books," *New York Times Book Review* (June 21), 1: 33-35.
1993 "Hyperfiction: Novels for the computer," *New York Times Book Review* (August 19), 1: 8-12.

DELANY, P., AND LANDOW G.P. (EDS.)
1991 *Hypermedia and Literary Studies*, Cambridge (Mass.): MIT Press.
1994 *The Digital Word*, Cambridge (Mass.): MIT Press.

EARNSHAW, R.A., GIGANTE, M.A., AND JONES, H. (EDS.)
1993 *Virtual Reality Systems*, London: Academic Press.

EISENSTEIN, E.L.
1980 *The Printing Press as an Agent of Change: Communications and Cultural Transformations in Early-Modern Europe*, Cambridge: Cambridge University Press.

GIGANTE, M.A.
1993 "Virtual reality: Definitions, history and applications," in Earnshaw, Gigante, and Jones (eds.) (1993).

HEIM, M.
1987 *Electric Language: A Philosophical Study of Word Processing*, New Haven: Yale University Press.

JOYCE, M.
1988 "Siren shapes: Exploratory and constructive hypertexts," *Academic Computing*, 3: 10-14, 37-42.
1993 *The Metaphysics of Virtual Reality*, New York: Oxford University Press.

KERNAN, A.
1987 *Printing Technology, Letters & Samuel Johnson*, Princeton: Princeton University Press.

LANDOW, G.P.
1992 *Hypertext in Hypertext*, Baltimore: Johns Hopkins University Press.
1992 *Hypertext: The Convergence of Contemporary Critical Theory and Technology*, Baltimore: Johns Hopkins University Press.

LANDOW, G.P. (ED.)
1995 *Hyper/Text/Theory*, Baltimore: Johns Hopkins University Press.

LANHAM, R.A.
1993 *The Electronic Word: Democracy, Technology, and the Arts*, Chicago: University of Chicago Press.

MCLUHAN, M.
1962 *The Gutenberg Galaxy: The Making of Typographic Man*, Toronto: University of Toronto Press.

MOULTHROP, S.
1991 "Beyond the electronic book: A critique of hypertext rhetoric," in *Hypertext '91*, New York: Association of Computing Machinery.
1989 "Hypertext and 'the hyperreal,'" in *Hypertext '89: Proceedings*, New York: Association of Computing Machinery.

NELSON, TH. H.
1987 *Computer Lib/Dream Machines*, Seattle: Microsoft Press.
1981 *Literary Machines*, Swarthmore: Self-published.

WEXELBLAT, A. (ED.)
1993 *Virtual Reality Applications and Explorations*, Boston: Academic Press Professional.

YANKELOVICH, N., MEYROWITZ, N., AND VAN DAMM, A.
1985 "Reading and writing the electronic book," *IEEE Computer*, 18: 15-30.

Electronic materials

JACKSON, SH.
1995 *Patchwork Girl*, Cambridge: Eastgate Systems. Environment: Storyspace.

JOYCE, M.
1991 *Afternoon*, Cambridge: Eastgate Systems. Environment: Storyspace.

LANDOW, G.P.
1992 *Hypertext in Hypertext*, Baltimore: Johns Hopkins University Press. Environment: DynaText.

LANHAM, R.A.
1993 *The Electronic Word: Democracy, Technology, and the Arts*, Chicago: University of Chicago Press. Environment: Voyager Expanded Book.
1993 *Microsoft Art Gallery: The Collection of the National Gallery, London*, N.p. Microsoft, CD-ROM. Environment; Cognitive Resources.

MILLER, RAND AND ROBYN
1993 *Myst*, Novato, California: Broderbund, CD-ROM using QuickTime and Sound Manager.

MOULTHROP, S.
1991 Victory Garden, Cambridge: Eastgate Systems. Environment: Storyspace.

ROSENZWEIG, R., BRIER, S., AND BROWN J.
1993 *Who Built America? From the Centennial Celebration of 1876 to the Great War of 1914*, Santa Monica, California: Voyager, CD-ROM. Environment: Voyager Multimedia.

Raffaele Simone

THE BODY OF THE TEXT[1]

1. Presuppositions regarding the term "text"

The book is normally the graphic materialization or physical container of an object quite different from it: of a text, that is to say of a structured discursive body according to particular laws of composition. The two entities (the book and the text therein contained) are quite separate. Indeed a variety of texts ranging from a telephone directory to a balance sheet, a code of laws, and a historical novel may be accommodated in a book. In several languages the two entities are normally subsumed under the single term "book," through a sort of brachylogy. However, they are still distinct and should be carefully separated in specific circumstances.

Such is the case in point. In referring to the "future of the book" one should not only consider the book container's destinies or the relationships between the book container and the users (readers), but also what might happen to the textual body which is stored in the book. I shall concentrate on the possible evolution in the near future of the textual body which is contained in the book independently of the destiny of the book as a physical object.

A certain amount of terminology is necessary to indicate clearly the objects in question. The phenomenon which I intend to deal with will be referred to by the expression *articulation and disarticulation of the body of the text*. I shall describe it thus: disarticulation of the body of the text occurs when the text generated by an author is not perceived as closed to external interventions, an entity to which the author can have access only to read (or, to use an information science image, in the manner of ROM, that is "read only"), but as an open entity to which one has access – for purposes of both reading and writing. When the text is disarticulated it is perceived as an entity which can be disaggregated (broken apart), manipulated, and reaggregated (reassembled) without damaging the text per se or the author.

I would also propose the following: in the history of culture the opinion that the text had a body defined by a protective, invisible but insurmountable membrane is somewhat contested, betraying strong diachronic oscillations. Sometimes the text is in no way considered and treated as an impenetrable body, whereas at other times its uniform body and intangibility are observed and preserved with respect and even veneration. The former class of phases can be referred to by the term *moments of interpolation* and the latter by *philological moments*, given that philology is the discipline which has contributed the most to creating and spreading the idea that the text is a body which cannot be penetrated except by interpretation. My intention is to illustrate some fragments of this historical oscillation and to suggest what the tendency is likely to be in the near future.

In the present age we almost all intuitively believe that the text should be considered a closed entity, or rather that it is a closed entity (even when dealing with an open work in the strict and perhaps deliberate sense). Thus we also believe the reader is constitutionally in a ROM position, except of course for his or her rights to interpret. The reader reads the text and interprets it at great liberty. The interpretation however is an immaterial act because the physical body of the text is untouchable.

However this idea – which seems intuitive to us – that the text is a closed entity is far from natural and taken for granted. On the contrary, it is riddled with theory and is the result of one of the most important cultural evolutions. Whoever accepts this, takes on *ipso facto* a series of important presuppositions which we tacitly assume every time we pick up a book, being as we are, well-educated and equipped with metalinguistic capacities. Let me give a short list.

(a) The first is the presupposition of the *pre-eminence of the author*. If the text is closed, it generally has an author (or a definite number of authors). Not only is the author the pure and simple generative source of the text but he or she also acts judicially, as it were, because he or she assumes specific rights and duties by the pure and simple fact of making him or herself author of that text. First, as the author generates the text, he or she is responsible for it. This means the author is owner of that text and is therefore obliged to distinguish the original parts (= resulting entirely from his or her own invention) from those which are not original (= resulting from the invention of others). Furthermore, only the author is recognized as having the right to touch the text and above all to decide when it is *perfectum*. At the precise moment when the text is *perfectum,* and then only, is it closed to others and can the reader gain access in ROM modality. The closing of the text moreover applies only to others; for the author (while alive and therefore still owner of the text) the text can endlessly be reopened. The author can change, supplement, adapt, and modify it as often as he or she wishes. The author can even copy him or herself alone, as in the case of Pirandello, who continuously reworked parts of his novels for the stage and vice versa: the idea of plagiarism cannot be applied to the author who copies him or herself; only by plagiarizing someone else does plagiarism exist.

It is not incidental that we give considerable importance to philology in this conceptual framework. This discipline has the explicit task of defining the form the author has given to his or her text – the last form used in handing over the text to the reader, or more precisely, the way he or she closed it. Obviously philology could not exist without the idea of the closing and unicity of the text, linked to the idea that it is necessary to go back to the "true" form of the text, and that this form enjoys a very definite legitimation. In such an atmosphere, as that described by Orwell in *1984*, where the authorship of the text is of no importance, the texts could be indefinitely modified by others. Thus they have no true form but can be manipulated at will as needed.

(b) The second presupposition supposes that the text is handed over to the reader by the author in a state of *perfection*, or rather completeness. The idea of the closed text implies the presupposition that the text is presented to the reader in the *final* version intended by the author, or at least in a single, final, and *ne varieteur* form. Not even the author recognizes the right to leave the text "open," that is, incomplete. The text may be incomplete only if the author did not have the practical and physical opportunity to close it. Incomplete productions should at any rate be declared as such. At most the author can reopen his or her text to change it, but once it is changed he or she must close it and hand it over again to the ROM reader; as I have already said, our current culture only acknowledges the ROM reader's right to interpret the text but not to touch it, that is to alter the body. The example of authors such as Fernando Pessoa, who left several possible drafts of different parts of his texts, is disconcerting to philologists and readers alike. In such circumstances it behooves the author to choose one of the many different solutions facing him or her.

(c) A third important presupposition concerns the required *originality* of the text. The text, inasmuch as it is due to a recognizable author and on presentation is assumed to be *perfectum*, has also to be original, and the well-educated reader takes it for granted that this is the case. The reader assumes that the text derives wholly or mainly from the author's ideational effort and that the author has distinguished himself or herself from the work carried out by others, even if he or she cannot disregard the existence of texts by others. We tend to consider texts which fail to state and document their own originality as "common" or "base," and it is not fortuitous that plagiarism (worse if from that particular category we call "servile") is considered an offense in various legal systems. This accounts for the existence in the European legal-critical tradition of a plethora of expressions implicitly condemning every intentional form of lack of originality: "slavish imitation," "plagiarism," "unoriginal plagiarism," and so on. This is also why we are inclined to eye with suspicion texts by "anonymous" authors, in which it is impossible to identify the author, probably because we do not know what source the originality of the text can be ascribed to. Likewise, as well-educated readers (equipped with an implicit theory of what a text should be), we treat a wholly original book differently from one which is the result of compilation – that is, the assembling of the stuff of others (an anthology, work of consultation, a list or repertory).

As a result of these presuppositions the text has a body, or rather an actual *habeas corpus* which prevents others (apart from the author) from touching it and protects it from being interfered with. Even the Western culture of print (and, earlier, the tradition of writing) gradually devised diacritic marks to define this body: the title (which, as is well-known, is a relatively recent invention), the name of the author, the margins which on the page define the space of the text circumscribing and closing it, and even quotation marks (inverted commas which would seem to be Aldo Manuzio's invention, thus far closer to ourselves than to antiquity) which allow words to be isolated from the others correlatively distributing responsibility and qualities. It should however be clear that in this creation of the idea of the body of the text the well-educated European class plays an essential role. It constitutes a truly *textwise* social class who invented this idea and protect the textual *habeas corpus* from any sort of violation.

2. The closed-text idea is not a primitive

This presuppositional analysis regarding the term *text* should be clear to the well-educated present-day consciousness. However, we all know well that in reality this stratification of meanings is far from self-evident and did not come about at one go; neither is it acknowledged at all levels of culture. I shall come back to this point.

The devising of a notion of the text as a closed entity protected from external interventions has taken place over a long period, Western cultural tradition being, as it is, several centuries old. At all events this conviction never established itself definitively. Rather it has always oscillated between supremacy and the opposite conviction according to which the text is a typically open entity. At the beginning and for some time the text was now and then perceived as a space of possible and even legitimate interferences. In early European textual production the texts were very probably created closed; indeed the earliest Western texts were transmitted orally by professionals and were inevitably exposed to the possibility of being changed as they were handed down through generations. A well-known example of this fact is seen in the genesis of Homer's poems where one takes for granted that different parts of the text may have been included in an initial structure for the intervention of subsequent authors. The text was therefore open and due to the work of multiple authors who did not even have the right to sign. Homer can perhaps be seen as a sort of poetic Bourbaki – a multiple author whose legitimacy is explained precisely by the perception of current texts prevalent in his time.

If we consider how the idea of the text as a unified and closed body and therefore characterized by the author's unicitity, originality, and impenetrability (therefore by a radical corporality, guaranteed by the *habeas corpus* previously mentionned) was formed, the first explanation we meet is inevitably the birth of writing. It is permissible to think that it was actually writing which brought about a change in the intuitive idea of "text" and which resulted in the belief that the text, which was open, authorless, and devoid of originality, was really in fact a stable, crystalized entity generated by a single author who handed it on to a reader unable to change it in any way.

As is often the case in dealing with complex cultural perceptions, the description of this passage is found in Plato. In the most famous pages of *The Phaedrus* devoted to writing, Plato describes this very moment,

> once a thing is committed to writing it circulates equally among those who understand the subject and those who have no business with it; a writing cannot distinguish between suitable and unsuitable readers. (275D)

The written discourse detaches itself from the author who composed it and passes into the reader's hands. The author hands over to the reader a text which has reached a level of stability. Plato actually speaks of *bebaiótes*, of "stability" of the text, as an effect of the writing. In describing this passage he dwells considerably on the fact that it is bristling with dangers. Once written, the text can end up in the hands of individuals unable to understand it and moreover it cannot be defended or commented on by its author. This is due to the fact that the text, once in black and white, becomes stable.

However, the stability of the written text does not exclude the possibility of its being tampered with. This possibility also seems a thing of dubious value to Plato. The discourse, which is already perfect, does not need to be reshaped. Hence Plato at a certain point distinguishes two types of creators of texts (278 D-E): on the one hand the philosopher who "possess things which are of greater value compared to those which he has composed or written," and on the other the poet or a speech writer and maker of laws who rather

> has devoted his time to twisting words, pasting them together and pulling them apart this way and that.

The expression "pasting" (*kollao*) or pulling apart (*aphaireo*) "this way and that" clearly alludes to the operation of "cut and paste" (or, more traditionally, of "scissors and glue") which any writer before the advent of the computer remembers as laborious physical operations. These were procedures rendered possible by the appearance of writing and the invention of its technical procedures. The difference between the two types of authors lies in the fact that the former does not resort to dialectics to elaborate his or her discourses, whereas the latter uses physical procedures of composition.

Let us consider for a moment the risks connected to the stability of the text. The stability of the body of the text (the setting up of its *bebaiótes*) is in no way a positive conquest; rather it is described by Plato as a dangerous and terrible thing. He affirms that writing has a "terrible" (*deinón*) property in common with painting. The

> productions of painting look like living beings, but if you ask them a question they maintain a solemn silence. The same holds true of written words; you might suppose that they understand what they are saying, but if you ask them what they mean by anything they simply return the same answer over and over again. (275D)

The written text, in actually taking on stability and in becoming closed, loses its capacity to meet the receiver's questions and becomes inert.

The phenomena which Plato describes can be directly linked to the evolution of writing, namely, the separation of the text from author with the resulting consignment to the reader and the "crystalization" of the text and the loss of the text's expressive richness compared to the oral version. What Plato describes is the moment in which the text, in being set down in writing, also becomes intangible.

3. Medieval interlude

Plato represents a very clear-cut stand in the establishing of the process whereby writing renders the body of the text impenetrable and it is bestowed with an invisible membrane which protects it from others' interventions. Despite this stand it cannot be said that Plato's formulation sufficed to create and spread the awareness of the intangible nature of the text. For a long time the text, although written, was perceived as a penetrable and modifiable entity by other individuals apart from the author.

I shall mention some fundamental moments of this situation in the history of our culture, especially with reference to the Middle Ages.[2] Saint Bonaventure, in a frequently quoted passage, states the typology of textual production in his time:

> To write a book means different things. To limit oneself to transcribing into a book others' writings without adding or changing is what the copyist actually does. The work of the editor is rather that of collecting others' texts in a book, therein introducing reasonable order. The annotator's book is still more different: it reproduces others' work as an essential part, and he adds his own work when it serves to clarify. The real author writes instead what he himself knows about Learning and cites others only in confirmation. (*Commentarium in Librum Sententiarum*)

Such distinctions are frequently repeated in the Middle Ages. They constitute the theoretical base of a variety of types of books which are the actual symbol of the disarticulation of the text, as they involve an absolute lack of perception of a closed body. I shall refer to compilations (in which parts of texts by various authors are assembled together with the optional accompaniment of a commentary), the miscellaneous books (in which several texts by different authors are assembled together), and the commentaries (which are to the modern eye little more than extended summaries of the original text).

Seen from this point of view, the whole so-called scholastic method relies on a colossal industry of textual manipulation. The texts are divided into parts, annotated, expounded; their pithy platitudes are organized in collections and *corpora*. Even hermeneutic practices are formed according to the possibilities of disarticulating the text. This incredible, systematic, and theorized work of dismemberment goes as far as finding a particular physical home in universities where these practices prevail and were to be called *compilationes*. The dismembered and reassembled text is mainly used for learning and study. Amazingly, even today the set texts used in the education system are often only *compilationes*.

Historians of the book, culture, and philosophy have thoroughly documented the variety of these forms of the book and textual production. I shall therefore avoid examining these problems more closely. These phenomena are of interest from our point of view in that they possess one fundamental common element: all three negate the presuppositions that we associate today with the idea of the text, that is, that it should be unified, the work of a single author, and *perfectum*. Thus this idea is not native and does not originate together with the texts (not even the written ones), but intermittently disappears and reappears in the history of culture, continuously arousing interest.

Another field in which the capacity of the text to be disarticulated can be clearly seen is translation. Works on the history of translations including those into the vernacular also abound. It is clear from history that for several centuries within Europe and outside, translating a text from one language into another implied the right taken for granted of the chance to change the text with additional material, cuts, modifications, and the like. It was only towards the end of the nineteenth century that the principle, according to which the translator no longer had the right to interpolate or modify the text he or she was translating due to the text being closed, actually took root. The sole exception is the category of religious texts which enjoy a particular status as they are dictated (or even written, as in the Koran for example) directly by God.

4. Copy and interpolation

At this point I suggest that the idea of the text as a closed entity (and therefore of the book as object incorporating a closed entity), albeit seemingly difficult, late, and unstable to the well-educated, is inaccesible to the uneducated and to anyone whose grasp of metatextual elaboration is insufficient. Without embarking on considerations of psychosociology of the texts (which on the other hand would be useful and which in fact is already under way elsewhere),[3] it will suffice to remember that, when students start their degree dissertation, they almost invariably have to be made to follow certain ideas on the nature of the text they are about to write, the relationship with other preexisting texts, and their own status as author of the text itself. Among these notions are the following: (a) the text has an author and is not the result of an assemblage of opinions and teaching of various earlier authors; (b) the author is expected to express his or her own ideas in the text and to scrupulously distinguish them from those of others (hence the concept of "quotation" which is also far from obvious); (c) the text must be closed by the author alone and not by anybody else.

Indeed, individuals not used to dealing with texts have no compunction about occasionally resorting to textual procedures which are typical of a general philosophical concept that we are inclined to consider strictly linked to the idea of the text. These procedures are respectively copying and heterogeneous interpolation, that is, owing to someone other than the author. Whoever rejects the closed text idea (either out of lack of culture or out of refusal of the assumptions of the "well-educated" Western class) considers it quite normal that other texts can and should be copied. Copying, which the maintainer of the closure of the text considers an offense, is on the other hand quite in order for whoever does not believe in closure. "We masters are annotators of the ancients; we do not think up personal inventions," affirmed William of Conches[4] so as to render the idea that a statement which comes from the copy of a previous author, preferably famous, who has formulated, argued, and written it down, is stronger. Theoretic and doctrinal innovation is created only through small increases, *per additamenta*, through additions, always gradual and suitably apportioned. If the text is original and evinces its own claim to originality, it risks being untenable. Originality is dangerous. (Incidently, this stance witnesses the concordance of the European medieval tradition and the Confucian oriental tradition, where innovation and originality are viewed with suspicion.) Such a mechanism of textual production explains, for instance, why classical authors were so frequently quoted in the history of European culture, almost up till the end of the nineteenth century, and why the idea itself of *auctores* has actually survived. The presence of an excerpt from a classical author is not only an elegant decoration of a text, but also spares the author having to prove and reason what he is saying.

Interpolation is a variant of copying. As the text is closed rather than open, and as its protective membrane is not a barrier but a lightly drawn border, anyone can penetrate the text introducing their own fragments or those of others: the outcome will still be a text. From this point of view the classical and medieval commentaries are perfect examples. Indeed they are almost always distinct intentional interpolations in the texts which they comment. A famous case among many during the medieval period is that of Boethius' commentaries on Aristotle. Tradition calls them commentaries and we also use this expression, but the term hardly had the meaning it has today. According to the definition of Bonaventure, already cited, the commentaries were merely summaries interpolated from pages of Aristotle. The same holds true for other important series of commentaries, such as those on Virgil's *Aeneid* or the *Divine Comedy*.

It is not for nothing that such texts induce boredom in the contemporary reader. In the "modern age" we seek in vain interpretations, hermeneutic leaps, and semantic disparity between text and commentary, only to find summaries, hence the boredom. The contemporary reader is bored by the textual repetition because he or she fails to accept the basic premise of such a text. In other words, he or she does not accept that knowledge may progress through a gradual and very slow accumulation of interpolated summaries. He or she even wishes or expects that the break between commented and commentator were greater and that the new text were innovative compared to the previous one.

Written culture throughout the world is based to a great extent on the two procedures of copying and interpolation. It would therefore be of great interest to reconstruct the history of culture not as a succession of original discontinuities but as an uninterrupted chain of imitations and of textual interferences. Pierre Ménard, author of *Don Quixote*, according to Jorge Luis Borges, neither represents a textual pathology nor a chance meeting of textual destinies. Rather, he is the symbol of a civilization built on the basis of copied and revised texts, interpolations, and copies, which has followed this path in the firm belief that only in this way could knowledge progress. Moreover, he has opted for the avenue of copying and interpolation with complete confidence owing to the belief that the original text is not closed but accessible to changes and to being reworked.

5. The future

At the risk of generalizing I believe it can be convincingly claimed that the descending part of the curve (previously mentioned) of the book (and in general textual knowledge to which it is inextricably linked) will stand out clearly in the near future. Our intuitive idea of the text is again changing rapidly. It is no longer that of a closed and protected entity but that of an open and penetrable object which can be copied and interpolated without limits. To put it differently, the time is heralded when the protective membrane of the texts will decompose and they will once more become open texts as in the Middle Ages with all the standard concomitant presuppositions. Let me substantiate this prediction as I draw this analysis to a close.

Many signs lead us to believe we are entering an era (here I formally adhere to the traditional jargon of historians) in which the text will appear essentially disarticulated and the book will witness a change in the nature of the discourse it contains. I shall point out some of the premonitory signs of this change. The most obvious one is the world explosion of nontexts which is in keeping with the growth of nonbooks: collections of expressions, short stories, quotations, jokes, and famous proverbs of various authors. We are plainly dealing with a modernized version of the *compilationes*, no longer dedicated to doctrinal texts but to texts of a different kind. Besides these nontexts, there are other typologies, including in particular the massive reference section. The manual for computer applications is the most obvious example. It exists not for nonstop reading but to be consulted at intervals, for occasional forays; changes are to be expected: "updating" and a constant incorporation of new passages of text, even without an author.

One can add the vast range of new textual structures, such as the book-game, the electronic book, and the massive typology of interactive books in which the reader can enter, so as to choose the solution from those which the author (that is if one can speak of an author) makes available, but also to write parts which will be merged into the book itself.

As during the time of Plato, the creation of these new textual typologies is considerably boosted by a means of writing – the computer. The computer as a writing tool is the very symbol of the open text and perfectly illustrates Plato's vision. The means used for fixing the text in written symbols contributes to the creation of the intuitive conception which one has of the same text. I do not propose to go into the different ways in which the computer influences the nature of the text which it contributes in creating.[5] I emphasize one alone: the computer, as soon as it gives the impression of stabilizing the text, of conferring on it the *bebaiòtes* which Plato spoke of, and therefore of closing it in a polished and *perfecta* form, actually leaves it open, and indefinitely open at that, to the point that the text recorded on computer disk is a virtuality of text rather than a stable text. Above all, the text becomes immaterial. Second, it suffices to fix the pointer somewhere in the text to be able to reintervene, indefinitely reopening something which was presumed closed. In the end, the computer honors the two properties which Plato attributed to the bad writer of texts, he or she who cobbles together discourses (the *logon syngraphés*), or rather the operation of sticking (Plato's *kollao*) and carrying away (Plato's *aphaireo*).

All these operations can be carried out not only by the first author of the text, but by anyone else (the typesetter at a printer's, the reader of an electronic book, the forger who willfully wishes to change the text). In this way the text gradually loses its authorship and the perception that it is the product of an author dwindles in the general consciousness. At any time the computer can let the text be taken up again (by anyone), reopened, be submitted to drastic changes ranging from destruction to total interpolation, to the copying of pieces of other texts, and so on. The movement of "violators of the body of the text" is so extensive that the well-educated European class is gradually losing its power of being textwise and is yielding to the old idea that texts can be handled and changed by others as well.

It is strange that the consciousness of textuality produced in this way is exactly the same as that described by Saint Bonaventure in the passage I mentioned earlier. Writing a book is quite another thing from commenting, copying, or annotating it. However, in the near future it will be increasingly difficult – even impossible – to say who is the author of a text.

It remains to be seen, as is always the case when considering the periods of oscillation of a pendulum, if what is about to take place is positive or not. Plato devoted almost an entire dialogue to analytically defining his regret over spoken dialectic discourse, still attached to the mouth and mind of the speaker. On the other hand the Middle Ages has showed unrelentingly that it was the *sententia* of the text which carried weight. If one accepts this, it suffices to appropriate it, without even stating the quotation. Today we find ourselves faced with several possible choices and it is up to us to decide. However, we may well soon be relieved of this task too. Writing technology will bring about changes in the collective consciousness and sooner or the closed and protected text will be a thing of the past.

Notes

[1] Translation by Elizabeth Freeman.

[2] For what follows I am particularly indebted to the important work by Alessio (1988).

[3] See for example the works by Emilia Ferreiro, such as Ferreiro (1985).

[4] In Alessio (1988: 119).

[5] For an up-to-date summary consult Scavetta (1993).

References

ALESSIO, F.
1988 "Conservazione e modelli di sapere nel medioevo" in Rossi (ed.) (1988: 98-133).

FERREIRO, E.
1985 *La construcción de la escritura en el desarrollo del niño*, Siglo XXl, Mexico City.

ROSSI, P.
1988 *La memoria del sapere*, Bari-Rome: Laterza.

SCAVETTA, D.
1993 *Le metamorfosi della scrittura*, Florence: La Nuova Italia.

Jay David Bolter

EKPHRASIS, VIRTUAL REALITY, AND THE FUTURE OF WRITING

As Carla Hesse and James O'Donnell (this volume) remind us, speculation about the future of the book is nothing new. Trithemius in the fifteenth century offered strong opinions about the book-making technology of this day, and in the eighteenth century Condorcet had a utopian vision of the future of printing. Trithemius was responding to technological change, the invention of the letterpress; Condorcet was responding to enormous social change and perhaps also to improvements in print technology that suggested its coming industrialization in the nineteenth century. Our situation today seems more closely to resemble that of Trithemius than of Condorcet. For, like printing in the fifteenth century, the computer today is a technology that challenges the traditional definition of the book. Trithemius was openly skeptical of the changes brought about by print. Condorcet, at least at first, was optimistic: he hoped that print technology could liberate human communication, just as computer enthusiasts now see hypertext or virtual reality as liberating. Contributors to this volume could also be divided into skeptics and enthusiasts. Most are like Trithemius in being skeptical about the nature or the extent of the electronic revolution. A few are like the early Condorcet. (After the terror, Hesse argues, Condorcet himself turned conservative and favored institutional control of publication.)

For the skeptics, one danger in electronic writing is its apparent detachment from the material basis of all writing. Previous technologies of writing have all been grounded in material practice. Even print technology produces books that function as artifacts in a culture of artifacts. The computer is supposed to dematerialize writing, and this dematerialization threatens to isolate electronic writing from the traditions promoted by earlier technologies. Geoffrey Nunberg (this volume) suggests, for example, that the notion of information itself as defined in the nineteenth century depends in crucial ways upon the material properties of printed documents, dictionaries, and libraries; he concludes ironically that the computer is putting an end to the information age.

Although they emphasize the materiality of earlier technologies, the skeptics are not determinists. They do not believe that the physical characteristics of a writing technology determine its use, and so they criticize the enthusiasts of electronic writing as technological determinists. Indeed, the enthusiasts do argue that the nature of the computer gives electronic writing a unique flexibility, contingency, interactivity, and so on. Technological determinism is anathema to contemporary historiography and to postmodern theory in general. Nearly all postmodern theorists agree that technologies are socially constructed. For them, therefore, the computer as a writing technology must be defined by social and economic needs and preferences, not the other way around.

The true technophiles (computer specialists, futurologists, and many in business and government bureacracy) are unconcerned by the charge of technological determinism – both because they do not read postmodern cultural criticism and because they approve of the direction in which, by their interpretation, our technological culture is heading. On the other hand, many humanists who work with computers do read cultural criticism. They are likely to be troubled by the fact that so many of their colleagues are so critical of electronic writing. One (rather obvious) reply is that the skeptics are setting up a false dichotomy. Technological constraints and social construction always interact in such a way that it is impossible to try to separate the two. The state of the engineering art does impose limitations on possible uses of a technology. There are many things one cannot do with contemporary computers, even things that our society would obviously like to do. For example, artificial intelligence has not provided machines with the capacity to write stories or create graphic worlds autonomously, though many technophiles dream of such machines. A technology can also render certain social constructions easier and therefore more popular. Electronic writing systems do promote flexibility and changeability, rather than monumentality and permanence. However, within these limitations and tendencies, there is a broad range of choices open to each culture or to each group.

Thus, when we talk about the future of the book, we are talking about subtle interactions between changing technological constraints and changing cultural needs. It is unwise to try to predict technological change more than a few years in advance. Many of the arguments against the widespread use of the computer as a reading technology depend upon assumptions about the physical size and clarity of the computer screen. Yet we do not know what computers will look like in the year 2000: we do not know how small they will be, how portable, how comfortable and convenient to read. It is even more difficult to make predictions about the social or cultural impact of technological change. We cannot know whether readers in the years 2000, 2010, or 2050 may come to prefer computers to printed books. Certainly cultural choices are keeping printed books and other materials in use today. For most purposes, print could be eliminated now, at least in the industrialized world, if readers and writers made a determined effort to do so. Most readers today are not prepared to replace their books with computers, but they might change their minds in the future. In the history of writing, some techniques and technologies have gone almost completely out of use. The codex practically replaced the roll in late antiquity. Parchment replaced papyrus in the European Middle Ages. More often perhaps, a new technology takes over one function and leaves other functions to an existing technology. Printing replaced handwriting for the distribution of most kinds of texts, but it did not make handwriting obsolete. Electronic technology has already taken over some functions that belonged to print or to handwriting (business communication, accounting, record keeping, and so on), and it seems likely to appropriate others. But we cannot predict whether there are certain functions that will indefinitely remain the province of the printed book.

In any case the mere survival of the printed book is not what matters. Other technologies have survived as mere relics. The roll as book form stills exists in the sacred Torah used in Jewish services, and there are still a few craftspeople who produce facsimiles of illuminated manuscripts for exhibits or wealthy collectors. But neither of these technologies occupies a place in our economy of writing, and their place in our culture's mythology is carefully circumscribed. (No aspiring writer today dreams of publishing her first novel on a roll of papyrus.)

What matters is whether the printed book will survive as a cultural ideal. For most of us today, perhaps, the printed book is still the embodiment of text. Both as authors and as readers, we still regard printed books and journals as the place to locate our most prestigious texts. However, the printed book as an ideal is already under challenge from various electronic media. The ideal has in fact been challenged by poststructuralist and postmodern theorists for decades. Now the computer provides a medium in which that theoretical challenge can be realized in practice.[1] We could argue that some groups – some academic researchers, particularly in the physical and social sciences, along with some in business and government – are in fact transferring their allegiance from the printed page to the computer screen. They think of the computer as the primary medium for verbal communication, print as a secondary or special medium. If our culture follows their lead, it will come to associate with text the qualities of the computer (flexibility, interactivity, speed of distribution) rather than those of the printed book (stability and authority). Printed books could remain abundant or even superabundant, as they are now, and still lose their status as a defining symbolic communication.

Some skeptics argue that computers will be used for technical communication and for home entertainment, but that literature (prose fiction and belletristic nonfiction) will continue to be printed. O'Donnell (this volume) quotes the novelist Annie Proulx's categorical claim that "no one is going to read a novel on a twitchy little screen. Ever." Taken literally, this claim is simply wrong. Such conventional novels as *Brave New World* and *Jurassic Park* have been digitized and read (or at least purchased) by an audience of hundreds or a few thousand. Such hypertext fictions as *afternoon* (Joyce 1987) and *Victory Garden* (Moulthrop 1992), written exclusively for presentation on the computer, have also won small audiences. Ms. Proulx may be right, if we take her to mean that there will never be a substantial audience for verbal fiction and nonfiction in the new medium. If she is right, if literature and humanistic scholarship are left in print, while scientific and technical communications move to electronic form, the result would only be the further marginalization of literature in our culture. For in that case the scientific and literary communities would not share an ideal of publication or a forum for dialogue.

1. The computer and the future of writing

Hypertext and other electronic writing systems are not the only, or perhaps even the most likely, candidates for replacing the book as a cultural symbol. Electronic technologies of representation also include digital graphics, animation, and virtual reality. If hypertext calls into question the future of the printed book, digital graphics call into question the future of alphabetic writing itself. The issue is not so much a conflict between ink on paper and pixels on a computer screen; it is rather a conflict between contrasting modes of representation.

The computer was designed about fifty years ago to solve numerical problems for scientists and engineers. But the early designers, such as A.M. Turing, soon realized that the machine could operate on other sets of arbitrary symbols. Led by artificial intelligence specialists, computer scientists came to regard the computer as a generalized "symbol manipulator." (This characterization, by the way, is the real achievement of the artificial intelligence movement in its classic period from, say, 1950-1980.) Applications in symbol manipulation, from numerical analysis to hypertext, remain the economically and culturally dominant uses of the machine. But the computer is also being used increasingly for perceptual presentation rather than symbol manipulation. Computer graphics began in the 1960s, but it is only recently that graphic techniques have become available to wide numbers of users (though inexpensive machines and software) and to a large audience of viewers (through high-quality animation in television and on film). Enhanced by synthesized or digitized sound, electronic graphics can deliver compelling perceptual experiences. As a symbol manipulator, the computer is a writing technology in the tradition of the papyrus roll, the codex, and the printed book. As a perceptual manipulator, the computer extends the tradition of television, film, photography, and even representational painting.

Computer graphics can enter into a variety of competitive or cooperative relationships with electronic writing. Graphics can be integrated into electronic documents, where they function more or less like graphics on a printed page. Computer graphics can serve as elements of a hypertext. They can function as icons, as they do in the conventional desktop metaphor. The computer can offer its users a multimedia space that combines text, numbers, static images, animation, and video. In current multimedia, however, the trend is not to integrate the textual and the perceptual. Instead, perceptual presentation is being used to displace or replace verbal text. Video and animation dominate the screen, while verbal text is marginalized. And the displacement of text is not limited to multimedia; something similar is happening in print. In fact, print and electronic technology seem to be moving along parallel lines as our culture revises its sense apparent in American newspapers and magazines, particularly ones associated with the new media.

2. The breakout of the visual

Every issue of the popular newspaper *USA Today* offers three or four "USA Snapshots," colorful little graphs that tell Americans "who we are." And in these graphs we can discern a struggle between textual and visual modes of representation. The struggle is apparent in the example below, which illustrates how often American men shave on the weekend (*USA Today*, June 24, 1994). This graph is a bar chart: its three bars represent from left to right the number of American men who shave twice on the weekends, once, and not at all. The bars are drawn as safety razors, apparently to convince the viewer that the graph is really about shaving. The designers also distrusted the viewer's faith in numerical abstraction; they decided to draw two razors for the number of men shaving on both days and one for the number shaving on one day. The number of those who do not shave on the weekend then poses a problem. It becomes an empty column; it

Copyright 1994, *USA Today*. Reprinted with permission.

reverts to the form of a conventional bar chart. Consider also the grid of white lines behind the razors. The lines seem to define a Cartesian coordinate system, but they do not correspond to obvious numerical divisions. The grid in fact represents the tiles that one finds in an American bathroom: here a pictorial representation has supplanted the graph. In all these ways, it is as if the designers no longer trusted the arbitrary symbolic structure of the graph to sustain its meaning. Writing as a texture of arbitrary signs is coming undone to reveal the motivated signs or icons that are assumed to lie "beneath" its surface.

Finally, the shaving man himself has no function in the graph. His presence seeks to transform the graph into a picture, yet at the same time he gives the picture much of its semiotic complexity. As he shaves, the man appears to be looking into a mirror. We as viewers are on the other side of the mirror, looking back at the man. Now, as in other *USA Today* graphs and graphics, the statistics embodied in this graph are supposed to be a mirror of American life. Thus, the shaving man turns the graph into a verbal/visual pun, although it seems unlikely that the designers had this in mind. For them, the humor probably lies in the Gestalt shifts between bars and razors, Cartesian coordinates and grout lines between bathroom tiles. The caption of the graph – "statistics that shape our lives" – is more ironic and appropriate than the designers may have realized.

The pun in this graph recalls another technique that has become common even in those newspapers considering themselves more traditional and verbally sophisticated than the *USA Today*. Headlines often draw out latent metaphors in their subject: "Turbulent times ahead for United Airlines"; "Tobacco stocks are smoking"; "Mercedes slips earnings gears." In such headlines there is usually a visual or tactile image, and the point is to turn the analytic content of the headline into something sensual. The prose itself is straining to become iconic: to call forth through punning rhetoric an image that confirms what is being referred to in words.

Yet another form of visualized rhetoric is common in glossy computer magazines like *Byte* or *MacWorld*, particularly in advertisements. The headline claims that a certain software product will give your company "a bigger piece of the pie." The picture shows an apple pie with a large slice being removed. The visual realization seems to lend the cliché greater conviction for the reader/viewer. In such advertisements the dialectic of word and image – what W.J.T. Mitchell has called the "imagetext" (Mitchell *Picture Theory*, 83 ff) – can be commonplace or sophisticated. But in each case the image both reaffirms and dominates the verbal text. Words no longer seem to carry conviction without the reappearance as pictures of imagery that was latent in the words.

Throughout the history of writing, there have been genres that combine words, icons, and pictures. Rebus and emblem poetry were popular in the Renaissance. Children today still enjoy rebus books, in which some of the nouns are replaced by stylized drawings. A young child can follow the story and become accustomed to the linearity of reading before he can actually decipher the letters that constitute alphabetic writing. The *USA Today* graphs are also connected to the long tradition of *technopaignia*, poems written in a shape that reflects their content. Panpipes and other shaped poems are as old as the *Greek Anthology*. However, the contemporary examples of visual play are more widespread and have greater significance, coming as they do after five hundred years of printing. They can be seen as part of a general trend to renegotiate the relationship between arbitrary signs and perceptual elements in communication.

The renegotiation is also apparent in the layout and content of the newspaper. In many American papers, for example, pictures are coming to dominate and organize the articles. In some cases a picture and its caption replace a verbal story altogether. The picture catches the reader's eye: he reads the caption and then searches the page in vain for the text that will add detail. The picture has broken free of the prose that would traditionally have explained and justified its presence. The newspaper is becoming a picture book. The situation is still different in Europe, where "serious" newspapers often contain fewer pictures and more prose and where the pictures are more often under the overt control of the text.

If, during the heyday of print in the eighteenth and nineteenth centuries, writers controlled the visual by subsuming it into their prose, writers today seem to be trying to become more visual and sensuous. Eventually, the visual element not only rises to the surface of the text, but escapes altogether and takes its place as a picture on the printed page. It is not only newspapers and magazines that are renegotiating the verbal and the visual. Other forms, including "serious" and popular fiction and academic prose, are also changing, and in all cases verbal text seems to be losing its power to contain and constrain the sensory. Each genre of writing is either experiencing a "breakout of the visual" or is reacting against it. It would be worthwhile, for example, to examine the history of artistic prose since the nineteenth century to watch how sensory elements at first suffused the prose in the late romantics and early modern writers and then began to bubble out of the writing altogether. One key to understanding this change would be to correlate it with the invention and spread of photography and then film.[2]

In the late twentieth century, the cultural importance of film and television (as heirs to photography) is certainly part of the explanation for the breakout of the visual. Media critics in the tradition of McLuhan have been arguing for decades that television offers an alternative to print literacy.[3] Television can be said to weaken traditional literacy both by offering an alternative to prose communication and by providing a competing paradigm of communication that prose writers may be inclined to follow. It is a truism (but still true) that television cannot display abstract concepts in a compelling fashion. It also seems true that the *USA Today* and other American newspapers are following television's tendency to replace words with images.

On the other hand, in graphic form and function, the newspaper is coming to resemble a computer screen rather than a television screen. The mixture of text, images, and icons turns the newspaper page into a static snapshot of a multimedia presentation. The page is laid out in numerous rectangles that resemble the windows or boxes of a multimedia screen. By contrast, broadcast television tends to keep the screen undivided. (Split screens and other special graphic effects are, however, beginning to appear on broadcast television, again under the influence of computer multimedia.) The display units in the newspaper allude to, although they cannot perform, the interactive functions of hypermedia. In many newspapers, for example, the index now consists of summaries in a column down the left-hand side of the page. In some cases a small picture is included with the summary. Anyone familiar with multimedia presentations can easily read such a picture as an iconic button: one would press the button to receive the rest of the story. The *USA Today* in fact makes considerable use of hypertextual links back and forth throughout its pages, and these links are often cued by small graphics.

The assimilation of newspapers to multimedia brings us back to the computer. The breakout of the visual has more scope in computer-controlled multimedia than in print, because computer applications do not feel the weight of the tradition of print, under which even the *USA Today* must still operate. In typical examples of multimedia, graphics dominate the verbal text. Words are often used either for titles or to identify buttons. The space of multimedia includes video and sound, which are particularly effective at displacing verbal text. This displacement is common in multimedia for business training and for information kiosks, and text is often displaced even in multimedia for education. A good example is provided by IBM's showcase hypermedia application called *Ulysses* (AND Communication 1990). The application is designed to help students understand Tennyson's poem *Ulysses* by providing definitions of unfamiliar words, historical background, literary comment, and so on. The program starts by presenting the student with the text of the poem in a window on the screen. But the strategy is to take students away from the text of the poem wherever possible: to replace written text with audio or video segments. Although audio and video have the ostensible role of explaining the text, these media soon reverse that relationship. Tennyson's poem becomes incidental to a story told in sound and moving pictures. The high quality of its video production makes *Ulysses* unusual, but the idea of translating printed works into multimedia has become common. Through such translations, computer-controlled video may come to play as important a role as television in realizing for our culture the breakout of the visual.

3. The natural sign

The relationship between word and image is becoming as unstable in multimedia as in the popular press, and this instability seems to be spreading. Even when words and perceptual media are brought together in the same space, they seldom achieve the harmony that existed in the classic age of print. That harmony was based on the subordination of the image to the word, and we are no longer certain that words deserve the cultural authority they have been given. In this volume Geoffrey Nunberg points out that information is a historically determined category, determined for us in the age of print. Perhaps the current anxiety over the "information explosion" comes from a breakdown of that traditional category. It is unclear what now counts as information. If graphics and video are as informative as (or even more informative than) verbal text, then we do indeed confront enormously more information than previous generations. At the same time alphabetic text itself is breaking apart, if not exactly exploding. When we see graphics and animation slipping out of the semantic reach of the text, we no longer know what codes to apply or whether the very notion of coding is appropriate.

The use of images for cultural communication is certainly not new. Before the invention of the printing press, the Middle Ages had developed a sophisticated iconography that served in the place of words for a largely illiterate audience. A medieval cathedral was a complex text displayed in a sacred space for the community to read. However, there are important differences between the visual culture of the Middle Ages and our visual culture. One difference is the sheer ubiquity of images today. In the Middle Ages, images must have had a sanctity not only because of their religious themes, but also because of their inaccessibility. A major source of such images, such as a cathedral or minster, would have been available only to a fraction of the population. Most peasants would have attended parish churches that could hardly afford much stained glass and sculpture, and might have seen the interior of a cathedral only a few times in their lives. Even town dwellers fortunate enough to live near a religious center would have dragged themselves to church before or after an exhausting day's work and received a glimpse of the rich imagery. The images must have had a different status for them than the endless barrage that confronts the contemporary television viewer. Furthermore, medieval society as a whole had a different relationship to verbal literacy: there was a small literate elite and a large class of illiterates. Our culture is by comparison postliterate, emerging out of the enormous experiment in mass literacy of the nineteenth and twentieth centuries. In this historical context, visual representation too can be seen as emerging out of the alphabet and other symbol systems. The visual puns in the *USA Today*, for example, depend upon centuries of exposure to statistical analysis and the Cartesian coordinate system. It is interesting to speculate how photography, film, television, and multimedia might have been developed and used, if Western culture could somehow have jumped over the technology of printing and gone directly from medieval iconography to chemical and electronic visual presentation. What did happen is that these visual technologies had to define themselves in a culture of printed materials, and in particular in a literary culture dominated by the printed novel. They had to assume the task of subverting the dominant model of prose, of breaking free of the constraints of verbal rhetoric.

Thus, the renegotiation of word and image that is taking place in our traditional and new media is leading to a crisis in rhetoric. For both ancient and modern rhetoric have depended upon subordinating images to words. In ancient rhetoric it was the spoken word that controlled the image; in modern rhetoric it has been the written or printed word. Now when neither the written nor the spoken word can exert effective control, the result is an inversion of traditional rhetorical practice. In particular, the effect of turning a newspaper into a multimedia screen can be seen as an inversion of the classical device of the *ekphrasis*. *Ekphrasis* is the description in prose or poetry of an artistic object or striking visual scene; it is the attempt to capture the visual in words. Today, as the visual and the sensual are emerging out of verbal communication, images are given the task (as in the *Ulysses* program) of explaining words, rather than the reverse.

For ancient rhetoric, *ekphrasis* was in the first instance the description of a work of visual art; *ekphrasis* set out to demonstrate the superiority of the rhetorical art to painting or sculpture. Yet there was also a highlighting of the visual artwork in ekphrastic description. There is a sense of trying to get beyond the words to the thing itself, which literary critic Murray Krieger has identified as the "desire for the natural sign":

> In speaking of ekphrasis, or at least of the ekphrastic impulse, I have pointed to its source in the semiotic desire for the natural sign, the desire, that is, to have the world captured in the word... This desire to see the world in the word is what, after Derrida, we have come to term the logocentric desire. It is this naive desire that leads us to prefer the immediacy of the picture to the mediation of the code in our search for a tangible, "real" referent that would render the sign transparent. (Krieger 1992: 11)

Krieger documents the desire for the natural sign through centuries of the practice in *ekphrasis*. If, as Krieger suggests, we connect this desire with Derrida's logocentrism, then we could say that the desire comes into existence with the invention of writing itself. According to Derrida, as soon as culture invents an arbitrary sign system, there arises a yearning to close the gap between the sign and the signified. However, this yearning can take different forms depending on the available technologies of representation. In Plato's Greece, when oratory and drama were the defining arts, the spoken word was treated as the natural sign. In one sense Plato himself created the dialogue form in order to bring his writing closer to the natural sign. Printed literature since the Renaissance has faced a different and more difficult situation, because the techniques of representation to which print has been responding have been visual rather than oral. Print managed to establish an equilibrium with representational painting, but that equilibrium perhaps began to erode with the invention of photography. Just as photography precipitated a crisis in painting – what could the painter do now that painting could not compete in fidelity with the illusion offered by the photograph? – so photography and the inventions that followed (film, television, and computer graphics) also called into question the power of prose. Thus, in the nineteenth and twentieth centuries, the desire to see the world in the word has been gradually supplemented by the more easily gratified desire to see the world through technologies of perceptual illusion. In this period, *ekphrasis* became a greater and greater challenge. *Ekphrasis* may still be found in various guises, but in order to compete with film, television, and computer graphics, popular prose now seems determined to attempt to "speak the language" of these media – that is, to turn back to picture writing or to pure imagery. The breakout of the visual in contemporary prose and multimedia is a denial of *ekphrasis*. Popular prose and multimedia are striving for the natural sign in the realm of the visual rather than through heightened verbal expression.

Krieger suggests that the desire for the natural sign is another manifestation of Derrida's metaphysics of presence, the conviction that a reader can pass through the sign to the thing represented by it. The natural sign is supposed to be perspicuous. The sign should dissolve and leave the reader in the presence of the thing itself. The ideal is to have no sign at all, but only the things signified; a method of representation is preferable to the extent that it brings us closer to that ideal. Written fiction can not perhaps get very close at all. The reader must forget about the words on the page as a structure of signs and treat the page instead as a window onto a fictional world. The notion of the book as window was in fact employed for decades as a film device. The movie would begin with a written introduction on the page of a book. The page would turn, the viewer would see the imagined scene, and the story would continue in visual mode. (This is precisely what happens in the new and very successful computer game *Myst*, which is consciously cinematic.)

Pictures or moving pictures seem to have a natural correspondence to what they depict.[4] They can satisfy more effectively than prose the desire to cut through to a "natural" representation that is not a representation at all. So the desire for the natural sign leads to the desire to abolish symbolic representation altogether. One only needs a sign system if signs are *not* natural. If signs are natural, they need not be organized into a code, and the conception of language and writing as a set of coded oppositions can be abandoned.

4. Text as a window

The convention of beginning a narrative film by showing the opening pages of a book deserves further attention. The convention belonged to movies of the thirties and forties; it is hardly used today. Yet the popular belief remains that there is an easy correspondence between visual and verbal texts – that to read a novel is to run a movie inside one's head and so to visualize each setting, scene, and character. In this view, it is the reader's capacity to visualize that renders the novel intelligible. The technology of the cinema made this analogy powerful. When there were only static paintings and photographs, the novel or any written text was perhaps more obviously a different form of representation. Certainly in the eighteenth and nineteeth centuries, an analogy could have been made to the stage: the novel could have been thought of as a drama in prose. But the invention of film made it much easier to regard a written narrative as a script for visualization. The novel could become a mental movie, and reading could be construed as the act of *looking through* the written text to the visual experience that lay behind and validated the words.

Richard Lanham (1993: 43 ff) argues that much of twentieth-century art is a self-conscious reflection on two kinds of engagement with the viewer: looking at and looking through. In painting, looking through means accepting the illusion that the painting is really a window onto a perceived world. Looking at means focusing one's attention on the painting as an artifact, a surface covered with paint, a manipulation of color, shape, and texture. In literature, looking through means losing oneself in the story. When a reader is called back to the text and examines it for its rhetorical and structural properties, he is looking at rather than looking through that text. When a reader treats a text as a film, she is looking through the text and not at it. In all cases, perhaps, the viewer or reader must oscillate between looking at and through. Even in the most effective illusionistic painting or in the most compelling "page-turner," we must occasionally be reminded that we are looking at paint on a canvas or at ink on paper. Twentieth-century verbal and visual art maintains a vigorous oscillation between looking at and through and so reminds us repeatedly of the painting as painting or the novel as novel.

In current culture, however, works that oscillate in this fashion – for example, hypertextual fictions like *afternoon* (Joyce 1987) – are bound to be "unpopular." The popular notion remains that art or writing should aim at "realism." Art or writing is realistic in this sense when it generates a compelling illusion. The viewer or reader is supposed to fall through the frame or the page into another world, one that is either continuous with our world or has its own convincing logic. The work of art or literature is supposed to describe an *environment* that the viewer or reader can inhabit for the time in which she is enjoying the work.

5. Virtual reality and the natural sign

Computer specialists have used the term "environment" for many years. A computer environment is a suite of software tools. Thus, a text-editing environment might consist of a word processor, a spelling checker, an electronic dictionary, and a bibliographic database. The metaphor of environment suggests that the software defines a space that the user can inhabit: she can move among the tools and grasp and use the ones needed. A computer environment does not necessarily imply a graphical interface. However, given the current trends, it becomes natural for computer users to think of these environments as graphical and eventually as three-dimensional.

The ultimate graphical environment is provided by the technology of *virtual reality*. In a typical virtual reality system, the user wears a head-mounted display, a helmet with eyepieces covering each eye. The computer controls the user's entire field of view. A tracking device senses movements of the helmet, so that when the user turns her head, the computer adjusts the image accordingly. Virtual reality provides an illusion rather different from that of photography, film, or video. Nevertheless, in terms of the oscillation between looking at and looking through that we have just been discussing, virtual reality is another

technology for looking through. In traditional computing, the user sits at a keyboard and looks at a monitor. But with virtual reality, there is nothing to look at, because the user is wearing the machine and her eyes can now see only what the computer draws in her field of view.

Virtual environments offer an apparently unmediated perception of another world. They achieve what in the popular view narrative fiction and films have always sought to achieve: total empathetic involvement in a created world. As the VR enthusiast Meredith Bricken puts it:

> [In virtual reality] you don't need a body; you can be a floating point of view. You can be the mad hatter or you can be the teapot; you can move back and forth to the rhythm of a song. You can be a tiny droplet in the rain or in the river; you can be what you thought you ought to be all along. You can switch your point of view to an object or a process or another person's point of view in the other person's world. (Bricken 1991: 372)

The user has fallen through the frame and is now located in a graphic world. Occupying any location in that world, she can also inhabit the point of view of any person, animal, or object.

One does not need full, immersive virtual reality to evoke in the viewer the sense of falling through the frame. Even on a conventional monitor, computer graphics can create a sense of surround. The best video games can draw the user into an environment that in fact consists only of changing pixels on a computer screen. Of course, television, film, and perspective painting could also succeed in convincing the viewer to project himself into the scene. Yet each medium accomplishes the task of projection somewhat differently. The key to such projection in virtual reality is that the user can control her perspective and sense of movement through the scene. In film, video, and animation, the shifts in perspective are under the control of the director, editor, or animator. In virtual reality, and in computer environments generally, the shifts are under the user's control.

In this respect, virtual reality can be understood as a paradigm for the whole realm of computer graphics. And in turn the technology of computer graphics is gaining more and more cultural importance. Computer graphics and animation have already reached a wider audience than hypertext or even word processing, and they may soon surpass print. Tens, perhaps hundreds of millions of people have seen *Jurassic Park* or *Aladdin* – far more than the entire population of users on the Internet. One does not have to put on a helmet to appreciate the new self suggested by virtual reality: animated films and conventional television are also experiments in shifting points of view, both technically and thematically. It is no mere coincidence that Disney films, the best in popular animation, are adopting computer technology and that the space inhabited by Disney characters is beginning to take on the surreal look of a demonstration produced on the latest Silicon Graphics hardware. Computer graphics greatly expands the capacity for animation to simulate camera shots and therefore to define a shifting perspective.[5]

In redefining the notion of perspective, computer graphic environments are reinforcing our culture's desire for the natural sign. They suggest that the computer-controlled media can provide a kind of representation without words, in which the user inhabits and experiences the world through immediate perception. The unstated assumption in Bricken's remarks above is that mediation itself is evil, because it gets in the way of pure, empathetic experience. This same assumption can be found not only among enthusiasts for computer graphics and virtual reality, but also in a variety of other manifestations of popular culture. It is the assumption behind the breakout of the visual in popular prose and in multimedia. The pictures jump out of the text in an effort to provide their readers with "pure" visual experiences – in effect to turn them away from reading and toward apparently unmediated forms of perception.

6. Virtual silence

I suggested earlier that the breakout of the visual in print and in multimedia was the inversion of the rhetorical device of *ekphrasis*. Enthusiasts seem to construe virtual reality too as the denial of *ekphrasis*. *Ekphrasis* depends upon a written or spoken text. But virtual reality is often, perhaps always, silent; it achieves its mobile point of view without text, almost without voice. I do not mean of course that sound or even recorded human voices are absent from the virtual environment. What is absent is any resonance between the human voice as part of the perceived environment and the written sign. Without this resonance, the ekphrastic impulse is stilled, and there cannot be an oscillation between looking at and looking through. Electronic virtual environments seem to constitute a final phase in the desire for the natural sign, the phase in which the sign itself is eliminated.

The arbitrary sign cannot, however, be eliminated from all electronic environments. For electronic technology does not promote a single mode of representation; it promotes instead radical heterogeneity. All sorts of relationships between word and image are being defined in various corners of the electronic network – everything from apparently pure perceptual environments to textual and mathematical representations that avoid graphics altogether. Although enthusiasts for virtual reality may dream of eliminating writing, they cannot succeed. Even their virtual reality systems rest on layer after layer of writing, of arbitrary signs in the form of computer programs. What can happen, perhaps, is the cultural devaluation of writing in comparison with perceptual presentation. It is possible that writing will be identified more and more as an "elite" activity, while the more popular modes of communication will be ones that strive to restrict or eliminate the arbitrary sign. This is an elaborate way of saying that both conventional novels and hypertextual fictions will be less popular than interactive soap operas.

The new media also threaten to drain contemporary prose of its rhetorical possibilities. Popular prose responds with a desire to emulate computer graphics. Academic and other specialized forms respond by a retreat into jargon or into willful anachronism. ("No one will read novels on a computer screen – ever.") In all cases, the silence, the lack of resonance, of electronic media seems to be descending upon prose too. Since ancient times, the rhetorical voice has been a primary instrument for defining point of view. Now the ability to define a mobile, visual point of view in electronic media seems to be replacing our culture's rhetorical voice.

This silencing may ultimately constitute a new beginning, the forging of a kind of written communication in which the primary mode of imitation is visual rather than oral. Rather than defining a new orality, as McLuhan (1964) and Ong (1982) predicted, electronic technology seems to me to be moving us toward an increasing dependence upon and interest in the visual. The most popular new electronic writing system is the Internet's World Wide Web. The protocol of the Web invites users to write and post hypertextual documents that can then be examined by other users from around the world. Although it is possible to create purely verbal documents on the Web, no one does so. Graphics and even video are included along with words. Such Web documents are experiments in the integration of visual and verbal communication. The hypertextual character of these documents – the fact that text, graphics, and video may be linked electronically – defines a space in which arbitrary signs can coexist with perceptual presentation. However, it is not a peaceful coexistence. The verbal text must now struggle to assert its legitimacy in a space increasingly dominated by visual modes of representation.

Notes

[1] See Landow 1992.

[2] Jonathan Crary's *Techniques of the Observer* (1990), for example, would be a starting point for charting the complex cultural interactions between writing and photography and other early forms of imaging technology

[3] See McLuhan (1964) and, for example, Postman (1985).

[4] For extended discussions of this venerable idea, see Mitchell (1986) (1994).

[5] See Bolter (1996).

References

AND COMMUNICATION
1990 "*Ulysses* and beyond: Knowledge prototype system. Computer software," presented by James E. Dezell in a lecture on "Restructuring education through technology," IBM Schools Executive Conference, February 2, 1990, Palm Springs (videotape).

BOLTER, J.D.
1996 "Virtual reality and the redefition of self," in L. State, R. Jacobson, and S. Gibson (eds.), *Communication and Cyberspace: Social Interaction in an Electronic Environment*, New York: Hampton Press Inc.

BRICKEN, M.
1991 "Virtual worlds: No interface to design," in M. Benedikt (ed.), *Cyberspace: First Steps*, Cambridge (Mass.): MIT Press: 363-82.

CRARY, J.
1990 *Techniques of the Observer: Vision and Modernity in the Nineteenth Century*, Cambridge (Mass.): MIT Press.

HAYLES, N.K.
1993 "The materiality of informatics," *Configurations,* 1, 1: 147-70.

JOYCE, M.
1987 *afternoon, a story*, Watertown: Eastgate Systems (computer program).

KRIEGER, M.
1992 *Ekphrasis: The Illusion of the Natural Sign*, Baltimore: Johns Hopkins University Press.

LANDOW, G.
1992 *Hypertext: The Convergence of Contemporary Critical Theory and Technology*, Baltimore: Johns Hopkins University.

LANHAM, R.
1993 *The Electronic Word: Democracy, Technology and the Arts*, Chicago: University of Chicago Press (also available in diskette version as electronic text).

MCLUHAN, M.
1964 *Understanding Media: The Extensions of Man*, New York: McGraw-Hill.

MITCHELL, W.J.T.
1986 *Iconology: Image, Text, Ideology*, Chicago: University of Chicago Press.
1994 *Picture Theory*, Chicago: University of Chicago Press.

MOULTHROP S.,
1992 *Victory Garden*, Watertown: Eastgate Systems (computer program).

ONG, W.
1982 *Orality and Literacy*, New York: Methuen.

POSTMAN, N.
1985 *Amusing Ourselves to Death: Public Discourse in the Age of Show Business*, New York: Viking Penguin.

Michael Joyce

(RE)PLACING THE AUTHOR: "A BOOK IN THE RUINS"[1]

A dark building. Crossed boards, nailed up, create
A barrier at the entrance, or a gate
When you go in. Here, in the gutted foyer,
The ivy snaking down the walls is wire
Dangling. And over there the twisted metal
Columns rising from the undergrowth of rubble
Are tattered tree trunks. This could be the brick
Of the library, you don't know yet, or the sick
Grove of dry white aspen where, stalking birds,
You met a Lithuanian dusk stirred
From its silence only by the wails of hawks.

The poet stands in the ruins, it is the modernist moment. But, no, this is not what we see. The poet makes his way into the ruins, and in so moving the movement in itself reads barrier as gate. What he reads he writes. Against the unassigned space of the dark building – let us call this space the screen – crossed boards read as sign and juncture, axis and nullification, light on light. A gutted foyer no longer opens to another space but is the space of its own opening. Yet in movement the outward dark gives way to memory and metonymy, to multiplicity, the one continually replacing the other. In this crossing "here" and "there" are interwoven as if ivy. Or wire. Shifting light, dusk or dawn, yields what I have called elsewhere the momentary advantage of its own awkwardness, a slant illumination in which we are allowed to see each thing each time interstitially, in the moment before it assumes its seamlessness in the light of day, the dark of night. The electronic age now enjoys the time of awkwardness before the age itself disappears along with the mark of its name into the day to day of what at Xerox PARC they call "ubicomp," ubiquitous computing.[2] For now, in the shifting light of the present awkwardness, even though the figures move asymmetrically (ivy is wire, column is tree), each thing nonetheless remains itself even in the displacement, the chiasmus, of its form. What's changed is not the thing but its placement. Print stays itself, electronic text replaces itself. Electronic text is as apt to evolve before it forms, as apt to dissolve before it finishes. On the screen it takes our constant and attentive interaction to maintain even the simulacrum of static text.

The future, too, requires as much of us, and has for some time.

There is a play on words in this formulation, since whatever the future has for some time required of us it incorporates the past, or rather pulls it through as through the wormhole of a singularity. The future won't stay still but instead keeps on replacing itself. The page becomes the screen, the screen replaces the page. We could call this placement "history." Electronic texts present themselves in the medium of their dissolution: they are read where they are written, they are written as they are read. What "this could be," the poet tells us, "you don't know yet." The boy who stalked birds himself is stalked, circled by history. Only wailing hawks have the perspective of memory and in memory they are said to circle a sick grove, although one whose locus, we know extratextually, is the golden age, the childhood land, of the poet who here – the year is 1941 and it is Warsaw – is a young man, a janitor in a bombed library, who "carted books from the University Library to the National Library, and from the National Library to the Krasinki Library."[3]

I want to speak carefully. In reading this poem of Milosz as a meditation on electronic text, I do not wish to appropriate the horror of this scission, to trivialize what the space of the Warsaw library opens into or what, in slicing through, it replaces. Alexander's sword cut through the topological manifolds which gave meaning to the Gordian knot – we could call these twined strands ivy or wire, word or superstring – and in this movement he both read and wrote his own fate. "There was a sense then that all cultural values were undergoing tremendous destruction, the total end of everything," says Milosz in Czarnecka and Fiut (1987). The hole replaces the whole, they carted books behind not before the storms. And yet the book in the ruins is always the book of the ruins. We live in a time when the book itself is in ruins, *eskhate biblos*. I want to read this poem as if the young poet knew that he both read and wrote the space he moved through. The young poet's war was about the end of hierarchy, hierarchy blasted away under the stolen aegis of a bent cross. The war was the second in a series – or the seven times seven hundredth, it does not matter; topologically number furls into metaphor – an infinitely divisible series of forays of movement into form. It is an ancient movement, this cross which both annuls and becomes form. Under its sign the idea of everything is no more privileged than the idea of any thing.

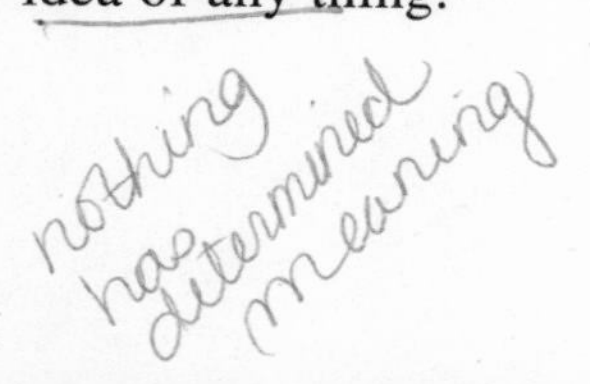

In the more recent interviews collected in Czarnecka and Fiut (1987), Milosz speaks of his "incredible fastidiousness and [his] need for a strict hierarchy." The old man the poet has become might not like this reading of the young poet. "Literature," he says, "is very hierarchical." Yet what was cut was released into meaning, his poem knows this. "Our hope is in the historical," says Milosz in Czarnecka and Fiut (1987), "because history as time, but time remembered, is something different from nature's time." Yet nature's time, too, we are finding is time remembered. "History is important," says the social theorist Sandra Braman (1994): "In a topologically mapped universe, the location of a point is less important than how it got there... systems also have memories, and when they unravel will retreat by the routes along which they had previously traveled in the self-organizing phase."[4] The knot springs to and from its form, rehearsing the manifold movements of its many tyings, knot on knot.

"Now walk carefully," the next movement of the poem begins. The poem slows into present tense, the meaning in movement is discovered. The light is mixed, not Lithuanian dusk but "a patch of blue" through a "ceiling caved in by a recent blast" (later we will see this is noon as workmen sit and have their lunch upon a table made of books). The scene moves from the metonymic to the metaphoric. The pages of books are "like fern-leaves hiding/a mouldy skeleton, or else fossils." Every discovered thing is discovered as written on, inscribed: the skeleton etched by mold, the fossils "whitened by the secrets of Jurassic shells" (just as this line itself is now written on by popular culture, a whole epoch crossed over into sign, trade style, and copyright, the Jurassic marketed in every airport shop and shopping mall, cannot be retrieved to mean geologically until the market culture is done with it and still not then), and in turn inscribed by tears of rust. The whole space in turn is written upon by the movement of these lines.

Yet inscription as always is questioned: it isn't clear in these ruins whether the shadow of a dead epoch is a living form. The poem presents the ambiguous figure of a scientist already like the guardian mole of Milosz's later poem, *A Poor Christian Looks at the Ghetto*, who "distinguishes human ashes by their luminous vapor/ The ashes of each man by a different part of the spectrum." In the scission of the caesura in the poem at hand (the English translation is Milosz with Robert Haas) the scientist's mind is split:

> A remnant life so ancient and unknown
> Compels a scientist, tilting a stone
> Into the light, to wonder. He can't know

What at the start of the poem was the potential "you don't know yet" is now embodied, characterized, and denied, "he can't know." The stone must be replaced, tilted into light, before the scientist "looks again" and in this recurrence reads. The compulsion to wonder marks the figure of the scientist as no mere polar figure for the poet. A "rust of tears" simultaneously writes and erodes "chalk spirals" and the next caesura in the following lines ("Thus") is an engine, a compulsion to wonder:

> He looks again
> At chalk spirals eroded by the rain,
> The rust of tears. Thus, in a book picked up
> From the ruins, you see a world erupt

The idea of everything is no more privileged than the idea of any one thing. Following the catastrophic eruption of world from book, "[G]reen times of creatures tumbled to the vast/ abyss and backward." The one who reads the book in the ruins replaces the one who reads the space of the ruin in the book we read. In its unraveling the erupted world retreats by routes along which it had previously traveled. Thus beyond the abyss of the poem the paleontologist's fossil gives way to the poet's imagined "earring fixed with trembling hand, pearl button/on a glove." Seen is scene.[5]

In the course of what is seen the writer is replaced by the reader (the writer who will be). This is the claim of constructive hypertext, and by extension any system of electronic text, from hypertext to virtual reality to ubicomp. The fossil word, which on the computer screen is always tilted to the light and constantly replaced, again takes its place within the universe of the visible and the sensual. Print stays itself, electronic text replaces itself. With electronic text we are always painting, each screen washing away what was and replacing it with itself. The shadow of each dead letter provides the living form of what replaces it.[6]

The electronic text is a belief structure and the workaday reader is apt to believe that even the most awkward contemporary technology of literacy embodies the associational schema of the text which it presents. She sees herself there in its form as she finds it, and feels that the form trails behind her as she goes. Scene is seen: this is the shift from the book. Not that the storm of association around the book – the isobaric indexes, the note cards, the pages "scattered like fern leaves," or the tropic marginalia – could not encompass the associations within it (they have and wonderfully, this is the history of the book as remembered time); but rather that the electronic form now embodies the same latitudes which once encompassed the book. The storm circles inward and disperses, belief structures saturate the electronic text, raining down like manna, driving skyward through us like the graviton, sustaining and anchoring its continual replacement.

Likewise with electronic media the image again takes its place within the system of text, that is within narrative syntax, where as Braman (1994) reminds us "the location of a point is less important than how it got there." What's seen next: what's said next. The constructive hypertext is a version of what it is becoming, a structure for what does not yet exist. As such it is both the self-organizing phase of the reader who replaces the retreating writer, and the readable trace, time remembered in the unraveling retreat of this replacement. The one who will write will have to recall what the one before has written in such a way that the next one, the third self – you who writes after us – may find the one finding the other first. Else what either of us have done will be lost to you and to remembered time; in its retreat the space of the story will mark neither the form of its making nor the making of its form. There will be no knot.

Seen is scene. In the poem the erupting world "glitter[s] with its distant sleepy past." Seen through the poet's eyes, four chapters follow from the book in the ruins: three linked, a fourth marked by a scission and wounded. The first, as always, is light and lovers' meeting.

> The lanterns have been lit. A first shiver
> Passes over the instruments. The quadrille
> Begins to curl, subdued by the rustle
> Of big trees swaying in the formal park.
> She slips outside, her shawl floating in the dark,
> And meets him in a bower overgrown
> With vines. They sit close on a bench of stone
> And watch the lanterns glowing in the jasmine.

The big trees are twisted metal columns; we know this from the space where we entered; a bench of stone and glowing lanterns will become a table of heavy books dragged out by workmen in the light of a fire the sunlight kindles on a floor strewn with pages. You can't know this yet from the poem but you know it now from this particular reading. Or perhaps you already know this from the poem and mark it again in this reading. In hypertext each such point of a reading – what you know or don't know, tree or column, bench or table – potentially impinges upon another.

Yet we don't know where or in what form the world will erupt, whether for us, for the lovers, or for the poet who sees a book in the ruins. In *Treatise on Poetry* in Czarnecka and Fiut (1987) Milosz questions "whether Hegel's Spirit of History is the same spirit that rules the world of nature... in what respect history is a continuation of nature."[7] For him, naturally, it is a question of being versus becoming, Heraclitus flows into Hegel, the confluence overflowing the Thomist channel.

Or so the poet says outside the poem where he knows no other metric for nature or history. Inside the poem, however, there is, I think, the topological, a truly Heraclitian science.[8] "Space is best mapped topologically, rather than, as has been the Western habit, geometrically," writes Braman (1994),

> the latter is capable only of modelling linear movement or change... [describing] a system at a given moment only in terms of its earlier or later states, meaning geometric mapping can never describe the transformation of a system. Topology... describes qualitative transformations, including discontinuities so severe they transform the system itself.

The jasmine light cannot last, scene is seen but sound is a singularity, a discontinuity, space furled in on itself. The next chapter of the book in the ruins is a stanza that won't stand still. Sounds come to the fore, the curl of quadrille and rustle of trees giving way to what you hear here:

> Or here, this stanza: you hear a goose pen
> Creak, the butterfly of an oil lamp
> Flutters slowly over scrolls and parchment,
> A crucifix, bronze busts. The lines complain
> In plangent rhythms, that desire is vain.

The creaking goose pen, like the Escher hands which draw themselves (themselves now gone over into trade style and T-shirt, greeting card and wallpaper, an icon of recurrence), writes its own plangent lines, a genuine *autopoiesis*. In his *Treatise on Poetry* the butterfly serves Milosz as a sign of the power of recurrence; the boy in that poem (the section is a portrait of the artist as Lithuanian boy logician and poet) "looks upon the butterfly's colors with a wonder that is mute, formless, and hostile to art." Outside the poem Milosz (who is not afraid to say what something means outside the poem) says, "That means he admires the butterfly, but art which was supposed to be an incantation and break that cycle of recurrence... turns out not to have been very effective; the power of recurrence, of the natural order is very strong."[9] Whether this is so we cannot know, even holding it to the light, but it is clear that the butterfly in this poem flutters over icons of recurrence, from Horace's bronze bust to Jesus' cross, from scroll to book, and alights on desire.

I once wrote about electronic text that "our desire is a criticism that lapses before the form and so won't let form return to transparency."[10] I am not wise enough to be able to say what that means exactly but I know I was trying to think about how to talk about the replacement of the author in its double sense: the author moves to another place, the author is put in another place. "We need to surrender control and in that constant declination continually render control meaningless," I went on. The electronic text is such an oscillation, a strange clock which keeps track of space not time, or, if time, what Milosz in the *Treatise on Poetry* calls "Time lifted above time by time."[11]

Place to place within the electronic text place itself is replaced in something like Braman's "qualitative transformations... discontinuities so severe they transform the system itself." So too, in the next chapter of the book of Milosz's poem, "here" replaces "here" in just such a transformation. The earlier line "Here, this stanza" becomes

> Here a city rises. In the market square
> Signboards clang, a stagecoach rumbles in to scare
> A flock of pigeons up.

Not just the birds (these pigeons, like the hawks of the entrance to the poem), but everything (including time itself), is up in the air again. "Under the town clock/ In the tavern, a hand pauses in the stock/ Gesture of arrest" and meanwhile underneath (remember this is a clock in a poem in a chapter of a book in a ruin: remember, remember) meanwhile life goes on, "meanwhile workers walk/ Home from the textile mill, townsfolk talk." The scene here is another metric, the human drama seen as a mechanical clock, and though, as Jay Bolter (1984) reminds us, every such clock is a miniature universe, a recurrence machine, it cannot serve as a measure of mind. "The course of the planets seems unchanging and free of interference, so it can easily be mimicked by a clock," says Bolter, adding in his typical, understated calm, "But the human mind seems more changeable... responding in a variety of ways to new circumstances".

Now while the poem is stopped under the shadow of the outstretched hand, let us use this moment of calm as a place to talk about contours and new circumstances of mind. Previously I have talked about the qualitative transformations in electronic texts in terms of contours, borrowing a geometric term for what I now think I have always really understood topologically, sensually (as a caress) and outside the linear. I meant how the thing (the other) for a long time (under, let's say, an outstretched hand) feels the same and yet changes, the shift of surface to surface within one surface which enacts the perception of flesh or the replacement of electronic text. "If there is a name *surface*," asks the poet Erin Mouré, "then what else is there? is what is 'different' from the surface *depth* or is it *another surface*?"[12]

Contour, in my sense, is one expression of the perceptible form of a constantly changing text, made by any of its readers or writers at a given point in its reading or writing. Its constituent elements include the current state of the text at hand, the perceived intentions and interactions of previous writers and readers which led to the text at hand, and those interactions with the text that the current reader or writer sees as leading from it. Contours are represented by the current reader or writer as a narrative. They are communicated in a set of operations upon the current text which have the effect of transforming that text. Contours are discovered sensually and most often they are read in the visual form of the verbal, graphical, or moving text. These visual forms may include the apparent content of the text at hand; its explicit and available design; or implicit and dynamic designs which the current reader or writer perceives either as patterns, juxtapositions, or recurrences within the text or as abstractions situated outside the text.

Topology is sometimes called "rubber sheet geometry"; we can think perhaps of the supple and gelatinous movement of a jellyfish to animate it. In trying to formulate this provisional definition for contour, I meant to recover this surface to surface and transparent shift which Mouré suggests in lieu of depth as a name for difference. Narrative syntax, like Brancusi's curve, is a syntax of merging and emerging surfaces. Yet even now the whole thing gets caught up and sticks upon a barb, the so-called given point[13] in the claim that contour is "one expression of the perceptible form of a constantly changing text... at a given point in its reading or writing." A point at first, it seems, must be a metric, a measure of a state and not the transformation of a system. The poem senses this, and won't wait much longer for us to tarry in the talk of townsfolk or the calm of new circumstance. We will have to put off this point of transformation, time moves on.

> ... and the hand moves now to evoke
> The fire of justice, a world gone up in smoke,
> The voice quavering with the revenge of ages.

So ends the third of three linked chapters of the book read in the ruins in the poem *A Book in the Ruins*. *Eskhate biblos*. Doom descends in the figure of a man in a tavern whose hands show the final hour. Does this arm's span retrace Leonardo's man as "measure of everything"? Everything seen now smoke, all sounds a quaver.

We are talking about transformations. In his extraordinary, topologically based meditation upon Boccioni, Sanford Kwinter (1992) describes how "in topological manifolds the characteristics of a given mapping are not determined by the quantitative subspace (the grid) below it,"[14] which is, perhaps, to say that a jellyfish's course is not mapped by the seafloor, or by a world gone up in smoke, or by an arm's span or a stanza. Instead Kwinter suggests that the characteristics of the manifold are mapped "in specific 'singularities' of the flow space of which it itself is part." The jellyfish is a form of water we might say. "These singularities," according to Kwinter, "represent critical value or qualitative features that arise at different points within the system depending on what the system is actually doing at a given moment or place...". Scene is seen, the movement of the map makes the mark. Which brings us to the point, the barb of metric, where we left off before the fall of the hand of doom.

"Singularities," says Kwinter, "designate points in any continuous process (if one accepts the dictum that time is real, then every point in the universe can be said to be continually mapped onto itself)...". Print (we remind ourselves) maps itself against the geometric and so stays itself; electronic text, conversely and topologically, replaces itself. What happens at the point of a singularity, says Kwinter, is "that a merely quantitative or linear development suddenly results in the appearance of a 'quality' (that is, a diffeomorphism eventually arises and a point suddenly fails to map onto itself)." Contours, I have said, are discovered sensually and they most often are read in the visual form. "A singularity in a complex flow is what makes a rainbow appear in the mist," says Kwinter. "So the world seems to drift from these pages," the poem goes on

> Like the mist clearing on a field at dawn.
> Only when two times, two forms are drawn
> Together and their legibility
> Disturbed, do you see that immortality
> Is not very different from the present
> And is for its sake.

In an instant – the interstice of line to line in a poem, the turn of page in a book in the ruins – the smoke of a world gone up becomes a mist, last hours become the awkward light of dawn. We are back to the boy and the butterfly but now the problem of recurrence maps immortality on the present. Twin time is twined, and so less lonely.[15] The search is for the diffeomorphism: where the legibility of two drawn on two is derailed; where immortality differs, though not very much, from now; and where therefore the idea of everything is no more privileged than the idea of any thing.

When I was a boy, I spoke like a boy, Saint Paul reminds us. Previously I tried to speak of the diffeomorphism of electronic text in terms of coextensivity and depth, where coextensivity is our ability to reach any other contour from some point of a hypertext, that is, the degree of impingement and dissolution among elements of a hypertext. Borrowing from Deleuze and Guattari (1983), I suggested that coextensivity is the manner of being for space. As a boy in this, I didn't know the names for the topological, and probably meant the jellyfish.

Depth was a more difficult thing, and shows itself as such in this poem. I characterized it then as the contour-to-contour inscriptions or links which precede, follow, or reside at any interstice along the current contour of a hypertext. Depth, I wanted to suggest – borrowing the second half of Deleuze and Guattari's formulation – is the manner of being in space, the capacity for replacement among elements of a hypertext. Our eyes, I said, read depth as the dimension of absence or indefiniteness which opens to further discourse and other morphological forms of desire. Like any boy, I probably did not know what I meant by depth or desire; I meant the flow space or the jellyfish as a form of water, but instead named petals on the starfish, points upon a grid.

The poem, however, has the word right. We are talking about form. Smoke into mist is a morphogenetic system, which, as Braman explains, "because [they] destroy form as well as create it... are also described [following Prigogine] as dissipative structures." Braman points again to Kwinter and I look along with her (scene is seen):[16]

> Catastrophe theory recognizes that every event (or form) enfolds... a multiplicity of forces and is the result of not one, but many different causes... Any state of the system at which things are momentarily stable... represents a form. States and forms, then, are exactly the same thing... In fact, forms represent nothing absolute, but rather structurally stable moments within a system's evolution... paradoxically [emerging at] a moment of structural instability.

The electronic text is a dissipative (belief) structure, and the reader is apt to believe that its states and forms are exactly the same thing. The electronic text thus embodies a multiplicity of forces in the associational schema which it presents. Contours are not forms in the text, the author or the reader, but rather those moments which express relationships among them in the form of the reader as writer. Originally I wanted to isolate coextensivity and depth in order to locate the place where the reader truly writes the text, the interstitial, which I now see as the "diffeomorphism [where] a point suddenly fails to map onto itself." The ability to perceive this point (we can call it form) makes genuine interactivity possible. It gives us some place both to move in and move the text; it thus replaces the author in the double sense of replacement.

We are talking about interaction. Replacement is the interaction which occurs when what Umberto Eco (1989) calls the "structural strategy" of an open work[17] becomes available for reinscription. For Eco, writing about interactive media in its earliest, serial epoch

> the possibilities which the work's openness makes available always work within a given field of relations... the *work in movement* is the possibility of numerous personal interventions, but it is not an amorphous invitation to indiscriminate participation. The invitation offers the performer the chance of oriented insertion into something which always remains the world intended by the author.

Eco's author places us, "the author offers... the performer... a work to be completed... It will not be a different work... a form which is [the author's] form will have been organized, even though... assembled by an outside party in a particular way he could not have foreseen." Electronic text can never be completed; at best its closure maps point on point until time is linear and the text stays itself, becoming print.

But when a point suddenly fails to map onto itself, the author is replaced. Replacement of the author turns performer to author. The world intended by the author is a place of encounter where we continually create the future as a dissipative structure: the chance of oriented insertion becomes the moment of structural instability, the interstitial link wherein we enact the replacement of one writing by another.

Seen through the poet's eyes, I said earlier, four chapters follow from the book in the ruins: we have seen three linked, now comes a fourth, marked by a scission and wounded. The fourth as we reach it is, like the first, lovers' meeting outside time. What cuts the caesura here, however, is shrapnel, an actual fragment

> Disturbed, do you see that immortality
> Is not very different from the present
> And is for its sake. You pick a fragment
> Of grenade which pierced the body of a song
> On Daphnis and Chloe. And you long,
> Ruefully, to have a talk with her,
> As if it were what life prepared you for.

I want to speak carefully. I do not mean to suggest a cheap analogy, or to misappropriate the form of what might seem a fairly straightforward and romantic, even classic, poem; but what follows with Chloe is directly interactive. You can see it as a trope, an apostrophe; it is nonetheless the singularity which follows (here quite literally) a catastrophe, what life prepares us for. "How is it," the poet asks the woman in the fragment of the poem in a book in the ruin fragmented by a real grenade, "How is it, Chloe, that your pretty skirt/Is torn so badly by the winds that hurt/Real people...?"

This is a question of forms beyond the book. Thus in the verse which follows, unscathed by what wounds her, Chloe – "who, in eternity, sing[s] / the hours, sun in [her] hair appearing/ And disappearing" – here runs beyond the book and through the actual landscape, where real oak groves burn beside forests of machinery and concrete, pursued by the voice of the poet (a Daphnis we could say gone daffy with longing and grief):

> How is it that your breasts
> Are pierced by shrapnel, and the oak groves burn,
> While you, charmed, not caring at all, turn
> To run through forests of machinery and concrete
> And haunt us with the echoes of your feet?

In the old forms it is supposed to end in a wedding, this pastoral. The lovers are supposed to be replaced in their homes, restored to their parents, wedded and fed. The poet, sure enough, attempts it. "If there is such an eternity, lush/ Though short-lived, that's enough," he says, but his own question cannot sustain the possibility of this form and muffles himself, "But how... hush!" the line ends.

Though not the poem. A marriage still took place here, albeit an ambiguous one, and so the banquet which follows is equally ambiguous. It is a marriage of life and forms beyond the book, writer and reader (the writer who will be). The groom makes a formal speech, it isn't clear to whom (it isn't clear now to whom he's been talking all along):

> We were predestined to live when the scene
> Grows dim and the outline of the Greek ruin
> Blackens the sky. It is noon, and wandering
> Through a dark building, you see workers sitting
> Down to a fire a narrow ray of sunlight
> Kindles on the floor. They have dragged out
> Heavy books and made a table of them
> And begun to cut their bread. In good time
> A tank will rattle past, a streetcar chime.

It isn't clear. Scene is seen. Noon is made dark by a ruin other than the one the poet is wandering through, a ruin in a romance outside time. Its darkness is illuminated by a fire kindled by sunlight other than that which, appearing and disappearing, marks the hours in the hair of the girl who lives beyond time. Perhaps the books are burning. Perhaps the books become an altar where the workmen cut their bread. Perhaps "in good time" the books (in time) lift time above time like sacramental bread. Who can know? Ask Milosz, perhaps he will tell you what this means. In Polish the poem ends on fingersnap, two words: *Tak Proste*, "that simple," which the Milosz/Haas translation folds into the ambiguity of "in good time."[18] Scene is seen but sound is a singularity, a discontinuity, space furled in on itself. Tank rattles, streetcar chimes, that simple.

I should end this there, borrowing against the rhythm and parabola of the poem, its apparent closure. I should end this here but I won't yet (though soon enough) because print stays but electronic text is spaces. Again I want to speak carefully. Again I want to speak of forms beyond the book. I want to leave off (not end) in another space, it too a library of sorts (though some would say a ruin), one in which I confess, though I am in some sense among its authors, I am as baffled and multiple and lost, as much replaced as Milosz is here in my reading of him.

Hotel MOO is an electronic space, a textual virtual reality (VR) if you will (MOO stands for MUD Objected Oriented, and MUD in turn for Multi-User Dungeon or Dimension).[19] There are literally hundreds of these virtual spaces throughout the world where anyone who has a computer connected to the Internet can come and move through the written space in real time in the presence of others who write the space they read with their actions, their objects, and their interactions with each other on the screen. This particular virtual space is the creation of a Brown University student programmer and poet named Tom Meyer, who built a structure (of words, everything I talk about from now on is made of words) upon the structure (the programming language for LambdaMOO) created in turn by Pavel Curtis of PARC upon the structure created by another student, Steven White, at the University of Waterloo some years ago. What Tom Meyer did was build a way that hypertext structures created in Storyspace (a program developed by Jay Bolter, John B. Smith, and myself) could become rooms in a MOO, their links doors or corridors (or windows) between them, each room a text to be read as well as written, and a place where at any time a reader could encounter another and a text change (seen is scene) before one's eyes. Hotel, the eponymous structure for this MOO, is a hypertext created (and continuing to be created) by Robert Coover, his students and others over the past few years, first in a hypertext system called Intermedia,[20] now lost (these genealogies, as we have been reminded by Foucault, themselves inhabitable structures and open to time), and then in Storyspace. In the months since, other stories have appended themselves like ramshackle additions to the lobby. A hypertext critical edition of David Blair's videotape *WAX: Or the Discovery of Television among the Bees* is, hivelike, being built there; a women's collaborative hypertext project, Hi-Pitched Voices, has linked stories under a yonic roof with corridors made of sestinas.

But the first time I was there, in the place where I sat in what is called RL, real life, it was two in the morning (though the MOO has no obvious time). Hotel MOO was new and there were only the original stories. I entered the lobby of the hotel by typing my character name and typing where I wished to go. I was alone there at that hour. I went to the Penthouse Bordello where a man and a woman both propositioned me (in fully developed, comically obscene dialogue). Robert

Coover was also there (but, like the man and woman, in a story, a written self). I declined the advances of both man and woman, left the virtual Coover to eternally tell his life story, and took one of the "obvious exits," finding myself, surprisingly, delightedly, in a place between the walls of the hotel rooms, inhabited only by the rats (one of whom has written his or her own epic in another space) and by the hotel engineer, a man named Crotty, whose story I unexpectedly found myself in (a story which was written, in the pseudo-Joycean protolingo of chaosmos, by me nearly a year before when I had visited Brown and was invited to put my mark in their hypertext). It was a shock to see myself there and I was still in it when suddenly someone in real time asked me a question. She had come upon me without my knowing (you can find out who is in the MOO with you by typing a question, but when I'd come in there was no one; now too when you enter a room you can ask it to tell you how many authors it has had and what their names are).

"Hi, I'm new here," the person said, we will call her Chloe (though this is the truth and she did really appear there, the reader as writer, typing somewhere elsewhere in the real of what once was my text), "Can you show me around?"

James Joyce could not be here with us today. Pavel Curtis wants to call the MOO a "social virtual reality" and in his current effort at PARC, Project Jupiter, a multimedia MOO, to approach Joyce's ineluctable modality of the visible. "Every space within the virtual world would be a place where people could display text, bulletin boardstyle," the *Wired* reporter (the ambiguity is their trade style) reports, "But people who were present in the same virtual room, no matter where they were in the physical world" ("Chloe," I say, though it could be Gerty McDowell), "could choose to be in audio or video contact." "Signatures of all things I am here to read, seaspawn and sea wrack, the nearing tide, that rusty boot," that last is my cousin Stephen Daedalus speaking in a book, it too a library of sorts (though some would say a ruin).[21] Actually he's writing in his mind there, moving along a strand and thinking of signs. What he reads he writes.

"In the course of what is seen the writer is replaced by the reader (the writer who will be)," I said this in another time (it was now, earlier in the space of this text), extending the claim of constructive hypertext to any system of electronic text, including virtual reality or (Russell's paradox notwithstanding) ubicomp. This claim is not merely meant to extend the dominion of the word within the universe of the visible and the sensual. It means also to point toward an inherent paradox, built into both the conception and the technology of virtual reality (both, of course, mapping onto themselves as one point), and which for now, and perhaps forever, makes it an alchemy. (Though there will ever be alchemists, a scientist in Texas even now attempts to work mercury to gold[22] and in a recent book Michael Heim [1993] suggests that "ultimate promise of VR" – "the Holy Grail" he says later – "may be to transform, to redeem our awareness of reality – something that the highest art has attempted to do.")

More calmly, Jay Bolter claims that in VR "the viewer gains in a mathematical sense more degrees of freedom. Like hypertext, virtual reality invites the user to occupy as many perspectives as possible."[23] Yet VR in some sense diminishes whatever the mathematical gain of degrees of freedom by insisting on the unification of all these perspectives within self-generating computer spaces meant to reproduce the illusory seamlessness of the aural, visual, and psychological world as thing. Freedom in my construction comes from replacement, the ability to scan and skip. VR attempts to subsume the point where point fails to map into the seamless. Against the backdrop of VR's infantile seamlessness, on the hierarchical stage set of the sensorium, the old drama plays, meaning by gaps (Lacan) or defamiliarization (Schlovsky), by "betweenus" (Cixous), by situated knowledges (Haraway), or by my interstitial.[24]

The interdeterminability of points of perception[25] argues against a virtual reality which depends, as most do, upon successive disclosures of self-generating spaces. The last time I was in actual virtual reality,[26] no sooner had I donned the helmet than I went running full speed for the edges of the representation, boundary testing, bursting through, blowing away the whole wire-frame world into a landscape of countless, brilliant ruby dice, each spinning letter or numeral a particle of the code, each an error exception.

To be sure, before long there will be (there already are) virtual worlds which can contain us wherever we run. But they too will be a structure of words, everything we will see from now on is made of words: scene is seen, text is useless, thus its use. On a Vassar farm in virtual space, or on a Dublin strand, a woman walks toward me and passes, for all I know wordlessly, yet I believe that she too creates the space she walks through and that it is somehow different from mine.

That is, there is no point from which to see, even in three space, each new point in its own multiple perspectives. Gridded VR, driven by vision, misses the point which fails to map upon itself, the new thing, Milosz's barrier at the entrance, or the gate when (not where) you go in.

Notes

[1] This paper was given as a talk on July 28, 1994 in San Marino at "The Future of the Book," a conference cosponsored by Umberto Eco's International Center for Semotic and Cognitive Studies and the Rank Xerox Research Centre of Grenoble. I am grateful to Vassar College, and especially Professor Barbara Page and Dean of Faculty Nancy Schrom Dye, who welcomed and housed me as Randolph Distinguished Professor of English while, among other things, I completed this paper. All quotations from *A Book in the Ruins* are from Milosz (1988) and, as noted in the text above, this poem was translated by Milosz with Robert Haas.

[2] In Rheingold (1994).

[3] In Czarnecka and Fiut (1987).

[4] I wish to note here my deep indebtedness to Sandra Braman's paper. For years a number of people I respect (especially John McDaid and David Porush) have tried both directly and indirectly to get me to understand second-order cybernetics, catastrophe theory, and autopoiesis. Perhaps all this tutoring finally took when I read Braman's paper, though I think it was something more than this. I not only owe my discussion of topology to her paper, I also owe my reading (chapter and verse, her citations mine) of Kwinter (1992). In a similar acknowledgment in his *Electronic Word* (1993), Richard Lanham suggests that he "does not come by [a certain quotation] honestly," a statement which (however tongue in academic cheek) puzzled me in a book which addresses the nature of electronic text, which is nothing if it is not that prickly flower, the clinging nettle. I came by my discussion of Kwinter quite honestly from Braman; I learned from her poetic and incisive writing and continue to do so.

[5] My EESLA encyclopedia entry, "Hypertext and Hypermedia," collected in Joyce (1994) begins, "Hypertext is, before anything else, a visual form." Bolter (1991) is by far the best introduction to electronic writing issues. Landow (1992) builds upon and extends Bolter's framework in important ways.

[6] Much of the discussion of electronic text in this vicinity (and indeed much of the language) has migrated from other texts and talks (especially "A feel for prose: Interstitial links and the contours of hypertext"), many of them collected in Joyce (1994). In the "Introduction" to that collection I argue as follows (aware that some might see such an argument for electronic text as an apologia for well-wrought sloth): "What is... increasingly characteristic of the late age of print... is that before, during, and after they were talks or essays, these narratives were often email messages, hypertext "nodes," and other kinds of electronic text which, as will be seen, moved nomadically and iteratively from one talk to another, one draft to another, one occasion or

perspective to another. The nomadic movement of ideas is made effortless by the electronic medium which makes it easy to cross borders (or erase them) with the swipe of a mouse, carrying as much of the world as you will on the etched arrow of light that makes up a cursor. At each crossing a world of possibility can be spewed out in whole or in kernel, like the cosmogonic dragon's teeth of myth. Each iteration 'breathes life into a narrative of possibilities', as Jane Yellowlees Douglas says of hypertext fiction, so that in the 'third or fourth encounter with the same place, the immediate encounter remains the same as the first, [but] what changes is [our] understanding'. The text becomes a present tense palimpsest where what shines through are not past versions but potential, alternate views."

[7] In the following pages Czarnecka brings up the confluence of Hegel and Heraclitus (and the Thomist contrary) directly, asking whether the poet means "Becoming" in the Heraclitian sense of the word as constant flow. To which Milosz replies, "It's pure Hegelianism" and then quotes a section from the poem which begins "O Antithesis which ripens into Thesis."

[8] Kwinter (1992) suggests that "catastrophe theory is a fundamentally Heraclitian 'science' in that it recognizes that all form is the result of strife and conflict."

[9] In Czarnecka and Fiut (1987).

[10] Collected in Joyce (1994). "The momentary advantage of our own awkwardness" was presented as a performance piece at the 1992 MLA convention session "Hypertext, hypermedia: Defining a fictional form."

[11] Kwinter (1992) discusses how with Poincaré: "Time... reappeared in the world as something real, as a destablizing but creative milieu; it was seen to suffuse everything, to bear each thing along, generating it and degenerating it in the process."

[12] In *Furious* (Mouré 1988) the collection of poems is followed by a section "The Acts," which is both an extraordinary poetic manifesto ("it's the way people use language makes me furious") and also a protohypertext linked to various poems by footnotes. The quotation here is from this linked section (and underlining is as it is in the original). Mouré's poetry seems to me hypertextual, especially the poems in Mouré (1989).

[13] Caught upon such a point, it is natural to think of Derrida's meditation on the question of style: "It is always a question of a pointed object. Sometimes only a pen, but just as well a stylet, or even a dagger. With their help, to be sure, we can resolutely attack all that philosophy calls forth under the name of matter or matrix, so as to stave a mark in it, leave an impression or form; but these implements also help us to repel a threatening force, to keep it at bay, to repress and guard against it – all the while bending back or doubling up, in flight, keeping us hidden or veiled... Style will jut out then, like a spur, like the spur of an old sailing vessel: like the rostrum, the prong that goes out in front to break the attack and cleave open the opposing surface. Or again, always in the nautical sense, like the point of a rock that is also called a spur and that 'breaks up waves at the entrance to a harbour'." (Derrida 1985)

[14] The quotations from Kwinter (1992) woven through this and the following paragraph are from the same page (58) and (I wish to note again) I first found cited so in Braman (1994). Lanham (1993) also goes back to the Futurists. His essay "Digital rhe-

toric and the digital arts" (29-52) launches itself Marinetti's *Futurist Manifesto* (and a less well-known tract *La cinematografia futurista* from which he translates the following malediction: "The book, the most traditional means of preserving and communicating thought, has been for a long time destined to disappear, just like cathedrals, walled battlements, museums, and the ideal of pacifism...") and works his way in almost effortless, and copiously illustrated, fashion to a discussion of why electronic text is like Christo's *Running Fence*.

[15] This sentence plays on a literal translation of the Polish metaphor which I owe to personal communication with the Milosz scholar and translator Regina Grol-Prokopczyk, professor of comparative literature at Empire State College in Buffalo, NY. The verb (*splota*) has the sense of twisting strands of a cord around together (twining) until their legibility is blurred. The twining is also (re) enacted in the Polish where eternity is said never to be lonely because it connects with the day in a double-stranded way: the phrase (*i po to*) having both the sense of "connected with day and for it(s sake)" as well as "connected with day just as well ('for that too')." That Milosz and Haas chose a metaphor of inscription for the English here seems telling.

[16] The quotation which follows is from Kwinter (1992). The italics are in the original.

[17] For over a decade now (beginning with my first writing on these matters, "Selfish interaction: Subversive texts and the multiple novel" collected in Joyce 1994), I have proposed in a number of talks and papers that Eco's open work and the notion of "oriented insertion" prefigure the transformation of reader to writer in constructive hypertext. Following one such talk – to the infamous, unruly, and influential CHUG group at Brown University – Robert Scholes' persistent and generous questions prodded me (rather unsuccessfully I must say, since I remained cheerfully utopian and dim about it all) to account for differences between the open text and the constructive hypertext. Even so I was (and am) grateful for his prodding, so much so I tried to account the differences more clearly here. The truth is that when I wrote "Selfish interaction" I foresaw no difference between Eco's open work and the multiple fiction; but we had not built a hypertext system then. Nor had I experienced my students' apprehension of constructive hypertext or myself written hyperfiction.

[18] Again I owe this insight to Regina Grol-Prokopczyk. She also points out that in the Polish the workmen place (rather than, as here, cut) the bread upon the table of books. The Milosz/Haas translation thus emphasizes the scissions of this poem of scissions.

[19] Hotel MOO is an electronic space, a textual virtual reality and you can go there, if you know how, with Crotty and Coover and Chloe and Tom Meyer and HI-Pitched Voices by telnet to <count.cs.brown edu8888>.

[20] See Landow (1992) for a rich account of this Atlantis.

[21] My cousin Stephen Daedalus speaking in a book and seeking "signatures of all things I am here to read" appears, one hopes it goes without saying, in James Joyce's *Ulysses*, a different family of Joyce in every way (he, the master) from me.

[22] See Mangan (1994) for the (fleet-footed) frontier details.

[23] Personal communication (1994).

[24] These instances of notions of interdeterminability (scan and skip) are cited above (except for Lacan, who like Foucault earlier, is cited from the aether – while the unseen and surrounding Chaos is, of course, Nietzsche). The specific essays are Haraway (1991) and Cixous' "Clarice Lispector: The approach" in Cixous (1991). Benjamin Sher, making the stone stony, wants to translate Shlovsky's neologism (Russian: *ostraniene*) with the neologism "enstrangement" though no one much wants to follow, including Gerald Bruns who writes the introduction. (As an aside, Derrida, in the process of being called upon to defend, among other things, the study of his own death in the *New York Times Magazine* interview in January 1994, reports that the best translation is, as one might have guessed, deconstruction.)

[25] I first used this neologism in a very similar sentence in "What happens as we go? Hypertext contour, interactive cinema, virtual reality, and the interstitial arts of Jeffrey Shaw and Grahame Weinbren" in Joyce (1994). Perhaps I had in mind Haraway's *Situated Knowledges* (1991): "All these pictures of the world should not be allegories of infinite mobility and interchangeability, but of elaborate specificity and difference and the loving care people might take to learn how to see faithfully from another's point of view, even when the other is our own machine".

[26] The last time I was in actual virtual reality was at Andy Van Dam's Brown University Computer Graphics Group, which is managed by a wonderful friend of artists, Daniel Robbins who was very tolerant, and even a little amused by my cheap trick of ruby dice, which I must emphasize did not in any way really "break" their program but rather simply went outside the events it was prepared to handle visually.

References

BOLTER, J.D.

1984 *Turing's Man: Western Culture in the Computer Age*, Chapel Hill: University of North Carolina Press.

1991 *Writing Space: The Computer, Hypertext, and the History of Writing*, Hillsdale: Lawrence Erlbaum and Associates.

BRAMAN, S.

1994 "The autopoietic state: Communication and democratic potential in the net," *Journal of the American Society of Information Scientists*.

CIXOUS, H.

1991 *Coming to Writing and Other Essays*, Cambridge (Mass.): Harvard University Press.

CZARNECKA, E., AND FIUT, A.

1987 *Conversations with Czeslaw Milosz*, New York: Harcourt Brace Jovanovich.

DELEUZE, G., AND GUATTARI, F.

1983 "The smooth and the striated," in *A Thousand Plateaus: Capitalism and Schizophrenia*, Minneapolis: University of Minnesota Press.

DERRIDA, J.
1985 "The question of style," in D.B. Allison (ed.), *The New Nietzsche*, Cambridge (Mass.): The MIT Press.

ECO, U.
1989 *The Open Work*, Cambridge (Mass.): Harvard University Press.

HARAWAY, D.
1991 "Situated knowledges: The science question in feminism and the privilege of partial perspective," in *Simians, Cyborgs and Women*, New York: Routledge.

HEIM, M.
1993 *The Metaphysics of Virtual Reality*, New York: Oxford University Press.

JOYCE, M.
1994 *Of Two Minds: Hypertext Pedagogy and Poetics*, Ann Arbor: University of Michigan Press.

KWINTER, S.
1992 "Landscapes of change: Boccioni's *Stati d'animo* as a general theory of models," *Assemblage*, 19: 55-65.

LANDOW, G.
1992 *Hypertext: The Convergence of Contemporary Critical Theory and Technology*, Baltimore: Johns Hopkins University Press.

LANHAM, R.
1993 *The Electronic Word: Democracy, Technology and the Arts*, Chicago: University of Chicago Press.

MANGAN, K.S.
1994 "A&M's alchemy caper," *Chronicle of Higher Education*, January 19: A19.

MILOSZ, C.
1988 *The Collected Poems*, New York: The Eco Press.

MOURÉ, E.
1988 *FURIOUS*, Toronto: Anansi.
1989 *WSW* (*West South West*), Montreal: Véhicule Press.

RHEINGOLD, H.
1994 "PARC is BACK!", *Wired* 2.2: 90-95.

SHKLOVSKY, V.
1929/1990 *Theory of Prose*, Elmwood Park, N.J.: Dalkey Archive Press.

Umberto Eco

AFTERWORD

Since my arrival at the symposium on the future of the book I have been expecting somebody to quote "Ceci tuera cela." Both Duguid and Nunberg have obliged me. The quotation is not irrelevant to our topic.

As you no doubt remember, in Hugo's *Hunchback of Notre Dame*, Frollo, comparing a book with his old cathedral, says: "Ceci tuera cela" (The book will kill the cathedral, the alphabet will kill images). McLuhan, comparing a Manhattan discotheque to the Gutenberg Galaxy, said "Ceci tuera cela." One of the main concerns of this symposium has certainly been that *ceci* (the computer) *tuera cela* (the book).

We know enough about *cela* (the book), but it is uncertain what is meant by *ceci* (computer). An instrument by which a lot of communication will be provided more and more by icons? An instrument on which you can write and read without needing a paperlike support? A medium through which it will be possible to have unheard-of hypertextual experiences?

None of these definitions is sufficient to characterize the computer as such. First, visual communication is more overwhelming in TV, cinema, and advertising than in computers, which are also, and eminently, alphabetic tools. Second, as Nunberg has suggested, the computer "creates new modes of production and diffusion of printed documents." And third, as Simone has reminded us, some sort of hypertextual experience (at least in the sense of text that doesn't have to be read in a linear way and as a finished message) existed in other historical periods, and Joyce (the living one) is here to prove that Joyce (the dead and everlasting one) gave us with *Finnegans Wake* a good example of hypertextual experience.

The idea that something will kill something else is a very ancient one, and came certainly before Hugo and before the late medieval fears of Frollo. According to Plato (in the *Phaedrus*) Theut, or Hermes, the alleged inventor of writing, presents his invention to the pharaoh Thamus, praising his new technique that will allow human beings to remember what they would otherwise forget. But the pharaoh is not so satisfied. My skillful Theut, he says, memory is a great gift that ought to be kept alive by training it continuously. With your invention people will not be obliged any longer to train memory. They will remember things not because of an internal effort, but by mere virtue of an external device.

We can understand the pharaoh's worry. Writing, as any other new technological device, would have made torpid the human power that it replaced and reinforced – just as cars made us less able to walk. Writing was dangerous because it decreased the powers of mind by offering human beings a petrified soul, a caricature of mind, a vegetal memory.

Plato's text is ironical, naturally. Plato was writing down his argument against writing. But he was pretending that his discourse was related by Socrates, who did not write (it seems academically obvious that he perished because he did not publish). Therefore Plato was expressing a fear that still survived in his day. Thinking is an internal affair; the real thinker would not allow books to think instead of him.

Nowadays, nobody shares these fears, for two very simple reasons. First of all, we know that books are not ways of making somebody else think in our place; on the contrary they are machines that provoke further thoughts. Only after the invention of writing was it possible to write such a masterpiece on spontaneous memory as Proust's *Recherche du temps perdu*. Second, if once upon a time people needed to train their memory in order to remember things, after the invention of writing they had also to train their memory in order to remember books. Books challenge and improve memory; they do not narcotize it.

One is entitled to speculate about that old debate every time one meets a new communication tool which pretends or seems to substitute for books. In the course of this symposium, under the rubric of "the future of the book," the following different items have been discussed, and not all of them were concerned with books.

1. Images versus alphabetic culture

Our contemporary culture is not specifically image oriented. Take for instance Greek or medieval culture: at those times literacy was reserved to a restricted élite and most people were educated, informed, persuaded (religiously, politically, ethically) though images. Even *USA Today*, cited by Bolter, represents a balanced mixture of icons and letters, if we compare it with a *Biblia Pauperum*. We can complain that a lot of people spend their day watching TV and never read a book or a newspaper, and this is certainly a social and educational problem, but frequently we forget that the same people, a few centuries ago, were watching at most a few standard images and were totally illiterate.

We are frequently misled by a "mass media criticism of mass media" which is superficial and regularly belated. Mass media are still repeating that our historical period is and will be more and more dominated by images. That was the first McLuhan fallacy, and mass media people have read McLuhan too late. The present and the forthcoming young generation is and will be a computer-oriented generation. The main feature of a computer screen is that it hosts and displays more alphabetic letters than images. The new generation will be alphabetic and not image oriented. We are coming back to the Gutenberg Galaxy again, and I am sure that if McLuhan had survived until the Apple rush to the Silicon Valley, he would have acknowledged this portentous event.

Moreover, the new generation is trained to read at an incredible speed. An old-fashioned university professor is today incapable of reading a computer screen at the same speed as a teenager. These same teenagers, if by chance they want to program their own home computer, must know, or learn, logical procedures and algorithms, and must type words and numbers on a keyboard, at a great speed.

In the course of the eighties some worried and worrying reports have been published in the United States on the decline of literacy. One of the reasons for the last Wall Street crash (which sealed the end of the Reagan era) was, according to many observers, not only the exaggerated confidence in computers but also the fact that none of the yuppies who were controlling the stock market knew enough about the 1929 crisis. They were unable to deal with a crisis because of their lack of historical information. If they had read some books about Black Thursday they would have been able to make better decisions and avoid many well-known pitfalls.

But I wonder if books would have been the only reliable vehicle for acquiring information. Years ago the only way to learn a foreign language (outside of traveling abroad) was to study a language from a book. Now our children frequently learn other languages by listening to records, by watching movies in the original edition, or by deciphering the instructions printed on a beverage can. The same happens with geographical information. In my childhood I got the best of my information about exotic countries not from textbooks but by reading adventure novels (Jules Verne, for instance, or Emilio Salgari or Karl May). My kids very early knew more than I on the same subject from watching TV and movies.

The illiteracy of Wall Street yuppies was not only due to an insufficient exposure to books but also to a form of visual illiteracy. Books about the 1929 crisis exist and are still regularly published (the yuppies must be blamed for not having been bookstore goers), while television and the cinema are practically unconcerned with any rigorous revisitation of historical events. One could learn very well the story of the Roman Empire through movies, provided that movies were historically correct. The fault of Hollywood is not to have opposed its movies to the books of Tacitus or of Gibbon, but rather to have imposed a pulp- and romancelike version of both Tacitus and Gibbon. The problem with the yuppies is not only that they watch TV instead of reading books; it is that Public Broadcasting is the only place where somebody knows who Gibbon was.

Today the concept of literacy comprises many media. An enlightened policy of literacy must take into account the possibilities of all of these media. Educational concern must be extended to the whole of media. Responsibilities and tasks must be carefully balanced. If for learning languages, tapes are better than books, take care of cassettes. If a presentation of Chopin with commentary on compact disks helps people to understand Chopin, don't worry if people do not buy five volumes of the history of music. Even if it were true that today visual communication overwhelms written communication the problem is not to oppose written to visual communication. The problem is how to improve both. In the Middle Ages visual communication was, for the masses, more important than writing. But Chartres cathedral was not culturally inferior to the *Imago Mundi* of Honorius of Autun. Cathedrals were the TV of those times, and the difference from our TV was that the directors of the medieval TV read good books, had a lot of imagination, and worked for the public benefit (or, at least, for what they believed to be the public benefit).

2. Books versus other supports

There is a confusion about two distinct questions: (a) will computers made books obsolete? and (b) will computers make written and printed material obsolete?

Let us suppose that computers will make books disappear (I do not think this will happen and I shall elaborate later on this point, but let us suppose so for the sake of the argument). Still, this would not entail the disappearance of printed material. We have seen that it was wishful thinking to hope that computers, and particularly word processors, would have helped to save trees. Computers encourage the production of printed material. We can imagine a culture in which there will be no books, and yet where people go around with tons and tons of unbound sheets of paper. This will be quite unwieldy, and will pose a new problem for libraries.

Debray has observed that the fact that Hebrew civilization was a civilization based upon a book is not independent of the fact that it was a nomadic civilization. I think that this remark is very important. Egyptians could carve their records on stone obelisks, Moses could not. If you want to cross the Red Sea, a book is a more practical instrument for recording wisdom. By the way, another nomadic civilization, the Arabic one, was based upon a book, and privileged writing upon images.

But books also have an advantage with respect to computers. Even if printed on acid paper, which lasts only seventy years or so, they are more durable than magnetic supports. Moreover, they do not suffer power shortages and blackouts, and are more resistant to shocks. As Bolter remarked, "it is unwise to try to predict technological change more than few years in advance," but it is certain that, up to now at least, books still represent the most economical, flexible, wash-and-wear way to transport information at a very low cost.

Electronic communication travels ahead of you, books travel with you and at your speed, but if you are shipwrecked on a desert island, a book can be useful, while a computer cannot – as Landow remarks, electronic texts need a reading station and a decoding device. Books are still the best companions for a shipwreck, or for the Day After.

I am pretty sure that new technologies will render obsolete many kinds of books, like encyclopedias and manuals. Take for example the Encyclomedia project developed by Horizons Unlimited. When finished it will probably contain more information than the *Encyclopedia*

Britannica (or Treccani or Larousse), with the advantage that it permits cross-references and nonlinear retrieval of information. The whole of the compact disks, plus the computer, will occupy one-fifth of the space occupied by an encyclopedia. The encyclopedia cannot be transported as the CD-ROM can, and cannot be easily updated; it does not have the practical advantages of a normal book, therefore it can be replaced by a CD-ROM, just a phone book can. The shelves today occupied, at my home as well as in public libraries, by meters and meters of encyclopedia volumes could be eliminated in the next age, and there will be no reason to lament their disappearance. For the same reason today I no longer need a heavy portrait painted by an indifferent artist, for I can send my sweetheart a glossy and faithful photograph. Such a change in the social functions of painting has not made painting obsolete, not even the realistic paintings of Annigoni, which do not fulfill the function of portraying a person, but of celebrating an important person, so that the commissioning, the purchasing, and the exhibition of such portraits acquire aristocratic connotations.

Books will remain indispensable not only for literature, but for any circumstance in which one needs to read carefully, not only to receive information but also to speculate and to reflect about it.

To read a computer screen is not the same as to read a book. Think of the process of learning how to use a piece of software. Usually the system is able to display on the screen all the instructions you need. But the users who want to learn the program generally either print the instructions and read them as if they were in book form, or they buy a printed manual (let me skip over the fact that currently all the manuals that come with a computer, on-line or off-line, are obviously written by irresponsible and tautological idiots, while commercial handbooks are written by intelligent people). It is possible to conceive of a visual program that explains very well how to print and bind a book, but in order to get instructions on how to write such a computer program, we need a printed manual.

After having spent no more than twelve hours at a computer console, my eyes are like two tennis balls, and I feel the need to sit comfortably down in an armchair and read a newspaper, or maybe a good poem. It seems to me that computers are diffusing a new form of literacy but are incapable of satisfying all the intellectual needs they are stimulating. In my periods of optimism I dream of a computer generation which, compelled to read a computer screen, gets acquainted with reading from a screen, but at a certain moment feels unsatisfied and looks for a different, more relaxed, and differently-committing form of reading.

3. Publishing versus communicating

People desire to communicate with one another. In ancient communities they did it orally; in a more complex society they tried to do it by printing. Most of the books which are displayed in a bookstore should be defined as products of vanity presses, even if they are published by an university press. As Landow suggests we are entering a new samizdat era. People can communicate directly without the intermediation of publishing houses. A great many people do not want to publish; they simply want to communicate with each other. The fact that in the future they will do it by E-mail or over the Internet will be a great boon for books and for the culture and the market of the book. Look at a bookstore. There are too many books. I receive too many books every week. If the computer network succeeds in reducing the quantity of published books, this would be a paramount cultural improvement.

One of the most common objections to the pseudoliteracy of computers is that young people get more and more accustomed to speak through cryptic short formulas: *dir*, *help*, *diskcopy*. *error 67*, and so on. Is that still literacy? I am a rare-book collector, and I feel delighted when I read the seventeenth-century titles that took one page and sometimes more. They look like the titles of Lina Wertmuller's movies. The introductions were several pages long. They started with elaborate courtesy formulas praising the ideal addressee, usually an emperor or a pope, and lasted for pages and pages explaining in a very baroque style the purposes and the virtues of the text to follow. If baroque writers read our contemporary scholarly books they would be horrified. Introductions are one-page long, briefly outline the subject matter of the book, thank some national or international endowment for a generous grant, shortly explain that the book has been made possible by the love and understanding of a wife or husband and of some children, and credit a secretary for having patiently typed the manuscript. We understand perfectly the whole of human and academic ordeals revealed by those few lines, the hundreds of nights spent underlining photocopies, the innumerable frozen hamburgers eaten in a hurry...

But I imagine that in the near future we will have three lines saying "W/c, Smith, Rockefeller," which we will decode as "I thank my wife and my children; this book was patiently revised by Professor Smith, and was made possible by the Rockefeller Foundation." That would be as eloquent as a baroque introduction. It is a problem of rhetoric and of acquaintance with a given rhetoric. I think that in the coming years passionate love messages will be sent in the form of a short instruction in BASIC language, under the form "if... then," so to obtain, as an input, messages like "I love you, therefore I cannot live with you." (Besides, the best of English mannerist literature was listed, if memory serves, in some programming language as 2B OR/NOT 2B.)

There is a curious idea according to which the more you say in verbal language, the more profound and perceptive you are. Mallarmé told us that it is sufficient to spell out *une fleur* to evoke a universe of scents, shapes, and thoughts. It is frequently the case in poetry that fewer words say more things. Three lines of Pascal say more than three hundred pages of a long and tedious treatise on morals and metaphysics. The quest for a new and surviving literacy ought not to be the quest for a preinformatic quantity. The enemies of literacy are hiding elsewhere.

4. Three kinds of hypertext

It seems to me that at this time we are faced with three different conceptions of hypertext. Technically speaking, a hypertext document is more or less what Landow has explained to us. The problem is, what does a hypertext document stand for? Here we must make a careful distinction, first, between systems and texts. A system (for instance, a linguistic system) is the whole of the possibilities displayed by a given natural language. In this framework it holds the principle of unlimited semiosis, as defined by Peirce. Every linguistic item can be interpreted in terms of other linguistic or other semiotic items – a word by a definition, an event by an example, a natural kind by an image, and so on and so forth. The system is perhaps finite but unlimited. You go in a spiral-like movement *ad infinitum*. In this sense certainly all the conceivable books are comprised by and within a good dictionary. If you are able to use Webster's *Third* you can write both *Paradise Lost* and *Ulysses*. Certainly, if conceived in such a way, hypertext can transform every reader into an author. Give the same hypertext system to

Shakespeare and to Dan Quayle, and they have the same odds of producing *Romeo and Juliet*.

It may prove rather difficult to produce systemlike hypertexts. However, if you take the Horizons Unlimited Encyclomedia, certainly the best of seventeenth-century interpretations are virtually comprised within it. It depends on your ability to work through its preexisting links. Given the hypertextual system it is really up to you to become Gibbon or Walt Disney. As a matter of fact, even before the invention of hypertext, with a good dictionary a writer could design every possible book or story or poem or novel.

But a text is not a linguistic or an encyclopedic system. A given text reduces the infinite or indefinite possibilities of a system to make up a closed universe. *Finnegans Wake* is certainly open to many interpretations, but it is sure that it will never provide you with the proof of Fermat's Last Theorem, or the complete bibliography of Woody Allen. This seems trivial, but the radical mistake of irresponsible deconstructionists or of critics like Stanley Fish was to believe that you can do everything you want with a text. This is blatantly false. Busa's hypertext on the Aquinas corpus is a marvelous instrument, but you cannot use it to find out a satisfactory definition of electricity. With a system like hypertext based upon Webster's *Third* and the *Encyclopedia Britannica* you can; with a hypertext bound to the universe of Aquinas, you cannot. A textual hypertext is finite and limited, even though open to innumerable and original inquiries.

Then there is the third possibility, the one outlined by Michael Joyce. We may conceive of hypertexts which are unlimited and infinite. Every user can add something, and you can implement a sort of jazzlike unending story. At this point the classical notion of authorship certainly disappears, and we have a new way to implement free creativity. As the author of *The Open Work* I can only hail such a possibility. However there is a difference between implementing the activity of producing texts and the existence of produced texts. We shall have a new culture in which there will be a difference between producing infinitely many texts and interpreting precisely a finite number of texts. That is what happens in our present culture, in which we evaluate differently a recorded performance of Beethoven's Fifth and a new instance of a New Orleans jam session.

We are marching toward a more liberated society, in which free creativity will coexist with textual interpretation. I like this. The problem is in saying that we have replaced an old thing with another one; we have both, thank God. TV zapping is an activity that has nothing to do with reading a movie. Italian TV watchers appreciate *Blob* as a masterpiece in recorded zapping, which invites everybody to freely use TV, but this has nothing to do with the possibility of everyone reading a Hitchcock or a Fellini movie as an independent work of art in itself.

5. Change versus merging

Debray has reminded us that the invention of the photograph has set painters free from the duty of imitation. I cannot but agree. Without the invention of Daguerre, Impressionism could not have been possible. But the idea that a new technology abolishes a previous role is much too simplistic. After the invention of Daguerre painters no longer felt obliged to serve as mere craftsmen charged with reproducing reality as we believe we see it. But this does not mean that Daguerre's invention only encouraged abstract painting. There is a whole tradition in modern painting that could not exist without the photographic model: I am not thinking only of hyperrealism, but also (let me say) of Hopper. Reality is seen by the painter's eye through the photographic eye.

Certainly the advent of cinema or of comic strips has freed literature from certain narrative tasks it traditionally had to perform. But if there is something like postmodern literature, it exists because it has been largely influenced by comic strips or cinema. This means that in the history of culture it has never happened that something has simply killed something else. Something has profoundly changed something else.

It seems to me that the real opposition is not between computers and books, or between electronic writing and printed or manual writing. I have mentioned the first McLuhan fallacy, according to which the Visual Galaxy has replaced the Gutenberg Galaxy. The second McLuhan fallacy is exemplified by the statement that we are living in a new electronic global village. We are certainly living in a new electronic community, which is global enough, but it is not a village, if by that one means a human settlement where people are directly interacting with each other. The real problem of an electronic community is solitude. The new citizen of this new community is free to invent new texts, to annul the traditional notion of authorship, to delete the traditional divisions between author and reader, to transubstantiate into bones and flesh the pallid ideals of Roland Barthes and Jacques Derrida. (At least this is what I have heard said by enthusiasts of the technology. You will have to ask Derrida if the design of hypertexts really abolishes the ghost of a Transcendental Meaning – I am not my brother's keeper – and as far as Barthes is concerned, that was in another country and besides, the fellow is dead.) But we know that the reading of certain texts (let us say, Diderot's *Encyclopédie*) produced a change in the European state of affairs. What will happen with the Internet and the World Wide Web?

I am optimistic. During the Gulf War, George Lakoff understood that his ideas on that war could not be published before the end of the conflict. Thus he relied on the Internet to spell out his alarm in time. Politically and militarily his initiative was completely useless, but that does not matter. He succeeded in reaching a community of persons all over the world who felt the same way that he did.

Can computers implement not a network of one-to-one contacts between solitary souls, but a real community of interacting subjects? Think of what happened in 1968. By using traditional communication systems such as press, radio, and typewritten messages, an entire generation was involved, from America to France, from Germany to Italy, in a common struggle. I am not trying to evaluate politically or ethically what happened, I am simply remarking that it happened. Several years later, a new student revolutionary wave emerged in Italy, one not based upon Marxist tenets as the previous one had been. Its main feature was that it took place eminently through fax, between university and university. A new technology was implemented, but the results were rather poor. The uprising was tamed, by itself, in the course of two months. A new communications technology could not give a soul to a movement which was born only for reasons of fashion.

Recently in Italy the government tried to impose a new law that offended the sentiments of the Italian people. The principal reaction was mediated by fax, and in the face so many faxes the government felt obliged to change that law. This is a good example of the revolutionary power of new communications technologies. But between the faxes and the abolition of the law, something more happened. At that time I was traveling abroad and I only saw a photograph in a foreign newspaper. It portrayed a group of young people, all physically together, rallying in front of the parliament and displaying provocative posters. I do not know if faxes alone would have been sufficient. Certainly the circulation of faxes produced a new kind of interpersonal contact, and through faxes people understood that it was time to meet again together.

At the origin of that story there was a mere icon, the smile of Berlusconi that visually persuaded so many Italians to vote for him. After that all the opponents felt frustrated and isolated. The Media Man had won. Then, in the face of an unbearable provocation, there was a new technology that gave people the sense of their discontent as well as of their force. Then came the moment when many of them got out of their faxing solitude and met together again. And won.

It is rather difficult to make a theory out of a single episode, but let me use this example as an allegory: when an integrated multimedia sequence of events succeeds in bringing people back to a nonvirtual reality, something new can happen.

I do not have a rule for occurrences of the same frame. I realize that I am proposing the Cassiodorus way, and that my allegory looks like a Rube Goldberg construction, as James O'Donnell puts it. A Rube Goldberg model seems to me the only metaphysical template for our electronic future.